W9-CEZ-762

A Quarter Century on the Firing Line

The Best Writing from Americans for Religious Liberty's Journal, *Voice of Reason*

Edited by Edd Doerr and Albert J. Menendez

An Americans for Religious Liberty book

Copyright © 2009

All rights reserved under International and Pan-American Copyright Conventions. No part of this publication may be reproduced, stored in a retrieval system, or transmitted in any form or by any means, digital, electronic, mechanical, photocopying, recording, or otherwise, or conveyed via the Internet or a Web site without prior written permission of the publsher or copyright holder, except in the case of brief quotations embodied in critical articles and reviews.

Inquiries should be addressed to:

Americans for Religious Liberty
Box 6656
Silver Spring, MD 20916
Telephone: 301-260-2988
FAX: 301-260-2989
arlinc@verizon.net
www.arlinc.org

ISBN: 978-0-9821254-1-0

Printed in the United States of America

This book is dedicated:

- to the Jackson Social Welfare Committee of First Unitarian Universalist Church of Ann Arbor, Michigan, whose generous grants helped to make publication of this book possible;
- to the memory of Marie W. Schoch, whose generosity helped ARL at a critical time;
- to the thousands of wonderful contributors who have supported ARL's work for over a quarter of a century; and
- to Edward L. Ericson, the late Rabbi Sherwin Wine, and others, whose vision and efforts created Americans for Religious Liberty.

Table of Contents

Chapter 7 – ARL: Founders and History

Chapter 8 – Obituary Tributes

Introduction

The Americans for Religious Liberty (ARL) newsletter was named *Voice of Reason* (*VOR*) partly because that was the name of one of the two original organizations that merged to become ARL and also because ARL has always espoused the importance of the applicaton of reason to the development of the secular democracy that protects freedom of religion and conscience for all its citizens.

This anthology includes what the two long-time editors, one of whom was present at the creation and the other for more than half of the organization's life, have selected as the most significant and timely articles to have appeared in ARL's quarterly journal.

VOR has always included news, analysis, commentary, feature stories and book reviews. *VOR* began as a four-page newsletter that could be folded into an envelope. By Issue 34 (Summer 1990) we expanded to 12 pages, though we occasionally published an eight-pager, depending on the volume of news. We took on a "new look" with Issue 57 (Fall 1996) with a cleaner, brighter typeface.

The press of news and the availability of more information via the Internet caused us to expand our coverage further. A rather updated look came with Issue 80 in 2002, when we expanded to 16 pages and adopted a format allowing the newsletter to be sent to subscribers without an envelope. This gave it a more permanent feel and a more magazine-like quality. We expanded again to 20 pages with Issue 88 in 2004 and to 24 pages with Issue 91 in 2005. Occasionally, we publish a 28-page issue.

As always, we appreciate the skills and contributions of our long-time production manager, Teri Grimwood. And we appreciate the many contributions of our wives, Herenia Doerr and Shirley Menendez, to the success of ARL through the years, not to mention the contributed services of Helena Doerr.

Edd Doerr
Albert J. Menendez
May, 2009

Chapter 1
You Read It Here

It is not often that a small newsletter/journal can claim journalistic "scoops," but some of our articles are more complete and thoroughly researched than most others on the same topic. If not exactly scoops, they represent years of experience, research and analysis as we try to unravel and make sense of some of the often hidden dimensions in church-state stories.

Many of the feature stories are examples of our own investigative journalism and represent significant contributions to the church-state debates of the past quarter century.

Military Tackles Religious Conflicts

The U.S. Air Force issued new guidelines on August 29 that discourage public prayer at official functions and urge commanders to be sensitive to personal expressions of religious faith. The guidelines apply to the entire Air Force, not just to the Air Force Academy in Colorado Springs, which has come under heavy fire for allowing the promotion of evangelical Christianity at the expense of other faith traditions. An earlier Task Force report found some evidence of discrimination and harassment against non-evangelicals at the Academy, though critics saw it as an ineffective response to a pervasive problem.

The draft says that members of the Air Force "will not officially endorse or establish religion, either one specific religion or the idea of religion over non-religion." It also says that "abuse or disrespect" based on religious belief is unacceptable. The guidelines allow "a brief nonsectarian prayer" at special ceremonies or in "extraordinary circumstances" such as "mass casualties, preparation for imminent combat and natural disasters." Rabbi Arnold Resnicoff, a Navy veteran who was hired as a special assistant to the Air Force and who helped write the guidelines, said, "We support free exercise of religion, but we do not push religion."

Lt. Gen. Roger Brady, Air Force deputy chief of staff for personnel, noted that religious diversity is a hallmark of the U.S. military, especially "at a time when many nations are torn apart by religious strife."

Air Force chaplains must "respect the rights of others to their own religious beliefs, including the right to hold no beliefs." Individual discussions of religion between commanders and subordinates are still allowed, though members must be "sensitive to the potential that personal expressions may appear to be official expressions."

On October 11 the Air Force announced that it had "withdrawn for further review" an "ethics code" that gave its chaplains permission to evangelize or attempt to convert military members who are "not affiliated" with any faith. The change apparently came in response to the federal lawsuit filed by Air Force graduate and former Reagan Administration official Mikey Weinstein. The Air Force claimed that the code was issued in January 2005, but former chaplain MeLinda Morton told the *New York Times* that she had received a similar statement while attending chaplain training school at Maxwell Air Force Base in Alabama several years ago. Morton is a Lutheran minister who recently left the Air Force chaplaincy after complaining of evangelical domination and discrimination.

The guidelines received cautious praise from two congressional critics, Steve Israel (D-NY) and Lois Capps (D-CA), but Weinstein charged that the guidelines meant little because no officers who engaged in discriminatory activities were disciplined. In October, alleging that the Academy coerced attendance at evangelical services, Weinstein filed suit. His two sons are or have been students there.

The Washington Post expressed a tepid endorsement in a September 3 editorial. The guidelines, the paper said, "sound like a sensible balancing of interests" and "say all the right things," but "it's important that the public prayer exceptions don't end up swallowing the general rule."

The Air Force statement may just be the tip of the iceberg. *Washington Post* writer Alan Cooperman noted, "The growing influence of evangelical Protestants is roiling the military chaplain corps, where their desire to preach their faith more openly is colliding with long-held military traditions of pluralism and diversity."

Evangelical chaplains, who are becoming more and more dominant as mainstream military clergy are in decline, are pressing their demands, often in federal courts. At the Chaplain Training Schools, evangelicals and "pluralists" frequently clash over the styles of public prayer and the requirements of pluralism in public ceremonies.

Evangelicals are mounting a counterattack against these guidelines. Air Force Chief of Chaplains Maj. Gen. Charles C. Baldwin, sent a videotaped message to all active duty and reserve chaplains, saying the guidelines should recognize and support those with "belief systems that require us to tell others of our faith." Baldwin, a Southern Baptist, said the rules should prevent coercion but should allow proselytizing, prayers at staff meetings, and discussion of religion between senior officers and subordinates.

Seventy U.S. House members asked President Bush to issue an executive order protecting "the constitutional right of military chaplains to pray according to their faith" and 35 members signed a similar letter to the Air Force acting secretary. An orchestrated campaign is coming from religious conservatives. Cooperman reported in *The Washington Post*: "The Christian Coalition, Focus on the Family and other Christian advocacy groups have deluged the White House and Pentagon with thousands of phone calls, letters and e-mails denouncing the Air Force guidelines as an infringement of religious freedom."

According to the Pentagon's Defense Manpower Data Center, Catholic chaplains have declined to only 355 for 295,324 Catholic service members, a ratio of 832 personnel per chaplain. The 2,344 Protestant chaplains serve 652,529 members, a ratio of only 278 to one. The 22 Jewish chaplains have a 181 to one ratio, serving as they do 3,990 Jewish service personnel. There are also 20 Eastern Orthodox chaplains, 41 Mormons and 11 Muslims serving as chaplains. There are more Southern Baptist chaplains (451) than Roman Catholics. Of the 1,373,868 active duty personnel, only 112,166 (8%) claim no religious affiliation.

Air Force Downplays Religious Discrimination Evidence

A 16-member military panel that examined the heated religious climate at the U.S. Air Force Academy found that there was no "overt discrimination" against non-evangelical Christians but rather "a failure to fully accommodate all members' needs." The 100-page report issued on June 22 found that some officials were guilty of "a lack of awareness over where the line is drawn between permissible and impermissible expression of beliefs." The report admitted several instances in which cadets and professors were "overly aggressive in the expression of their faith."

General Roger Brady, the Air Force deputy chief of staff for personnel, told a Pentagon press conference that Academy commanders have not been given "useful operational guidance" as to the appropriate boundaries. Students were harassed for not attending "voluntary" prayer meetings during basic training, were pressured to attend the film "The Passion of the Christ" in 2004, and were harassed by over-zealous evangelicals on the faculty and in the sports programs.

While Abraham Foxman, national director of the Anti-Defamation League (ADL), praised the report, many critics remain unconvinced. Representative Lois Capps (D-CA), who asked for a high level investigation of the charges, commented, "I continue to have severe concerns. The report downplays the full extent of an environment consumed by religious intolerance. I am offended and shocked by the proselytizing that has been going on." Representative Steve Israel (D-NY) said the report "could have been more forthright than it is" and urged Academy officials to take decisive action to remedy the situation. Academy superintendent Lt. General John Rosa Jr. told the executive committee of the ADL on June 3 that religious intolerance did exist and that "it's going to take a while to fix, perhaps a half-dozen years." Rosa, who shortly after decided to leave the Academy and become president of The Citadel, singled out his second in command, Brigadier General Johnny Weida, for "inappropriate actions," especially his open endorsement of the National Day of Prayer activities in Colorado Springs.

The report ignored the transfer of Lutheran Chaplain MeLinda Morton after she protested against religious discrimination at the Academy. Morton resigned from the military on June 20 rather than accept transfer to Okinawa. Her attorney, Eugene R. Fidell, issued a statement which said, in part, "Chaplain Morton has been an outspoken critic of the academy's willingness to tolerate a pervasive evangelical climate that is threatening to members of other faith groups and disregards the constitutional separation of church and state, . . . It is clear that the academy has a lot of work to do to rectify the numerous First Amendment problems that have become a matter of public concern over the last several months. I think Chaplain Morton, because of her outspokenness and leadership on these issues, had concluded that it would be difficult for her at this point to contribute in the way she would like to the academy's transition to a better and more constitutional environment."

Morton is not the only chaplain who ran afoul of the evangelicals, who increasingly dominate the U.S. military. In a letter in *The Washington Post* on July 9, former Lutheran chaplain Christine Miller, of Waldorf, Maryland, wrote: "Having been a Lutheran chaplain in the military, I can tell you that the issues at the Air Force Academy are not new. They may be pervasive there now, but even when I was serving on active duty in the 1970s and '80s as the first female Lutheran chaplain (Navy) in any of the military services, there was an attitude among many evangelicals, both chaplains and non-chaplains, that Catholics and liturgical Protestant (especially Lutheran and Episcopal) churches were not "Christian." It has only gotten more confrontational as many feel that (finally!) their views are dominant."

The task force that issued this report has also been criticized for not meeting with two outspoken critics whose allegations sparked the inquiry. One was Kristen Leslie, a Yale theology professor who highlighted the evangelical domination of the chaplaincy and religion program at the Academy. The other was Mikey Weinstein, an Academy graduate and former Reagan administration official, who lamented the anti-Semitism at the tax-supported school, and said he had heard from 117 students and graduates who cited examples of religious intolerance. These 117 people included 98 non-evangelical Protestants, ten Catholics, eight Jews and one atheist. Leslie's 2004 report concluded, "There's one religious voice, the conservative evangelical Christian voice, that has decided that it has the right to lay claim to the environment, and it is able to do that by working with the Academy power structure."

As a response to Leslie's findings, the Academy rather half-heartedly established a "sensitivity training" program to teach tolerance. But the program was watered down at the request of top brass and chaplains, and references to non-Christian religions were eliminated.

The response to these allegations and reports by evangelical leaders and by Republicans has been lukewarm at best and occasionally hostile. House Democrats, led by Wisconsin's David Obey, tried to pressure the Air Force to mount a full-scale inquiry into the problems at the Academy. But his amendment to H.R. 2863 was defeated on June 20 by a vote of 210 to 198. Only eight Republicans joined 189 Democrats and one Independent in support of the amendment, while 207 Republicans and three Democrats blocked it. This roll call vote shows the stark difference between the parties on the issue of religious tolerance: 98.4% of Democrats and only 3.7% of Republicans voted for religious tolerance. The GOP, as former Senator John Danforth (R-MO) has observed, has become the political arm of conservative Christianity.

Evangelical leaders scoffed at the charges. An executive at Focus on the Family, the powerful evangelical lobby whose headquarters can be seen from the Academy, called the inquiry "a witch hunt." Focus vice president Tom Minnery twisted the report's findings in an interview with Conor O'Clery in *The Irish Times*. "We fervently hope that this ridiculous bias of a few against the religion of the majority—Christianity—will now cease." The Navigators, an evangelical group that has worked officially with the military since the 1930s, was not concerned by the inquiry. "I don't think there's a pervasive or major problem at the Academy," Jeffrey White, president emeritus of the Navigators and a former Academy instructor, said. "If anything, it's a bit of intolerance among the cadets who are young kids and sometimes say stupid things," he told Religion News Service.

One grudging admission that something might be wrong came from former Virginia Governor James Gilmore, chairman of the Academy's Board of Visitors. "Some people thought, apparently, that they were doing the right thing by expressing their faith, but they failed to understand the impact it would have on people with other faiths or with no faith. They understand that now. I think they recognize that some faculty members probably went over the line." (As Virginia's last Republican governor, Gilmore intervened in a right to die case similar to the Terri Schiavo spectacle in Florida and tried to force a Virginia woman to keep her brain-dead husband alive. His grandstanding was rejected by state courts.)

The Academy did name a rabbi, Arnold Resnicoff, former top chaplain in the U.S. military's European Command, to serve as a "special assistant for values and vision." The retired U.S. Navy captain will advise Acting Air Force Secretary Michael Dominguez on implementing recommendations made by Lt. General Roger Brady to "accommodate adherents to minority beliefs" at the Air Force Academy. New guidelines for appropriate religious expression and training in religious diversity and respect are goals of the Academy, according to a report in Reuters on June 27.

The New York Times remained skeptical. In an editorial, "Separation of Church and Air Force," it said, "Right now, it is hard to believe that there can be true reform from within. It is time for the higher chain of command to deproselytize this institution of national defense."

The conflict may represent a larger trend. As Laurie Goodstein pointed out in an article in *The New York Times* on July 12, "Evangelicals are a growing force in the military chaplain corps. Evangelical chaplains have more than doubled their numbers from 1994 to 2005, while Catholic chaplains declined from 167 to 94, Presbyterians from 30 to 16, Methodists from 64 to 50 and United Church of Christ chaplains from 11 to 3." These trends have intensified since historian Anne Loveland found a similar pattern in her book, *American Evangelicals in the U.S. Military, 1942-1993.* It was, therefore, not surprising that the Air Force paid $300,000 to bring hundreds of its chaplains to a fourday Spiritual Fitness Conference in June at a Hilton hotel in—where else?—Colorado Springs, the "evangelical Vatican" that delivered Colorado to George Bush in the 2004 election.

This controversy has not gone unnoticed overseas. Conor O'Clery, U.S. correspondent for *The Irish Times,* asked openly in a lengthy July 16 article in Ireland's leading newspaper, "Have evangelical organizations made the U.S. Air Force Academy a test case for the Religious Right agenda?" He concluded in the affirmative and cited an interesting fact. "The U.S. Air Force Academy registered 55 allegations of religious bias dating back to 2000, compared with just one complaint at West Point and none at Annapolis."

O'Clery also professed amazement that Pastor Ted Haggard of the huge New Life Church in Colorado Springs and defender of the Academy confers with the White House every Monday. "That would not go down well in Ireland if Catholic bishops called the Prime Minister's office every Monday to discuss policy," he observed.

Park Service Capitulates to Religious Right

In a series of recent decisions, the National Park Service (NPS) has approved the display of religious symbols and Bible verses, as well as the sale of creationist books giving a non-evolutionary explanation for the Grand Canyon and other natural wonders within national parks, according to documents released on December 30 by Public Employees for Environmental Responsibility (PEER), a national alliance of local, state and federal resource professionals working to protect the environment.

Also, under pressure from conservative groups, the Park Service has agreed to edit the videotape that has been shown at the Lincoln Memorial since 1995 to remove any image of gay and abortion rights demonstrations that occurred at the memorial.

"The Park Service leadership now caters exclusively to conservative Christian fundamentalist groups," stated PEER executive director Jeff Ruch. "The Bush administration appears to be sponsoring a program of Faith-Based Parks."

Last July NPS deputy director Donald Murphy ordered the Grand Canyon National Park to return three bronze plaques bearing biblical verses to public viewing areas on the Canyon's South Rim. Murphy overruled the park superintendent who had directed the plaques' removal based on legal advice from the Interior Department that the religious displays violated the First Amendment. In a letter to the Evangelical Sisterhood of Mary, the group sponsoring the plaques, Murphy apologized for "any intrusion resulting from" the temporary removal of the plaques quoting Psalms 68:4, 66:4, and 104:24 and pledged "further legal analysis and policy review" before any new action is taken.

This fall the Park Service also approved a creationist text, *Grand Canyon: A Different View,* for sale in park bookstores and museums. The book by Tom Vail claims that the Grand Canyon is really only a few thousand years old, developing on a biblical rather than an evolutionary time scale. At the same time, Park Service leadership has blocked publication of guidance for park rangers and other interpretive staff that labeled creationism as lacking any scientific basis.

The Park Service is also engaged in an extended legal battle to continue displaying an eight-foot-tall cross, planted atop a 30-foot-high rock outcropping in the Mojave National Preserve in California. PEER board member and former-Park Service manager Frank Buono filed suit to force removal of the cross. That suit is now pending before the Ninth U.S. Circuit Court of Appeals.

Newfoundland Endorses Public Education

Since its founding, the isolated Canadian province of Newfoundland and Labrador educated its citizens in separate school systems based on religion. (There were no nonsectarian public schools, and the religious schools were all tax-supported.) But by the 1990s many residents, themselves the products of a religion-based educational system, wanted a more inclusive, religiously-integrated school system. At that time most students attended either Roman Catholic, Pentecostal, or a kind of pan-Protestant school that appealed to Anglicans, Moravians, the United Church (a union of most Presbyterians, Methodists and moderate-to-liberal Protestants), and the Salvation Army, which is a separate religious denomination in Canada.

Why should this matter to Americans? For one thing, there is a sustained national campaign in the United States to weaken public education through voucher schemes that will fragment the educational enterprise and divide Americans into sectarian enclaves. "If this experiment was tried and failed in another part of North America that has demographic and historical similarities to the United States, we ought to be aware of it," explains ARL president Edd Doerr.

In two referendum elections, the last one in 1997 (approved by 73% of the voters), the province moved toward one public school system open to students of all religious persuasions and traditions. The new school plan also survived a legal challenge from die-hard supporters of the religious private schools. The province's Premier, Brian Tobin, and his Liberal Party, gave determined support to the implementation of a new school system that was clearly desired by the electorate.

How has it worked out? By all indications the public school system has been a resounding success and is supported by the residents. The new Progressive Conservative government, which took office in November after 14 years of Liberal rule, supports the new system.

Because of the historic divisions along religious lines which characterized the province, the new unified school system had to develop a religious education curriculum that was satisfactory to and accepted by all segments of the community. To do that required imagination, ingenuity, and a commitment to sound educational values. As it turned out, the curriculum may be a model for a religiously pluralistic culture in a western democratic society. Its values are inclusiveness, the importation of objective knowledge about religious customs and traditions, a respect for diversity, and an avoidance of anything that smacks of indoctrination or intolerance.

Bryce Hodder, the program development specialist for religious education in the province, says the new program is a great step forward from the kind of denominational education that most Newfoundlanders received under the old separate and sectarian system, which emphasized only the superiority of their own religions and imparted little if any objective information about other faith traditions.

The new religious education curricula are much more likely to promote interfaith harmony and to enable citizens to engage fruitfully with the realities of the 21st century world, Hodder suggested.

This is a major achievement since it challenges what award-winning journalist Michael Harris called "a fiercely sectarian society with a long history of denominational education." (Harris made this observation in his 1990 book *Unholy Orders: Tragedy at Mount Cashel*, which exposed the child abuse scandal at a Christian Brothers-run orphanage in the province.) This scandal was a factor in the decline of esteem for separate schools. A Royal Commission report on the lagging quality of education in the province also fueled discontent.

On September 2, 1997, the voters of the province were asked, "Do you support a single school system where all children, regardless of their religious affiliation, attend the same schools where opportunities for religious education and observances are provided?"

The question was supported by 73% of the voters, compared to 54% who endorsed it in a 1995 referendum.

The overwhelming passage of the 1997 referendum started the ball rolling. In an intensely religious and traditionalist province, the development of an academically sound and fair-to-all religious education program was essential to the success of the new unified school system.

Work began on a new "framework document" for religious education in October 1997 and curriculum committees, consisting of teachers and board personnel from the former denominational schools, were set up in January 1998. Focus sessions were held throughout the province in February to elicit suggestions and reactions to the proposals.

The federal Department of Justice examined the framework document and its recommended resources in March and April 1998. New religious education curriculum guides were then developed for each grade level.

The "Curriculum Framework for Religious Education" includes many components. Among these are the following:

• In a world that is truly multi-cultural and multi-faith, it is important that each person can value and celebrate his/her own faith (religious heritage or commitment). However, with accurate information about other religions, the individual should recognize that others have religious beliefs that they value and celebrate as well. Religious and denominational intolerance will be eliminated only when people are more understanding of the intrinsic worth of religious views and traditions that are not their own. An effective religious education program should give accurate information and demonstrate respect for all world faiths.

• Religion has been a determining factor in history and in our cultural heritage. Major decisions have been made in light of religious teachings. While it is true that, at times, religions have been responsible for conflicts in the world, it is also true that they have served to bring about resolutions, peace, and social justice. Students need to be aware of the role religion has played historically. An effective religious education program will enable the student to understand and appreciate the relationship between religion and history.

• Religion is also a large contributing factor in current national and international events. By coming to a realization of the importance of religion in these events, the students will better understand some of the underlying causes and complexities.

• This religious education curriculum is non-confessional. In such a program it is essential that faith, beliefs, doctrines, practices, and history of Christianity and other religions be covered with sensitivity and respect. No attempt to indoctrinate, proselytize or present a biased view would be appropriate.

Bryce Hodder explained, "The new program is inclusive in its approach, representing the major faith communities as well as some which would be considered minor. Resources have been produced in recognition of multi-culture and multi-faith and every attempt has been made to avoid stereotyping and to present unbiased accurate information."

Hodder added, "The Department of Education received co-operation from members of various faith groups (religions) in the reviewing process and many of these people often provided suggestions and photographs to be used in the resources. There was, for the most part, a feeling of good will and a recognition that it is important for students to appreciate their own faith background (those who have one) but to appreciate the faiths of other people as well. To begin this journey, students need to have an understanding of what people believe and what their traditions are. There is a real attempt to move beyond just tolerance to more of an appreciation or celebration of people's religious beliefs and traditions. There is no intention to negate the importance and value of the individual's own faith commitment but it is hoped that through the programs students will recognize that people with beliefs different than their own also value and celebrate their beliefs and traditions."

Program standards, evaluation techniques, resources, and appropriate age-level curricula have been developed and tested. At the present time, the schools are piloting a world religions program for high school.

Hodder explains what he hopes will be accomplished, "This has been and is a challenging venture but through the involvement of many people with a vested interest it is working and we are confident that students graduating from our schools will have an understanding of and an appreciation for many of the living belief systems around the world. Hans Küng said, 'There will be no world peace without peace between the world's religions: there will be no peace between the world s religions without dialogue between the world's religions.' Maybe in our little province we can make a beginning and a difference."

— Al Menendez

Blaming Blaine: A Distortion of History

The never-ending controversy over government funding of faith-based schools has begun to turn ugly as groups favoring such aid are now aiming their considerable guns at state constitutional provisions banning state aid. At least 37 states maintain some type of ban on the use of tax funds for "sectarian or denominational" schools. And a new, concerted effort by pro-voucher and right-wing conservative groups has been launched to repeal these amendments. The Becket Fund and the Institute for Justice are spearheading the movement to abrogate what they call "Blaine amendments."

They are called Blaine amendments because of a now forgotten U.S. Senator from Maine and Republican presidential candidate in 1884 — James G. Blaine. Senator Blaine proposed an amendment to the U.S. Constitution in 1875 that would have banned public support for church-related schools. It passed the House but fell four votes short of the necessary two-thirds majority in the Senate. (Constitutional amendments require a two-thirds majority in each house of Congress and then ratification by three-fourths of state legislatures.)

According to today's conservative propagandists, Blaine was some kind of reactionary anti-religious, or, at least, anti-Catholic bigot. But was he?

A careful review of the historical record, a search of his memoirs and letters, and of several biographies suggests a very different picture. By his own admission, Blaine was seeking to clarify the clearly implied doctrine of the religion clauses of the First Amendment by adding a provision to paragraph 10 of Article I of the Constitution. It provided:

"No state shall make any law respecting an establishment of religion, or prohibiting the free exercise thereof; and no money raised by taxation in any state, for the support of the public schools or derived from any public fund therefore, shall ever be under the control of any religious sect, nor shall any money so raised ever be divided between religious sects or denominations."[1]

Blaine explained his reasoning in a letter of October 20, 1875, "Just let the old Jefferson-Madison amendment be applied to the States. This does not interfere with any State having just such a school system as its citizens may prefer, subject to the single and simple restriction that the schools shall not be made the arena for sectarian controversy or theological disputation. This adjustment, it seems to me, would be comprehensive and conclusive, and would be fair alike to Protestant and Catholic, to Jew and Gentile, leaving the religious faith and the conscience of every man free and unmolested."[2]

James Gillespie Blaine was born in 1830 in West Brownsville, Pennsylvania, to a family with a Northern Ireland background. He was a precocious lad who finished college at 17, taught school at a military academy in Kentucky and at a school for the blind in Philadelphia before becoming a country newspaper editor and publisher in his wife's hometown of Augusta, Maine. Elected to the U.S. House of Representatives in 1863, he became successively Speaker of the House, U.S. Senator and twice Secretary of State. He sought the GOP presidential nomination three times, losing to Hayes in 1876 and Garfield in 1880, but won the nod in 1884. He lost a close election to Grover Cleveland. As a national leader, he was most closely identified with high tariffs to protect U.S. business and the expansion of American influence in world politics.

Blaine was considered one of the great orators in a time in history when oratory and eloquence were much admired in political discourse. Blaine was called "the plumed knight" in a flamboyant nominating speech at the 1876 Republican convention by Robert Ingersoll, perhaps the most noted orator (and an outspoken agnostic Republican!) of his time.

A touch of the Blaine eloquence can be seen in the closing passage of a eulogy for the slain President James Garfield: "Let us think that his dying eyes read a mystic meaning which only the rapt and parting soul may know. Let us believe that in the silence of the receding world he heard the great waves breaking on a farther shore, and felt already upon his wasted brow the breath of the eternal morning."[3]

Why did Blaine's amendment fail? Historians differ, but one possible explanation has been advanced by historian Gaines M. Foster. In his study of the attempts by "Christian lobbyists" (almost all of them evangelical Protestants) to enact federal legislation to achieve "moral reconstruction" from 1865 to 1920, Foster concluded that Congress was unwilling "to establish the religious authority of the federal government"[4] and hence refrained from enacting most of the proposed legislation that touched on religion or religious questions. That reticence may well have included the amendment on denominational school aid.

There was another reason why the Senate rejected an amendment that the House had passed overwhelmingly, writes historian Mark Wahlgren Summers. "The Senate expanded Blaine's proposal to shut religious instruction out of prisons and reformatories and to permit Protestant Bible-reading in the public schools. By then even Blaine had lost interest; he failed to show up when the Senate fell four votes short of the necessary two-thirds required to pass it, and when he wrote his memoirs (*Twenty Years of Congress*), he omitted the affair entirely."[5]

It may very well be true that some anti-Catholic prejudice influenced the passage of these anti-subsidy amendments in some states. Religious conflict, usually between Catholics and Protestants, was on the increase during the Gilded Age, and intolerance against Catholics reared its ugly head during the Know-Nothing agitation of the 1850s. But Blaine was clearly opposed to this nonsense. He opposed the attempt by some Protestants to pervade the public schools with Protestant-oriented hymns, Bible readings, devotions or slanted curricula. Undoubtedly, many of his fellow Republicans disagreed. The GOP then, as now, had a powerful evangelical wing that favored federal and state "morality" legislation in such areas as Sunday closing laws, bans on Sunday mail (and even newspapers), prohibition, and strict censorship laws affecting literature, entertainment and lotteries. This precursor of today's religious right favored the retention of a Protestant orientation in public education. But Blaine did not support their efforts.

Blaine's position on religious intrusions into public schools can be seen in his letter of October 3, 1875, to the Ohio Republican Committee. He wrote, "The issue forced upon you in regard to the public schools may have far-reaching consequences. In a government where every citizen is entrusted with political power, the importance of a free education cannot be exaggerated. The schools must be kept free, free in every sense, and especially free from sectarian influence or domination. The bitterest of all strifes is the strife between religious sects; and if that strife be permitted to cross the threshold of our public schools, free education in this country is at an end."[6]

In fact, Blaine refused to pander to the anti-Catholic elements in his 1884 presidential campaign or in his two previous attempts to secure his party's nomination in 1876 and 1880.

Blaine, whose father was Presbyterian and mother Catholic, explained his revulsion at religious prejudice in an 1876 letter. "My mother was a devoted Catholic. I would not for a thousand presidencies speak a disrespectful word of my mother's religion, and no pressure will draw me into any avowal of hostility or unfriendliness to Catholics."[7]

Ironically, it was a bigoted Presbyterian minister, Dr. Samuel D. Burchard, who sabotaged Blaine's presidential bid with an intemperate remark at a campaign appearance by the candidate in New York City during the closing days of the election campaign. Burchard's attack on the Democrats, calling them "the party whose antecedents have been rum, Romanism and rebellion," almost certainly shifted some New York Catholic voters from Blaine to his Democratic opponent, Grover Cleveland. Blaine lost New York, where he was favored, by only 1,149 votes.

It appears that a weary Blaine had not heard the preacher's remarks, or had decided that it would be impolitic to refute them. He was on the way to a final rally in Boston before returning to cast his ballot in his hometown of Augusta, Maine. The damage was done, however, and Blaine narrowly lost New York, Connecticut and a few other states where he had been favored. He thus became the first Republican since the party's first nominee, John Charles Fremont in 1856, to lose the presidency. (Ironically, many New York Irish Catholics associated with Tammany Hall admired Blaine and were planning to vote for him. If the "Blaine" amendment had been considered so anti-Catholic, they would hardly have supported him. It is probable, though, that the Burchard remarks dissipated this support in the campaign's closing hours.) One biographer argues that Blaine did make a last-ditch effort to separate himself from Burchard's remarks. Speaking in New Haven on the Saturday evening before Tuesday's vote, Blaine said, "I am the last man in the United States who would make a disrespectful allusion to another man's religion. I should esteem myself most degraded if I could in any presence make a disrespectful allusion to that ancient faith in which my mother lived and died."[8]

Blaine, himself a Presbyterian, acknowledged Burchard's gaffe as a major blow. In a letter to Murat Halstead on November 16, 1884, Blaine wrote, "As the Lord sent upon us an Ass in the shape of a Preacher and a rainstorm to lessen our vote in New York, I am disposed to feel resigned to the dispensation to defeat which flowed directly from these agencies."[1]

In one other area, Blaine was adamantly opposed to the kind of mixing of personal religion and politics, and to the near-Inquisition which presidential candidates in the past few decades have been subjected to by many evangelicals and religious rightists. In an 1876 letter Blaine wrote, "I will never consent to make any public declaration on the subject [religion] because I abhor the introduction of anything that looks like a religious test or qualification for office in a republic where perfect freedom of conscience is the birthright of every citizen."[10]

Blaine was noted for a magnanimity of spirit on religious matters. Tolerance and respect for differing religious views seem to have been an animating part of his personality. In an encomium for former president Garfield, Blaine said, "The world of religious belief is full of solecisms and contradictions. Men by the thousand will die in defense of a creed whose doctrines they do not understand and whose tenets they habitually violate. It is equally true that men by the thousand will cling to church organizations with instinctive and undying fidelity, when their belief in maturer years is radically different from that which inspired them as neophytes."

Blaine seems to have enjoyed serious religious debates and discussions. One of his biographers, Edward Stanwood, wrote, "Mr. Blaine was all his life inclined to theological speculation, and often held long and earnest discussion on the points of creeds, not only with his own ministers, but with visitors at his home, and with members of his family."[12] He was a life-long Presbyterian, but he also joined a Congregational church in Maine, perhaps for political reasons since the Congregationalists were then the strongest religious group in upper New England.[13]

The "blame Blaine" strategy is not new. It can be traced to the 1967 constitutional revision strategy in New York. Advocates of state aid to parochial and private schools mounted a campaign to remove that state's ban on such aid, which proponents of aid likened to alleged Blaine-style bigotry. In a spirited campaign, the parochaiders were trounced, by 72% to 28%. Voters in this 40% Catholic state did not want to jettison this provision. Senator Robert F. Kennedy agreed with them and opposed the proposed deletion.[14]

Two decades later voters in the second most Catholic state, Massachusetts, also refused to remove the Bay State's ban on aid to church-related schools. Twice the issue was submitted to the electorate and twice did they reject it, the second time, in 1986, by a 70% to 30% margin.

In fact, more than two dozen referenda held throughout the U.S. since the late 1960s have considered this question, and voters have overwhelmingly chosen, by an average margin of two to one, to reject schemes that will drain the public treasury for sectarian special interests.

Maybe the late Senator Blaine wasn't so wrong after all. What he proposed was sensible and in keeping with our best traditions as a nation. He was not a bigot, though many in his party were and are unfriendly toward religious diversity and pluralism. But a new kind of bigotry which insists on state subsidies and symbolic recognition for its religion alone is initiating a national campaign to deny state residents the right to retain policies that are in keeping with our progressive heritage. The likely beneficiaries of this campaign are schools which are religiously intolerant and often disdainful of other religious traditions.[15]

Those who mistakenly condemn Blaine in their misguided campaign to remake law by rewriting history are doing a disservice to themselves and to the body politic. For one thing, we have seen that there is no evidence that Blaine's motivation in advocating a ban on public funding of religious schools was influenced by bigotry. He felt that this proposal would aid in the development of religious harmony by limiting sectarian passions that threaten democracy's civility.

Then, is there really anything inherently wrong about the citizenry's wishing to deny churches and church-related schools access to the public treasury? It has been a long-standing

American principle that citizens should not be taxed for the dissemination of religious opinions that they themselves do not share. The "voluntary principle" which undergirds religious experience in U.S. history can be seen to be salutary and beneficial to all faith groups and has generally been accepted by all. It makes good sense. It is a long-standing, if implicit, recognition that Americans should only support the religious institutions of their free choice.

— Al Menendez

Endnotes

[1] Quoted in James P Boyd, *Life and Public Services of Hon. James G Blaine* (New York: Publishers' Union, 1893), p. 353.

[2] Ibid.

[3] Often called "The Garfield Memorial Address," it was delivered by Blaine before a Joint Session of both houses of Congress in the hall of the House of Representatives on February 27, 1882. The full text is found in Thomas H. Sherman, *Twenty Years with James G Blaine* (New York: The Grafton Press, 1928), pp. 166-194.

[4] Gaines M. Foster, *Moral Reconstruction: Christian Lobbyists and the Federal Legislation of Morality 1865-1920* (Chapel Hill, NC: The University of North Carolina Press, 2002), p. 229.

[5] Mark Wahlgren Summers, *Rum, Romanism & Rebellion: The Making of a President, 1884* (Chapel Hill: NC: The University of North Carolina Press, 2000), p.79.

[6] Quoted in David Saville Muzzey, *James G. Blaine: A Political Idol of Other Days* (New York: Dodd, Mead & Company, 1934), p.82.

[7] Quoted in Edward Stanwood, *James Gillespie Blaine* (Boston: Houghton Mifflin Company, 1905), p. 13.

[8] Muzzey, *op. cit.,* p. 317. Muzzey referred to Burchard as "a dull-witted Presbyterian minister" and cited a *New York Sun* description of the pastor as "an early Paleozoic bigot."

[9] Quoted in Stanwood, *op. cit.,* pp. 294-295.

[10] Stanwood, *op. cit.,* p. 13.

[11] Boyd, *op. cit.,* p. 609.

[12] Stanwood, *op. cit.,* p. 38.

[13] Stanwood, *op. cit.,* pp. 351-352; Sherman, *op. cit.,* p. 157.

[14] For a vivid account of the New York controversy, see Edd Doerr, *The Conspiracy That Failed* (Washington, DC: Americans United, 1968).

[15] See Albert J. Menendez, *Visions of Reality: What Fundamentalist Schools Teach* (Buffalo, NY: Prometheus Books, 1993); Frances R.A. Paterson, *Democracy and Intolerance: Christian School Curricula, School Choice, and Public Policy* (Bloomington, IN: Phi Delta Kappa, 2003).

House Chaplaincy Dispute Ends With a Whimper

The protracted conflict over the appointment of a U.S. House chaplain began with a bang last Thanksgiving but ended with a whimper at the end of March. House Speaker Dennis Hastert stunned his colleagues by announcing that he had appointed a Chicago Catholic priest, the Reverend Daniel Coughlin, to be the lower chamber's 59th chaplain and its first Catholic.

Hastert claimed that the previous nominee, Presbyterian minister Charles Wright, had asked to have his name withdrawn, though *Roll Call,* a House newspaper, reported that Wright had no such intention but was essentially forced out. The Republican leadership had mishandled the nomination from day one, after Hastert and Dick Armey refused to nominate the Rev. Timothy O'Brien, also a Catholic, even though O'Brien had been the first choice of an 18-member House panel that spent months interviewing prospective applicants.

Just before the surprise announcement, a group of 40 Catholic Republicans asked for a meeting with the Speaker and informed him in blunt terms that their constituents were furious about the manner in which Wright, the third choice of the bipartisan committee, had been selected. Many indicated that the GOP control of the House could be lost in November because of voter backlash on this issue. Front-page stories in Detroit, Boston, Chicago and Milwaukee newspapers confirmed that Republican hopes were fading, especially in heavily Catholic congressional districts in the North.

The nastiness intensified when Republican whip Tom Delay of Texas told an ABC television audience that Democratic minority leader Dick Gephardt had voted for Wright over O'Brien last fall, which Gephardt denounced politely as a "misrepresentation" of his actions. It was, in fact, an outright lie, according to House insiders.

The GOP leadership needed desperately to extricate itself from the embarrassment and potential political fallout, and Hastert apparently sought help from Chicago's Cardinal Francis George, who supplied him with a list of potential Catholic clergy.

Hastert's surprise selection of Coughlin, who has been a counselor and a seminary professor, may not cool the controversy completely. House Democrats were said to be "seething with resentment" over the entire process, including its finale, though most were happy that one of the last remaining religious monopolies in the U.S. had been ended.

The selection of the first Catholic chaplain has still failed to soften the feelings of Democrats and search committee members. Rep. Earl Pomeroy, Democrat of North Dakota, has introduced legislation requiring unanimous approval of future chaplains by the speaker and by the majority and minority leaders. Many other House members think the rancorous dispute suggests that paid chaplaincies should be abolished.

Coughlin got off to a rocky start when Republicans attempted to politicize the appointment by scheduling a public Mass and reception on Capitol Hill. The public worship service was sponsored by the Republican National Committee (RNC), and Democrats complained that they were not invited. A spokesperson for the RNC admitted that only members of its Catholic Task Force and three Catholic Republican senators received personal invitations.

The new House chaplain will receive a raise under the pay raise scheme approved recently. His salary is $138,900. The chaplain is considered an officer of the clerk of the House, and his secretarial and travel expenses are assigned to that office. The outgoing chaplain, Dr. Ford, took 29 foreign trips during his last six years in office, courtesy of U.S. taxpayers.

House Chaplaincy Dispute Reawakens Old Tensions

In an extraordinarily stupid modern rendition of the 19th century's "No Catholics Need Apply" slogan (newspaper ads designed to discourage Catholics from seeking employment), the Republican-dominated House of Representatives set off a firestorm of religious controversy that has raged since December.

The dispute, which exacerbates tensions along religious and partisan lines, centered on an obscure and secretive position, the House Chaplain, an officer of Congress with an annual salary of $132,100. With the exception of a six-year period preceding the Civil War, the House has selected an official chaplain to pronounce daily prayers and, in modern times, to engage in various counseling services. The trouble is that all 58 chaplains selected since 1789 have been Protestant. It is the last redoubt of religious exclusivity in the United States. (There was one Catholic chaplain in the U.S. Senate in 1832, out of 61 who have served in that post, a record nearly as bad.) All of the chaplains have been white males, and 39 of the 58 have been Methodists or Presbyterians. The outgoing chaplain, James Ford, who has been on the job for 21 years, was the first Lutheran ever selected.

Apparently, most of the previous chaplains were selected by the House Speaker. On March 25,1999, Speaker Dennis Hastert decided to depart from tradition by appointing an eighteen-member search committee to select a new chaplain. Nine Republicans. including co-chair Tom Bliley of Virginia, were appointed by Hastert, while nine Democrats, including co-chair Earl Pomeroy, North Dakota, were selected by Minority Leader Dick Gephardt. The committee included 14 Protestants, three Catholics and one Jew, which is somewhat less Catholic and more Protestant than the House as a whole. It included such Religious Right zealots as Steve Largent (R-OK), Zach Wamp (R-TN), Dave Weldon (R-FL) and Helen Chenoweth (R-ID). Over the course of many months, thirty-eight applicants were interviewed. Candidates were winnowed down to three finalists by October 20.

After exhaustive interviews, the committee sent three names to the final selection group, Armey, Hastert and Gephardt. Receiving the highest number of "ranking points," indicating the applicant regarded as the best qualified, was Father Tim O'Brien, a political scientist and pastoral counselor who directs the Marquette University Washington program. The runner-up was the Rev. Robert Dvorak, a leader of the tiny Evangelical Covenant Church. The third-ranking applicant was the Rev. Charles Wright, a Presbyterian minister long associated with the National Prayer Breakfast.

The result, announced at the end of November when Congress was in a two-month recess, was a shocker. Armey and Hastert blocked the Catholic nominee and instead opted for the committee's third choice, Charles Wright. Armey and Wright are both Presbyterians, and Armey is closely associated with the extremist religious and political views of the Rev. D. James Kennedy's Coral Ridge Ministries. Armey recently addressed the group's "Reclaiming America for Christ" conference. Speaker Hastert is a graduate of Illinois' Wheaton College, where Catholics are excluded from the faculty and board of trustees. Dick Gephardt voted for O'Brien.

This decision provoked a furor, especially from fellow committee member who felt that they had been used and had wasted hundreds of hours of valuable time on the selection, only to be ignored by the Republican leadership. Then the entire evaluative process was called into question when highly respected Washington columnist Mark Shields exposed the scandal. In a *Washington Post* article published on December 1, Shields revealed a conversation he had with rejected applicant O'Brien, who said he had been asked questions regarding his unmarried status and his wearing of a collar as a requirement of his priestly ministry. Both questions came from Oklahoma Republican Steve Largent, an ex-football player and a prominent spokesperson for the Religious Right, who regularly receives a 100% rating from the Christian Coalition. Largent's questions revealed the level of religious ignorance found in the U.S. Congress, since it is common knowledge that Lutheran, Episcopalian, and Eastern Orthodox Christian clergy, among others, regularly wear a distinctive religious garb, as do firemen, policemen and military personnel.

The present Lutheran chaplain, Jim Ford, has worn his collar for the past twenty-one years, suggesting, perhaps, that Largent has never had any dealings with Ford. Largent admitted his "naivete" to the *Tulsa World* newspaper a few weeks later. O'Brien also mentioned that Dick Armey had made oddly insulting comments about Lutheran-Catholic relations in his home state of North Dakota more than thirty-five years ago, as if they had any relevance to the selection of the first House chaplain of the 21st century. O'Brien told the *New York Times* that he was "a bit shocked" by Armey's "strange comments."

Rumors also surfaced that Armey had been besieged by calls from unnamed sources, urging the rejection of O'Brien. Armey spokesperson Michele A. Davis admitted that calls in opposition had been made to Armey's office.

O'Brien also told the *Times* that in his second interview he ran into "an evangelical Protestant line of questioning" from Republicans, who asked him to quote three Bible passages, and to explain how his "moral character could be judged if he was not married." One of the Republican committee members, Dave Weldon of Florida, is a former Catholic who now attends a Protestant church. It was Weldon who asked O'Brien to share Scripture verses with the committee.

Journalist Mark Shields concluded, "What is clear is that a bipartisan committee working conscientiously under bipartisan leadership reached near-unanimity in selecting the first Catholic House chaplain and the decision was then vetoed for reasons that are, to say the least, difficult to understand."

Rep. Lois Capps of California, a Lutheran Democrat and strong supporter of church-state separation, announced her deep disappointment with the leadership decision. She was a member of the search committee. A fellow California Democrat, Anna Eshoo, a Catholic, commented, "I am very resentful of what they did. These are people who feel they have a corner on morality. They do not."

Anger continued to rise when the nomination of Charles Wright was announced. Many Catholic Republicans expressed sorrow and dismay, though most essentially accepted the Armey-Hastert line that Wright was selected because of his "pastoral counseling skills" and because the Republicans were "looking for which one would be the guy members would be most comfortable with, who they could turn to when they needed personal counseling," according to Armey's press secretary, Michele Davis. Davis also told ARL associate director Al Menendez, "You don't hear any Catholics complaining, do you?"

Armey issued a snide, narcissistic letter to colleagues on December 2, which did not allay concerns that religious bias had intruded into the selection process. Armey's letter, which invoked his personal opinions seven times, concluded, "I found Reverend Charles Wright to be the most personable and approachable of the three finalists." Armey added, "I was looking for the person most able to inspire confidence among the members and provide comfort and spiritual guidance to members during a personal crisis." Armey also leveled charges that "partisan accusations" had caused the dispute, even though it was a Catholic Republican member from Illinois who initially labeled the decision an example of anti-Catholic prejudice.

Michigan Democrat John Dingell asked for the release of all relevant documents pursuant to the selection process. Armey and Hastert chose to ignore the request and did not even bother to answer Dingell's letter. Dingell said there is "a strong possibility of anti-Catholic bias or religious bigotry" that could only be addressed if all information is released.

Instead, Hastert and Armey sent a letter to the *Washington Post,* saying, in part, "We are disappointed and offended by accusations that anti-Catholic bias affected the choice of the next House chaplain." Refusing to answer the specific objections raised by critics, Hastert and

Armey were content to resort to pious platitudes, praising Charles Wright's "warmth and graciousness."

John Dingell rejected this approach, saying, "Many American Catholics believe that the manner in which the candidates were questioned and considered was contaminated with a prejudice which led to the decision not to accept the committee's recommendation of Father O'Brien."

Americans for Religious Liberty announced on January 3 that it was asking every member of Congress to reject the Wright nomination because the process is "deeply flawed" and "suggests the unconstitutional application of a religious test for public office." ARL reminded the members that "religious tests are specifically prohibited for any office or public trust in the United States by Article 6 of the U.S. Constitution."

ARL president John M. Swomley, in his letter to every member, urged Congress to "take a fresh look at the chaplaincy position and question whether it is good and reasonable public policy to continue to fund it." ARL believes that there is no constitutional requirement for either house of Congress to maintain a publicly funded chaplaincy position.

Even if Congress chooses to retain the position, said Swomley, the constitutional ban on religious tests must be observed. Swomley wrote, "A reasonable person could conclude that Mr. Armey and Mr. Hastert made their decision with reference to religious bias and chose to engage in religious discrimination in the selection of this candidate. It is unconscionable that taxpayers should finance a public office, which pays $132,100 per year, from which representatives of their religious tradition are excluded. The only way to rectify this grievous mistake and to inaugurate a genuine discussion of the chaplaincy issue is to reject Mr. Wright's nomination."

Frantic Republicans resorted to absurd examples of damage control. Resembling the Keystone Cops or the Three Stooges, Republican leaders called press conferences denying that they are anti-Catholic or given to occasional lapses of judgement in religious matters. Hastert even paid a call on Cardinal Francis George, the Catholic archbishop of Chicago. He also asked GOP members to talk privately with Catholic leaders in their districts to assuage fears of anti-Catholic bias, according to the Capitol Hill newspaper, *Roll Call. Roll Call* also reported that "Republicans are considering commissioning a poll to determine just how much damage this furor has done to them in areas with large Catholic populations."

Republicans are also considering releasing private letters to all members from some members of the selection committee. And, finally, documents relevant to the process were released on January 10.

These clumsy attempts to convince critics without really addressing the underlying issues have only added to the controversy. The seventy-five pages of documents released by the selection committee consist mostly of resumes by the candidates, "weighted voting" from early in the process, suggested questions for the chaplains, and other marginally significant data.

Congressman Bob Wexler of Florida, who is Jewish and a Democrat, asked Speaker Hastert "to reconsider your selection." Wexler, who said that "many constituents" from his South Florida congressional district "have expressed their outrage with respect to this decision," told Hastert that the selection "sends the wrong message to the American people — that religious discrimination is alive and well in the House of Representatives." Wexler added that he was "shocked and disheartened" by the decision.

Even the document released belatedly by the Republicans did not dampen the concerns, nor did their decision to postpone the January 27 confirmation vote. In the list of "chaplain's qualifications" is this odd statement: "While not a qualification, it is extremely beneficial that the chaplain have a strong family life, and is a dedicated spouse and parent." If this is not a qualification, why is it included in the list? Would this exclude all Catholic clergy?

Among the other qualifications is "an age that would allow an extended period of service." The eventual nominee, Charles Wright, is 65, the age at which most Americans retire and are eligible for Medicare and Social Security. Did Armey and Hastert conveniently overlook this point?

Wright is not without his supporters, however. The powerful National Association of Evangelicals, which represents millions of conservative Protestants and is close to Republican officialdom, called on its members to ignore issues of bias and to pray for fellow Protestant Charles Wright.

"America's Chaplain," Billy Graham, has also weighed in, seemingly supporting Wright, largely because Graham's wife and Wright's wife are close friends. Hastert and Graham later issued "corrections" about their versions of the event. A second vote was postponed in February because the bitterness has escalated, causing several national magazines to label the dispute "a religious war."

Republicans continued their clumsy attempts to make nice with Catholics, passing resolutions praising Catholic schools and voting a $30,000 congressional gold medal to New York's ailing Cardinal John O'Connor.

Religious Right Influence on Foreign Policy

William Martin, professor of religion and public policy at Rice University, has concluded that the U.S.' domestic Religious Right has "taken advantage of a Congress that has proved itself to be extremely assertive in its efforts to shape U.S. foreign policy and has also sought to widen the scope of their international agenda."

Writing in the spring 1999 issue of the prestigious quarterly *Foreign Policy*, a publication of the Carnegie Endowment for International Peace, Martin says that "the Christian Right not only sees the United Nations as a threat to the American family but as a mechanism that allows a secular elite to threaten family values worldwide." Martin continues, "The campaign against the United Nations has had an impact. In large measure because of opposition from the Religious Right, the United States did not contribute to the UN Population Fund in 1998, jeopardizing a program that provides contraceptives to nearly 1.4 million women in 150 countries."

Thanks to House Republicans and the Religious Right, the U.S. has refused to pay $1 billion owed to the UN, unless the federal government bars aid to all organizations which provide abortion services in the developing world. Martin adds that "Christian Right leaders have pressured Congress to withhold U.S. contributions to organizations such as the World Bank, the International Monetary Fund (IMF) and the United Nations. Delays in funding have jeopardized U.S. voting rights in the UN and threatened the IMF's ability to stabilize collapsing currencies in Asia and Latin America."

The Religious Right has sought to deny most-favored nation trading status to China, because of allegations of religious persecution against Christians, and has pressured the U.S. government to impose unilateral sanctions against many governments which are said to violate the International Religious Freedom Act passed by Congress.

Martin, a theologically informed observer, notes that the Religious Right is dominated by "isolationism and a fear of compromising American safety and economic interests and sacrificing national sovereignty to an international, liberal world order." Some of this hard-line isolationism stems, Martin argues, "from a conviction that increasing globalization is a fulfillment of dire biblical prophecies foreshadowing the return of Christ and the onset of Armageddon."

Martin warns, "It is patently mistaken to imagine that religious conservatives will soon give up the fight to reshape American domestic and foreign policy to fit their vision of what a godly nation should stand for.... [T]he Religious Right has an endurance that goes beyond the zeal of its activists."

Strange Goings-on at the Library of Congress

An exhibit that opened quietly at the Library of Congress (begun with Thomas Jefferson's personal library) in early June soon escalated into a major conflict, a cause celebre, provoking loud and often contentious debate over the meaning of separation of church and state in American life and history.

The Chief of the Library's Manuscript Division, James H. Hutson, unveiled an exhibit about "Religion and the Founding of the American Republic," which also included a two-day conference and the publication of Hutson's book on the subject. Two national foundations known for their conservative orientation, the Pew Charitable Trusts of Philadelphia and the Lilly Endowment of Indianapolis, were the primary funders of the exhibition.

The Librarian of Congress, James H. Billington, a Reagan appointee, hailed the program for its alleged "careful and balanced scholarship" and lamented the "general neglect" of religion as a factor in scholarly activity. The exhibition, he explained, "followed the fortunes of evangelicalism which became the dominant feature of American religion in the first three decades of the nineteenth century." He claimed that "viewers may be surprised by the extent to which federal facilities were placed at the disposal of religion after the Founders moved the government to Washington in 1800." Finally, he observed that "fresh interpretations and little known materials in the exhibition ought to stimulate wide interest."

They did that, but not quite in the manner expected. For one thing, Hutson, who is not a church-state specialist, and the views he expressed in his book *{Religion and the Founding of the American Republic,* University Press of New England) and in an official Library of Congress paper, "The Wall of Separation Between Church and State," strongly suggest a bias toward the accommodationist position espoused by the Religious Right.

Hutson is, in fact, quite hostile to the position that separation of church and state was intended by the majority of America's Founders and represented the crystallization of legal thought in this critical area.

Hutson argues that many lawmakers have "distorted" the religion clauses of the First Amendment by misinterpreting Jefferson's use of the phrase, "wall of separation between church and state" in a letter the president wrote to the Danbury Baptist Association on New Year's Day, 1802. Hutson remarked that the U.S. Supreme Court "had used Jefferson's 'wall' metaphor as a sword to sever religion from public life, a result that was and still is intolerable to many Americans."

Hutson's main argument is that Jefferson, who drafted his letter with the assistance of his attorney general, Levi Lincoln, and his postmaster general, Gideon Granger, both New Englanders, was acting solely as a politician and apparently did not mean to express policy. Such a view is naive in the extreme, say most Jefferson scholars, since all U.S. presidents have used letters and public addresses to express public policy concerns and to influence the political culture.

Jefferson's letter was indeed written to Baptist supporters in New England, who were surprised that Jefferson refused to proclaim official days of thanksgiving, prayer and fasting, as his predecessors, George Washington and John Adams, had done. The Jefferson letter explained why he believed such actions were inappropriate for the president and transcended the proper boundaries he believed should exist between the institutions of religion and government. (New England voted strongly against Jefferson in the 1800 election, and the clergy of the Congregational Church, the established church in Connecticut, Massachusetts and New Hampshire, were his bitterest foes.)

Hutson claimed that "Jefferson's strictures on church-state entanglement were little more than reworded phrases and ideas from his Statute Establishing Religious Freedom." Hutson also tried to make a big deal out of the fact that the original Jefferson first draft contains revisions! Hutson must assume that presidential documents are always issued without emendations of any kind, a curious view for a scholar. He said that Jefferson inserted the phrase "wall of eternal separation" and the words "merely temporal" with - in Hutson's angry phrase — "a clenched-teeth, defiant ring." Then Jefferson softened these expressions somewhat. Therefore, in Hutson's view, "The Danbury Baptist letter was never conceived by Jefferson to be a statement of fundamental principles; it was meant to be a political manifesto, nothing more." Apparently, Hutson believes that political statements invariably lack principle, a highly cynical view of American politics.

Hutson also claims to have uncovered new information that Jefferson, as president, allowed churches to use federal buildings for worship, and frequently attended these services. Most Jefferson scholars have known these facts. Washington was a newly-established town and few places of worship were available. Allowing church groups to conduct services on a temporary basis before construction began on their own properties was not considered controversial. Jefferson was a lifelong student of religion, who read the Bible avidly and in fact compiled his own edition or version of biblical texts. Like most political leaders of his time, conservative or liberal, he enjoyed the intellectual give and take of sermons and religious discussions. So it is a highly enigmatic and peculiar view that Hutson expresses when he writes, "Going to church solved Jefferson's public relations problems. His attendance at church services in the House of Representatives was his way of offering support to religious faith and for its beneficent role in republican government."

The Hutson thesis escalated to a major controversy when the Religious Right seized on this and claimed that the hallowed Library of Congress had suddenly adopted their view of American history. The Christian Coalition immediately issued a press release claiming "Library of Congress Skewers Wall of Separation Myth" and then called on the House to pass a constitutional amendment authorizing school prayer. Ultraconservative writer David Barton said, "The Library has confirmed that the Jefferson letter was never meant to be a national policy paper." The conservative *Weekly Standard* opined, "Americans should go see this marvelous new exhibition either now at the Library of Congress or when it travels revival-like around the country. If enough do, no one will ever be able to claim again that *Everson* represents the thinking of the founders. And perhaps even the Supreme Court's great wall of separation will at last come tumbling down."

This sinister course of events angered and alarmed both church-state separationists and a hardy band of Jefferson scholars and historians. Two dozen of them, led by the University of Richmond emeritus professor of humanities Robert S. Alley issued a statement blasting the

Library of Congress for an "unbalanced, biased and flawed" analysis.

The statement, prepared by such eminent scholars as Derek Davis, Norman Dorsen, Edwin Gaustad, Richard Pierard and former Congressman Robert Drinan, accused the Library of "presenting inaccurate conclusions as settled fact."

In a later interview with *The New York Times,* Robert M. O'Neil, director of the Thomas Jefferson Center and professor of law at the University of Virginia, said, "The fact that there may have been a political context for Jefferson's letter hardly disqualifies it as an assertion of principle, especially since it is so consistent with everything else he did or said on this issue."

In August, Librarian of Congress Billington, in a letter to Alley, denied that the Library "is nor has it ever aspired to be the equivalent of a High Court of American scholarship, promulgating definitive judgments on controversial matters. Nothing would be further from my or the Library's intention than to dictate dogma about the interpretation of historical documents."

This lame and tardy excuse has not stilled the acrimony. Alley has kept up the pressure, accusing the Library of "the outright falsification of a document by the Library in its exhibit" and has lamented pointedly that the exhibit constitutes "an enormous conclusion about Jefferson manufactured by an insidious interpretation on the part of the Library."

Hutson is a Yale graduate, a Presbyterian, and primarily an author of articles and books about Benjamin Franklin and about relations between the U.S. and Switzerland. He has been caretaker of manuscripts at the Library since 1982. Wittingly or otherwise, he has set off a storm of protest that has moved from the ivory towers of scholarship to everyday conversations among informed people who want to preserve America's basic liberties of freedom of thought and freedom of conscience.

This controversial exhibit can be seen in Dallas, Philadelphia, Indianapolis, and Southern California during the coming months.

The Library of Congress Misinterprets Thomas Jefferson

(The following is the text of the letter sent to the Library of Congress by 24 eminent scholars.)
On June 4, 1998, the Manuscript Division of the Library of Congress mounted an exhibit entitled "Religion and the Founding of the American Republic." It is an impressive collection beginning with the English colonization in the 17th century and reaching into the New Republic. It was developed under the direction of Dr. James Hutson, Chief of the Manuscript Division in the Library of Congress. Unfortunately the press, with apparent encouragement from Dr. Hutson, chose to focus on a single document, a letter from President Thomas Jefferson on January 1, 1802 to a Committee of the Danbury (Connecticut) Baptist Association. Concurrent with the press conference, Dr. Hutson released an essay, written on official stationery of the Library of Congress, entitled, "The Wall of Separation Between Church and State: What Jefferson Originally Wrote and What It Means."

Dr. Hutson's essay yields an unbalanced treatment of this important topic on the basis of a questionable analysis that has not, as far as is known, been subjected to independent scholarly review. The essay depends upon a flawed premise that since President Jefferson edited the original draft of the letter, it is possible, simply by comparing that original with the final version, for the reader fully to "discern Jefferson's true intentions in writing the celebrated Danbury Baptist letter." From there, the essay devolves into an assault on the phrase "separation of church and state" supported with tenuous inferences from Jefferson's excisions. Dr. Hutson also implies that intent and meaning can be derived from examining the document in isolation from related materials, including Jefferson's extensive, lifelong examination of the subject at hand. There is not even a reference to the text of the letter from the Danbury Baptists to Jefferson. The Library of Congress has chosen to interpret the meaning of "separation" from Jefferson's omissions from a single letter.

There may be several possible explanations for Jefferson's excisions of certain material, but the most obvious to any experienced writer is that he was editing while composing. Although scholars may differ as to the reasons for Jefferson's editorial selections, there is no basis for arguing that these omissions indicate that the reply was not "conceived to be a statement of fundamental principles," but rather, "was meant to be a political manifesto, nothing more."

It is also inaccurate to claim that the reply to the Baptists was "political" and not "a dispassionate theoretical pronouncement." Supporters of a broad understanding of Jefferson's Danbury letter have never denied the relevant and pertinent political considerations; however, that fact does not negate either the significance of this statement or his commitment to the principle. Jefferson's two most prized examples of his authorship — the Declaration of Independence and the Statute for Establishing Religious Freedom in Virginia — could not have been more political, even as every line was laced with principles concerning democracy and freedom.

Respecting the timing of the deletions, Dr. Hutson ignores the fact that we simply do not know when Jefferson struck the word "eternal" modifying "separation." Dr. Hutson compounds the problem by assuming that *he* does know. Scholars certainly can argue persuasively that the four deletions indicated by Jefferson in the circled sentence which he did omit occurred *before* the letter was sent to Attorney General Levi Lincoln for his comments.

Of course the debate about the Danbury letter is of current significance because of the connection the Supreme Court has made between it and the First Amendment. Unfortunately, in addressing that issue Dr. Hutson ignores the past sixty years of Supreme Court opinions that analyzed Jefferson's phrase. He chooses to cite only one case, *McCollum v. Board of Education* (1948), and argues, with no citation of evidence, that the Court used "Jefferson's 'wall' metaphor as a sword to sever religion from public life, a result that was and still is intolerable to many Americans." Absolutely nothing in the *McCollum* decision hints at severing religion from public life. It was focused on "public school buildings used for the dissemination of religious doctrines" during the school day, Indeed, Justice Hugo Black, writing for the majority, observed that the decision "does not, as counsel urge, manifest a governmental hostility to religion or religious teachings." Finally, Dr. Hutson makes no mention of the *Zorach v. Clauson* decision in which the Court, four years later, allowed released time for religious instruction.

Another problem with Dr. Hutson's reasoning is his failure even to mention the letter *from* the Danbury Baptist Committee. What was Jefferson answering? Analysis of that letter is absolutely essential to any understanding of the Jefferson response. The three authors of the letter "rejoice" in Jefferson's election. Their "Sentiments are uniformly on the side of Religious Liberty." They speak of "civil government" extending "no further than to punish the man who works ill to his neighbors." So why would Dr. Hutson suggest that Jefferson's phrase "merely temporal" to describe his duties has "a clenched-teeth, defiant ring"? Indeed, the letter from the Danbury Baptist Association Committee endorsed a distinction between "civil government" and the existing governmental practices in Connecticut. [Editor's note: The complete text of the Danbury Baptists' letter to Jefferson and an analysis of Jefferson's reply may be found in Dr. Alley's book, *Public Education and the Public Good,* published by ARL in 1996.]

The Baptists criticized the political leaders in Connecticut who had reproached the President by calling him "an enemy of religion, Law & good order because he will not, dare not assume the prerogatives of Jehovah and make Laws to govern the Kingdom of Christ." It is difficult to understand why Dr. Hutson thinks the Baptists would have been offended by the term "temporal." The religious establishment of Connecticut might have objected, but they were never Jefferson supporters anyway. On the other hand, Baptists were quite familiar with the distinction that Roger Williams made between the temporal and the eternal. "All civil states," Williams wrote, "are proved essentially civil, and therefore not judges, governors or defendours of the spirituall or Christian state and worship."

The Jefferson phrase "thus building a wall of separation between church and state" is familiar to millions of Americans and is regularly thought of as a convenient way to describe the scope and effect of the religion clauses of the First Amendment. We believe Jefferson's metaphor to be a significant part of understanding the matrix out of which that Amendment emerged. The historical record makes clear that he used his commitment to religious freedom with utmost deliberation in order to set forth both his philosophy and his view of public policy. We have no hesitation in asserting that it was an extraordinary affirmation "befitting the best spirit in our republican democracy. Pulitzer Prize-winning historian Leonard Levy, one of Jefferson's harshest critics, phrased it best. "Jefferson had powerful convictions on the subject of religious liberty which he always approached most solemnly."

We strongly disagree with the conclusions reached by the Library of Congress and urge Library staff to refrain from presenting those conclusions as settled fact.

Signed,

Robert S. Alley, Professor of Humanities, Emeritus, University of Richmond; Derek H. Davis, J.D., Ph.D., Director of the J.M. Dawson Institute of Church-State Studies, Baylor University, and Editor of *Journal of Church and State;* G. Scott Davis, Lewis T. Booker Professor of Ethics and Religion, University of Richmond; Norman Dorsen, Stokes Professor of Law, New York University School of Law; Robert F. Drinan, S.J., Georgetown University Law Center; Ronald B. Flowers, Chairman of Religion Department, Texas Christian University; Edwin S. Gaustad, Professor of History, Emeritus, University of California at Riverside; Phillip E. Hammond, D. Mackenzie Brown Professor, Department of Religious Studies, University of California at Santa Barbara; Peter Irons, Professor of Political Science, University of California at San Diego; Gregg Ivers, Professor of Government, American University; Isaac Kramnick, Professor of Government, Cornell University; Bill J. Leonard, Dean, Divinity School, Wake Forest University; Henry S. Levinson, Professor of Religious Studies, University of North Carolina at Greensboro; Robert S. Michaelsen, J.F. Rowney Professor of Religion and Society, Emeritus, University of California at Santa Barbara; James Robert Miller, Chair, Department of Philosophy and Religion, Eastern Kentucky University; R. Laurence Moore, Howard A. Newman Professor of American Studies, Cornell University; Robert M. O'Neil, Professor of Law, University of Virginia; Richard V. Pierard, Professor of History, Indiana State University; Robert A. Rutland, Professor of American History, Emeritus, University of Virginia; Senior Editor of the *Papers of James Madison,* 1973-1985; Robert E. Shepherd, Professor of Law, University of Richmond Law School; George Shriver, Professor of History, Georgia State University; Paul D. Simmons, Clinical Professor, University of Louisville; Ruti Teitel, Professor of Law, New York Law School; William Van Alstyne, William R. and Thomas C. Perkins Professor of Law, Duke University School of Law.

Richard John Neuhaus: Guru of the Religious Right

For Richard John Neuhaus, it's been a long journey from the pastorate of a predominantly African-American Lutheran parish in Brooklyn to the Roman Catholic priesthood and editorship of a prestigious monthly journey called *First Things.* This odyssey, spanning more than two decades, includes an intellectual shift from New Left gadfly to neoconservative apologist for the Religious Right.

Neuhaus, who was ordained to the priesthood by his friend Cardinal John O'Connor of New York, continues to function as editor-in-chief of the neoconservative magazine published by the Institute on Religion and Public Life, based at 156 Fifth Avenue in New York City. In his apostolate to writers and intellectuals, Neuhaus apparently is unencumbered by pastoral duties and is able to spend his time reading, writing and reviewing books and articles. His column, "The Public Square," is a highly personal view of whatever interests him and serves as a sounding board for the exposition of his strongly-held views on diverse and sundry issues facing the Church and the world.

Neuhaus has also become a catalyst for those who seek to reverse the pluralism and neutrality that characterize the state of religion and public life in America. Neuhaus made his first mark as a critic of recent trends in his 1984 book *The Naked Public Square,* written when he was still a Lutheran pastor and published by Eerdmans, a venerable evangelical publishing firm in Grand Rapids, Michigan.

In that volume, often cited as one of the seminal conservative books of recent decades, Neuhaus argued glibly and forcefully, though without much concrete evidence, that "the public square," the area where public debate over "the proper ordering" of government and cultural life (favorite Neuhaus terminology) had been denuded of religious sentiments and values. Neuhaus claimed that people who brought strong religious convictions to play on the formulation of public policy or legal decision-making were excluded from the debate. Their views were ignored and were branded, ipso facto, illegitimate. Neuhaus saw secularism as ascendant and triumphant and suggested that American public life was much the worse because of this alleged exclusion.

When Neuhaus published his controversial diatribe, he was addressing a nation already in the throes of cultural, religious and political upheaval. Jerry Falwell's Moral Majority and other Christian Right groups had already been around for five years, enlarging their role in the political realm. Religious liberals and moderates had expanded their lobbies in the nation's capital and had, indeed, been given much of the credit for the passage of meaningful civil rights legislation during the 1960s and for the success of the movement to end the Vietnam War during the 1960s and 1970s. Far from being "naked," the public square seemed to many observers to be cluttered and well dressed. Still, the Neuhaus argument gained many converts, especially on the Right, whose adherents lamented their loss of power and status in American life since the advent of the New Deal.

The arguments advanced by Neuhaus in that book and subsequent books and articles will be critically examined in this article. The common themes that emerge, and the likely consequences if his pronouncements ever become the law of the land, form the basis of this analysis.

The Mainline Churches

Neuhaus is fierce in his criticism of the moderate to liberal non-evangelical churches in the Protestant family, which are often called the mainline or mainstream because of their historic influence on American life and culture. He charges that they have departed from established moral and theological traditions and are consumed with left-wing trendiness.

He blames these churches for defending abortion rights and freedom of choice for women in this sensitive area of ethics and personal morality. "The doleful fact is that the liberal oldline churches are incapable of challenging — and in some instances are actively supporting — the unlimited abortion license imposed on the country by the[Supreme] Court."[1]

He castigates religious liberals for allegedly ignoring the plight of Christians overseas. In a recent issue of *First Things* he charges, "The National Council of Churches, following its shameful pattern during the years of the Cold War, has belittled and often denied the persecution of fellow Christians."[2] He sneers that "a wide array of Protestant and Catholic religious groups operating out of the United Methodist Building on Capitol Hill... have a long record of support for left-wing dictatorships in Latin America."[3]

Neuhaus cannot resist even trivial reasons for ridiculing mainline Protestants. When *Commonweal,* the grand old journal of progressive Catholicism, moved its office in 1997 to 475 Riverside Drive in New York's Morningside Heights district, Neuhaus sneered, "Morningside Heights is a veritable mount of memorials to the now departed cultural hegemony of liberal Protestantism."[4]

Neuhaus casts a critical, if guarded, look at the two former Lutheran communities to which he once belonged, having attended Concordia Seminary in St. Louis in his early Lutheran Church-Missouri Synod days and later joining the Evangelical Lutheran Church in America (ELCA). He claims that "the ELCA has vanished into the potpourri of liberal Protestantism and the Missouri Synod is increasingly hardened in its separation from everyone else."[5]

On another occasion he commented snidely, "Among Lutherans, as with other oldline churches, it was not long ago that divorce was cause for removal from the church's ministry. Today the divorce rate among clergy in such churches is about the same as in the general population. It is not unusual for pastors and seminary professors to be divorced several times, in some instances having swapped spouses. So what's the big deal about divorce?"[6]

Vouchers and Parochiaid

Neuhaus is unwavering in his support for vouchers and other forms of public assistance to private and religious schools, which he maintains, in spite of considerable evidence to the contrary, is perfectly constitutional. Once in a while, he invokes the hoary thesis (officially espoused by the Vatican) that the United Nations requires that all countries provide such aid. Neuhaus advanced this absurd claim in November 1997: "The question on which this argument should turn is the right of parents to chose the education they want for their children. It is a right explicitly guaranteed in the 1948 Universal Declaration of Human Rights and, at least theoretically, in American constitutional law. It is a simple matter of justice."[7]

Religion in Politics

Neuhaus made his intellectual mark, initially, by advancing the now shopworn argument that America's public square — its public, predominantly governmental realm — had been denuded of a religious voice. This inversion had been accomplished partly by the betrayal of the mainline religious bodies — a *trahison des clercs* accomplished by these religious groups' adoption of secular modes of thought and embrace of putatively radical and anti-American policies.

This may be why Neuhaus has become such an admirer of and apologist for the Religious Right and why he claims that their essentially benign aims are ignored by the media and opposed by religious moderates and liberals. He writes, "What happened in the past half century is a mutiny of the Christian voice in public not because of secularization but because of the reconfiguration of Christianity in America, meaning chiefly the ascendancy of Catholicism and evangelical Protestantism. More precisely, the Christian voice in its Catholic and evangelical expressions is not so much muted as it is viewed by the remaining liberal establishment as suspect, as another intrusion upon our public life."[8]

Majoritarianism

Neuhaus has little or no interest in the religious liberties or sensibilities of religious minorities. He argues that the majority in a given area or nation should be respected and, furthermore, that the Constitution was originally intended to protect the majority ethos. He writes, "Were it not for the Judiciary's mindless pronouncements on the 'establishment' of religion, it would have been possible for the overwhelming majority of citizens to publicly celebrate one of their really important festivals. [Editor's note: Christmas.] In fact, it happened quite naturally until the Supreme Court, beginning in 1947, took its 'strict separationist' turn of hostility to religion. Before that, Jews more or less gladly left Christmas to the Christians, recognizing that a minority of 2 percent is, well, in the minority."[9]

Neuhaus's insensitivity is exceeded only by his arrogance. There is abundant evidence that the Jewish community, as well as some Christian groups, did not appreciate the manner in which Christmas was celebrated in public schools and institutions, and the signals such celebrations sent that religious outsiders were second-class citizens, at best.

When some Christians dissent from Neuhausian majoritarianism, he sneers that "Christian leaders are inhibited from publicly addressing themselves to the Christian majority."[10]

Neuhaus continues to hammer this argument in the following: "The allegedly 'exploding' Muslim population is frequently cited by those who contend for the religio-cultural balkanization of America. Muslim organizations claim figures as high as seven million, and these claims are often cited in news stories. For perfectly understandable reasons, minority groups tend to inflate their figures, a relatively innocent vice except when it plays into the hands of those with a more dubious agenda. In this case the dubious agenda is to relegate Christian views to a marginal status in public discourse. Of course many Christians are no more than nominal, and of course there is no one view by Christians on a host of disputed questions, and of course a hundred other important qualifications. But one of the most elementary facts about America is that its people are overwhelmingly Christian in their own understanding, and that they and many who are not Christian assume that the moral baseline of the society is the Judeo-Christian ethic. Acknowledging that does not answer the many questions that vex our public life, but to ignore it is a guaranteed formula for getting the wrong answers."[11]

" [A]s we have said so often, American public life is best understood in terms of a *Kulturkampf,* a battle over the ideas, moralities, stories, and symbols by which we will order our life together." [12]

"Our public life is manifestly not characterized by Christian virtues. But demographically and culturally it is equally obvious that this is a Christian nation. Nearly 90 percent of the American people claim to be Christians."[13]

"[T]he overwhelming majority of Americans derive their moral vocabulary and moral judgments, directly or indirectly, from religion. Whether we like that or not, it is the social fact. And the religion in question is overwhelmingly Christian of a sort that is comfortable in affirming a Judeo-Christian tradition."[14]

"The reason Christians are tolerant is not because this is a pluralistic society. This is a pluralistic society because most Christians are tolerant. ... But what the ACLU, the National Education Association, and their like must some day learn is that the only available reservoir of public morality in this society is the dominant ethos, and that dominant ethos is, however confusedly, Christian."[15]

Criticism of the Supreme Court

Neuhaus argues, as do other religious rightists, that the Supreme Court began to remove religion from public life in 1947, usurping an allegedly limited constitutional role and engaging in activist jurisprudence that properly belongs to the legislative branch of government.

Neuhaus criticizes the Court for allegedly adopting what "... is truly a new born interpretation that has a provenance of no more than fifty years, its godfather being the formidable and self-described extreme separationist, Leo Pfeffer of the American Jewish Congress. . . . The Pfefferian inversion of the religion clause that continues to be promoted by the American Jewish Congress subordinates 'free exercise' (the end) to 'no establishment' (a means to that end). It does so by establishing a religion that is in conflict with the religion espoused by the great majority of Americans, and by propounding a profoundly anti-democratic interpretation of our constitutional order."[16]

This attack on Pfeffer, one of the country's leading authorities and litigators on religious liberty issues, is both churlish and inaccurate.

Abortion Rights

Neuhaus has made *First Things* a sounding board for his extreme anti-abortion views, in which he expresses no appreciation for the rights of conscience of women or for their right to autonomy in moral decision-making. In an editorial in the January 1998 issue on the twenty-fifth anniversary of *Roe v. Wade,* Neuhaus called abortion "the bloody crossroads where conflicting visions of the kind of people we are and should be will do battle." He claimed erroneously that American abortion rights law is "radical" and accuses "the pro-abortion media" of covering up the truth that abortion is "the unlimited right to the private use of lethal force against innocent human beings." He angrily writes, "We must never lose sight of the fact that the abortion regime of *Roe* was arrogantly imposed by the Court... that is what is meant by an act of raw judicial power."

In an apocalyptic finale, Neuhaus declares, "The cleavage in our society over abortion and related questions touching on respect for human life is deep and ominous, comparable only to the cleavage over slavery." The exercise of the right to reproductive freedom is, in Neuhaus's tortured logic, "a nightmare" that will one day end.

In a final appeal to unreason and meanness Neuhaus thunders, "The culture of death commands a formidable array of powerful institutions. With few exceptions, it has in its service the establishment media, the universities, the foundations, the corporate elites, the labor unions, the oldline churches, and, of course, the courts. More than any other question in public dispute, abortion on demand is the core commitment of the American establishment."

For all of his reputed sophistication and erudition, Neuhaus displays a profound ignorance of American constitutional law, judicial supremacy and the separation of powers, and chooses to overlook the enormous influence of the anti-choice lobby.

Neuhaus also sees the population issue through the narrow lens of his culture of death theories. He wrote, "[Population control is ideology disguised as science. There is no scientific measure of 'over-population,' but there is a powerful and ideologically driven dread of lesser breeds that threaten our advantaged way of life and, presumably, the planetary balance."[17]

What Kind of Catholic Church?

Neuhaus, like many converts to Catholicism, or to any religion for that matter, seems to have a decided preference for a particular view of the Church. And, what is more, any other view — even if held by life long members — is suspect. Neuhaus delights in ridiculing liberal or progressive Catholics, chiding them on their incapacity for holding fast to that which the official Church has unerringly proclaimed as truth.

Neuhaus repeatedly criticizes progressive Catholics like Sister Maureen Fiedler and the late Cardinal Joseph Bernardin, whose "Common Ground" project to bring conservative and liberal Catholics together on common issues was called "comatose" by Neuhaus.

It is significant that Neuhaus waited twenty-five years after the close of the Second Vatican Council to embrace Catholicism. He did so well into the pontificate of John Paul II, whom Neuhaus reveres.

While a newcomer to the faith, he sneers at progressive Catholics who have spent their lives working for a different kind of church. About the distinguished scholar Richard McBrien, Neuhaus wrote in December 1990, "Sorrow is in order for the immutable rebel who must now seek out the company even of the declared enemies of the church in order to vent their bitterness about a vision of Catholicism that was not to be." He dismisses resigned priests as "dysfunctional men who resigned the priesthood in order to marry or who wrecked their ministries on the rock of alcoholism or drugs." About progressive Catholics as a group, he observed sourly, "Off on the sidelines, in the ruins of a failed revolution, surrounded by a few aging and dispirited comrades, superannuated leaders poutingly protest." And he called the lively *National Catholic Reporter* "a kind of *National Enquirer* of American Catholicism."

Separation of Church and State

Two positions central to the Neuhaus argument are the following: "Because politics is a function of culture and at the heart of culture is morality and at the heart of morality is religion, there is a necessary and unavoidable interaction between politics and religion."[18] And, "The separation of church and state means the separation of the law from common decency."[19]

Having denounced the central American contribution to political culture—the principle of separation of church and state—Neuhaus is free to indulge the most lavish and absurd propositions.

This leads inexorably to Neuhaus's primary politico-religious cause: the erection of a grand alliance between evangelical Protestants and conservative Catholics, based on supposedly shared cultural assumptions and politically similar stances.

— Al Menendez

Endnotes

1. *First Things,* November 1997, p. 67; 2. Ibid., p. 74; 3. Ibid., p. 81; 4. Ibid., p. 74; 5. Ibid., p. 74; 6. J. Bottum, ed., *The Best of the Public Square* (New York: Institute on Religion and Public Life), 1997, p. 137; 7. *First Things, op. cit.,* p. 79; 8. Ibid., p.68; 9. *First Things,* December 1997, p. 70; 10. *First Things,* November 1997, p. 68; 11. J. Bottum, *op. cit.,* p. 18; 12. Ibid., pp. 23-24; 13. Ibid., p. 25; 14. Ibid., p. 26; 15. Ibid., p. 91; 16. Ibid., pp. 52-53. Neuhaus elaborated on this charge in an address entitled, "The Pfefferian Inversion," at a Williamsburg Charter Foundation conference in April of 1988. Pfeffer was invited to attend the conference only after intervention by ARL's Edd Doerr but was not invited to speak. Doerr, paraphrasing Shylock's speech in *The Merchant of Venice,* publicly responded to Neuhaus, intimating that he was scapegoating Pfeffer because he was Jewish. 17. Ibid., p. 29; 18. Ibid., p. 143; 19. Ibid., p. 154.

Vouchers and "White Flight"

A nationwide voucher program would further the already increasing racial separation in education, especially in the rural South. The disturbing finding is based on 1990 census data, which indicate that in dozens of Southern counties a majority, or nearly a majority, of white students attend private schools, while almost all black children attend public schools. In addition, the overwhelming majority of the public school student body is African-American. Finally, in these counties very few black children are welcome in the private academies, many of which were established since 1970 for the express purpose of avoiding racial integration in education.

In Wilkinson County, Mississippi, more than 95% of the public-school students are black, while 86% of white students attend private schools. Sixteen counties in the Deep South exhibit this phenomenon. All are rural and poor. The per capita income averages less than half of the national average of $14,000. Since private school attendance in most parts of the country is highly correlated with above average family and per capita income, the fact of high private school enrollment of many low income whites, especially in counties where an overwhelming majority of public school students are black, is highly suggestive of white flight to avoid integration.

This phenomenon also includes Orleans Parish (County), Louisiana (the city of New Orleans), where 86% of public school students are black, but where 65% of whites attend private schools. Orleans has a much higher per capita income ($11,372.00) than the rural white flight counties, but the pattern of racial segregation in education is similar. Because of New Orleans' historic Catholic orientation and its French Creole cultural base, a considerable number of blacks are Catholics who prefer private schools. Nearly half of the private school enrollment in Orleans Parish is black, even though 87% of black children attend public schools. New Orleans is predominantly black.

Another group of fourteen counties substantiates this pattern. In these counties between 40% and 50% of white students are enrolled in private schools. The vast majority of public school students are black. And the counties are largely rural and poor. In this second tier of counties, 44% of white children attend private schools, at least partially because 73.2% of public school students are black. One city, Richmond, Virginia, appears in this grouping. In Richmond, 49% of white children attend private schools, largely because the black percentage of the total public school population is nearly 86%.

There is a strong statistical correlation between the percentage of black students in public schools and that of white students who attend private schools in these white flight counties. For every one point increase in the black percentage of public school enrollment, there is a two point increase in the percentage of white students attending private schools.

White flight is evident in eight counties (seven of them in Mississippi) which have more than one school district. Those public school districts which are the most heavily black invariably have the highest percentage of white pupils who opt for private education. In Orangeburg County, South Carolina, for example, the 79% black district 2 has 52% of white children in private schools; the 40% black district 4 has only 9% of white children choosing private schools. In Yazoo County, Mississippi, the increase in the black percentage from 60% in one district to 91% in the other results in a corresponding increase in white flight to private schools from 39% of whites to 77% of whites.

There are also 31 additional Southern counties where between 20% and 40% of white children attend private schools. In all of these counties, a majority of public school students are African-American. These counties include such cities as Macon, Savannah, Baton Rouge, and Charleston (SC).

It should be stressed that in all 61 of these Southern white flight counties, a much higher percentage of the student population in public schools is African-American than is the percentage of black students in private schools. In all 61 counties, the majority of the public school population is African-American; in not one county is the majority of the private school population African-American. In only 18 counties are more than 10% of private school students black. In Baker County, Georgia, Sharkey County, Mississippi, and Wilkinson County, Mississippi, there are no blacks attending private schools. In Perry County, Alabama, less than 1 % of the private school enrollment is black. In 31 of these 61 counties (about half), less than 5% of the private school enrollment is black.

This situation has gone on right under our noses for two decades. It represents one aspect of the resegregation of American education, a return to the separate but unequal educational opportunities so long a part of the US educational scene.

Advocates of vouchers, who claim that such schemes will only permit parents to choose better or more diverse educational opportunities for their children, should realize that this kind of "choice" may only lead to sharper racial divisions in American education.

Should Tax Dollars Subsidize Bigotry?

Should public funds be used, through vouchers or other means, to support schools where material such as the following is routinely taught in history and literature classes?

• The Catholic Church "enslaves man," is a "wicked, corrupted system which insured the people's intellectual and spiritual ignorance by depriving them of God's infallible word and destroyed more Bibles than the pagan emperors." Catholic teachings and practices are continually labeled "blasphemous" and "pagan," and the contributions of Catholics to U.S. and European history are downplayed, ignored or distorted.

• The Episcopal Church, which has given our country the largest number of Presidents and two-thirds of the signers of the Declaration of Independence, is repeatedly ridiculed. It and its sister, the Church of England, are "dead in ritualism and rationalism," "serve mainly a ceremonial function," lost their "scriptural authority," and "without constitutional safeguard would destroy evangelical churches." "Such religion," we are told, "had little effect upon upper-class morality and left the masses little better than barbarians."

• Quakers are "unbiblical" and "dangerous to biblical Christianity."

• Religious liberalism is "only a modern form of the paganism of Christ's day." Theological liberalism "has steadily undermined the nation's religious inheritance," "attempts to accommodate Christianity to a godless modern view of the world," and "deliberately elevates man's mind over God's."

• The Greek Orthodox Church "claims to teach correct doctrine but many of her beliefs are contrary to Scripture."

• The Mormon Church is a "cult." The proliferation of many religions in a nation which cherishes religious freedom is not seen as a positive good. "All these false versions of true religion and worship contribute to the growing theological anarchy of a nation whose people do merely what seems right in their own eyes," says a 1991 American literature text published by Bob Jones University Press.

• Secular humanism is "a substitute religion, glorifying the creation rather than the Creator... like Satan's deception of Eve, secular humanism has tempted modern man with the false promise of becoming like God," trumpets the same text.

Most of America's major writers are treated with contempt. A newly published American literature text asserts that, "Having rebelled against Christianity and its promise of heaven or hell, writers lived only for the fleeting moment." Poet Robert Frost "rejected God's word as the standard for human life." Carl Sandburg's poems "served as vehicles for his socialistic views" and "his moral values and view of man are not those of the Word of God." H.L. Mencken "openly repudiated the nation's inherited system of values and beliefs." Emily Dickinson "clearly rejected traditional Christianity."

The above views are taught as history and literature in a series of textbooks published by Bob Jones University Press in Greenville, SC, the largest publisher of textbooks used in fundamentalist Christian schools, the fastest growing sector of American private education.

American and British writers are not judged on merit or from an accepted standard of universal interpretation. Instead, their religious views are dissected, and students are warned that literary craftspeople represent apostasy, pessimism, and despair. No appreciation is expressed for the literary life or the life of the mind.

Religious bias permeates the presentation of history. For example, the Bob Jones University textbook on world history has not followed the lead recommended by most Christian churches, including the Vatican, regarding the imputation of deicide to the Jewish people. This text still teaches the following: "The Jewish religious leaders, whose blindness and hypocrisy Jesus had denounced, sought to put Him to death. They brought Christ before the Roman governor Pontius Pilate, charging that Christ had disrupted the state.... Although Pilate found no fault in Jesus, he desired to maintain the peace. Giving in to the Jewish demands, he sentenced Jesus to death by crucifixion."

God is said to have used the Renaissance and the printing press to weaken Catholicism and then "used Luther to break Rome's hold by establishing biblical authority... and replacing Rome's pagan system of works." God caused the Reformation, the defeat of the Spanish Armada, and "refused to answer the prayers" of Spain's king, according to the widely used history text.

Here are some more unique views of history found in these fundamentalist textbooks:

• The French and Indian wars "were in part an effort to preserve biblical Protestantism in America."

• One reason for the Civil War was the South's desire to preserve its Protestant identity. (In fact, both North and South were predominantly Protestant, and Jefferson Davis's Cabinet included Catholics and Jews, unlike that of Lincoln.)

• Those who drafted the Constitution were "men of Christian principle, products of Puritanism, who accepted biblical principles ... as the basis for human law." Furthermore, "The hand of God was obvious in the adoption, ratification and support of the Constitution."

• The Louisiana Purchase "resulted more from God's providence than from Jefferson's ingenuity."

• Evolution, it is said, is "unsupported by scientific law or investigation.... The main selling point for evolution is not that it has abundant support, but that it explains the universe without referring to God, and so it relieves man of any responsibility to his Creator." The Scopes trial of 1925 is dismissed as "a mockery of those who believed that the Bible was the Word of God." Those who accept Darwin's explanations are called "sinful men [who] demonstrated their rebellion against God and His Word."

• The Puritans and their society are seen as models to be emulated. "They were able to establish a civil society that was governed by Bible-believing Christians." Their repression of dissenters is whitewashed as understandable in a society "that emphasized morality and respected the Bible." The Puritan colonies attracted pure Christians while Roger Williams' Rhode Island experiment in freedom "encouraged many religious malcontents to settle there."

• Most early immigrants to the U.S. were "hardworking and thrifty Protestants" but Catholic immigrants soon "poured in" and "aroused fear and resentment among Protestants and others who feared the potential political power of the Roman church." Immigrants "aggravated labor unrest."

• Black Americans are treated with relative indifference and are always referred to as Negroes, even in 1991 editions. Students are reminded that "the Bible does not specifically condemn slavery." The treatment of Dr. Martin Luther King, Jr. is far from friendly. "Because he couched his speeches in peaceful terminology, he gained a reputation as a man of peace; he was even awarded the Nobel Peace Prize in 1964. . . . King had become a symbol of civil rights; his death brought violence and destruction in several parts of the country. Like Kennedy, he was viewed by many as a martyr for human rights; his increasing shift to the left, especially in the last year of his life, was soon forgotten."

• Native Americans are treated with disdain. "The concept of sin was foreign to the Indian culture; discipline was intended to teach children to survive rather than to make them moral. This amoral philosophy was often discouraging to Christian missionaries, who found it difficult to teach Indians the difference between right and wrong. . . . The Indian culture typified heathen civilization—lost in darkness without the light of the gospel."

• The United Nations is "unbiblical."

• Imperialism is seen as a positive good because it was "a means by which the gospel was spread to the far corners of the globe."

• President Franklin D. Roosevelt was a failure. His programs "did more harm than good."

• The Peace Corps is "less than successful."

• Many of Senator Joseph McCarthy's "accusations were true" but "the liberal media soon discredited him."

• The Warren Court "attempted to remold society."

• Labor unions "create turmoil," and fail "to govern the greed of their members." Furthermore, "most of the major labor strikes in our history have been immoral."

If sectarian special interests, ultraconservative critics of public education (and sometimes even of the very idea of public education itself), and their political allies succeed in getting Congress and/or state legislatures to create voucher plans for supporting nonpublic schools, and if a Supreme Court dominated by Reagan and Bush appointees upholds such programs, American taxpayers will find themselves supporting the kinds of indoctrination and bigotry cited above.

Public subsidization of nonpublic schools using such textbooks would not only offend most taxpayers, but it would also stunt the education of hundreds of thousands of children and increase social and interfaith tensions. While the fundamentalist schools using these books might claim to be open to children of all faiths, few if any parents are likely to enroll their children in a school which systematically denigrates all faiths and world views other than Protestant fundamentalism. Nor would teachers of nonfundamentalist persuasions be likely to be hired by or comfortable teaching in such schools.

It is bad enough that fundamentalist schools offer such bigoted, slanted curricula to impressionable students, which is their legal right, but tax support for such institutions would add substantial injury to insult.

— *Al Menendez*

'Should Tax Dollars Subsidize Bigotry?'

The books analyzed are the following:

American Literature for Christian Schools, Book 1, {Early American literature and American Romanticism), by Raymond A. St. John, Greenville, SC: Bob Jones University Press, 1991; *American Literature for Christian Schools, Book 2 (Realism, Naturalism, and Modern American Literature),* by Raymond A. St John, Greenville, SC: Bob Jones University Press, 1991; *The American Republic for Christian Schools,* by Rachel C. Larson with Pamela B. Creason, Greenville, SC: Bob Jones University Press, 1988; *Beginnings of American Literature, Classics for Christians, Vol. 3,* by Jan Anderson and Laurel Hicks, Pensacola, FL: Pensacola Christian College, 1982; *Biology for Christian Schools, Book 1* (Teacher's Edition), by William S. Pinkston, Jr., Greenville, SC: Bob Jones University Press, 1991; *Biology for Christian Schools, Book 2* (Teacher's Edition), by William S. Pinkston, Jr., Greenville, SC: Bob Jones University Press, 1991; *British Literature for Christian Schools: The Early Tradition, 700-1688,* by Ronald A. Horton, Greenville, SC: Bob Jones University Press, 1980; *British Literature for Christian Schools: The Modern Tradition, 1688 to the Present,* by Ronald A Horton, Greenville, SC: Bob Jones University Press, 1982; *A Child's Story of America,* by Michael J. McHugh and Charles Morris, Arlington Heights, IL: Christian Liberty Press, 1989; *The Literature of the American People, Classics for Christians, Vol. 4,* Pensacola, FL: Pensacola Christian College, 1983; *Introduction to English Literature, Classics for Christians, Vol. .5,* by Jan Anderson and Laurel Hicks, Pensacola, FL: Pensacola Christian College, 1982; *The Literature of England, Classics for Christians, Vol. 6,* by Jan Anderson and Laurel Hicks, Pensacola, FL: Pensacola Christian College, 1983; *New World History and Geography in Christian Perspective,* by Laurel Elizabeth Hicks, Pensacola, FL Pensacola Christian College, 1982; *United States History for Christian Schools,* by Glen Chambers and Gene Fisher, Greenville, SC: Bob Jones University Press, 1982; *United States History in Christian Perspective,* by Michael R Lowman, Pensacola, FL: Pensacola Christian College, 1983; *World History for Christian Schools,* by David A. Fisher, Greenville, SC: Bob Jones University Press, 1984.

Child Care, Congress, and Sectarian Special Interests

After two years of wrangling, both houses of Congress have finally passed Child Care bills, the most far reaching social legislation since the Johnson administration. The bills (H.R. 3 and S. 5) are in conference committee to reconcile differences between the two versions.

S. 5 provides $1.75 billion in initial subsidies and increases tax credits for child care for millions of families of the middle and working classes. H.R. 3 increases Social Security Title XX funding, expands the highly regarded Head Start program, and provides grants for before and after school care. The House bill also increases tax credits.

The bills have gone through a tortuous process, with several versions having been debated in Congress. H.R. 3 enlarges existing grant funds for child care and requires states to set standards for providers. The final House bill, which received strong support from the Democratic leadership, passed 265 to 145 after members rejected a substitute bill by Rep. Charles Stenholm (D-TX) and Rep. Clay Shaw (R-FL). Their bill would have provided for less money, contained no requirements for standards, and offered nothing for "latchkey children."

The question now is the response of the Bush administration. The President has threatened to veto the bill because he does not like the cost or the provisions for latchkey children or the requirement for state standards. Bush and the Republicans consider this to be too much expansion of government involvement in what they feel should essentially be private. This was President Nixon's rationale for vetoing a more modest bill in 1971. Bush has endorsed the concept of federal assistance for child care but would prefer to do it indirectly through tax credits.

Most contentious is the church-state issue. Both final bills allow parents to use grant funds for child care provided by churches. After considerable wrangling in the House and Senate, the final versions bar federal funding for sectarian activities, except for care provided by a relative or paid for by voucher, which states would be required to offer if a parent requested one. The bill prohibits discrimination on the basis of religion in facilities which receive more than 80% of their funds from tax sources, although sectarian organizations could require that employees adhere to religious "tenets and teachings."

Facilities receiving less than 80% public funding could still give preference in hiring and admissions for nonpublicly funded slots to participating members of the religious organization. The bill also stipulates that such requirements would not supersede state laws regarding public funding for religious institutions.

But this is doubletalk. In the initial debates, Rep. Pat Williams (D-MT and a Catholic) offered an amendment to bar all funds for religious-based child care except where a separate governing board oversees the program. "Is religion bad? No. Should the state pay for it? No," said Williams. However, he was overwhelmingly rejected by his colleagues on the House Education and Labor Committee. A compromise amendment by Jim Jontz (D-IN), passed by voice vote, stipulated that no provider receiving money "shall engage in any sectarian activity, including sectarian worship and instruction." Tom Tauke (R-IA) said publicly, "There is the fundamental problem with the assumption that federal money can flow directly into a church." Still, intense pressure brought by religious care organizations and spearheaded by the U.S. Catholic Conference, resulted in the final outcome. An estimated 30%-40% of all child care providers are church-based or church-related, though not all engage in sectarian instruction or activities.

H.R. 3 prohibits use of financial assistance provided under the act "for any sectarian purpose or activity, including sectarian worship and instruction," except for care purchased by parents with a federal financed voucher and care provided by a relative. It prohibits expenditure of federal funds under the act "in a manner inconsistent with the Constitution," allows sectarian organizations to require that employees adhere to the religious tenets and teaching of such organization, generally prohibits discrimination in hiring on the basis of religion except that preference may be given to a person already participating on a regular basis in other activities of the church. It prohibits discrimination against children on the basis of religion, except that preference in admissions for slots not publicly funded may be granted to children whose family members participate on a regular basis in other activities of the organization. Notwithstanding the above provisions, H.R. 3 prohibits discrimination in hiring or admissions in any child-care program whose operating budget is 80% or more funded with public money and stipulates that none of the above requirements is intended to modify or supersede any provision of a state constitution or state law prohibiting the use of public funds in or by sectarian institutions.

The bill requires school districts to provide for the inclusion of children who attend private pre-school or elementary and secondary schools in the same manner as services provided to such children under the Chapter 1 program. This would seem to be an attempt to circumvent the Supreme Court decision in *Aguilar v. Felton,* which barred tax-paid teachers from serving in sectarian schools.

The best guess is that Bush will veto the bill, an example of a President doing the right thing for the wrong reasons. Bush and the Republicans, however, favor allowing church groups to participate in the programs and still teach religion. *Congressional Quarterly* reported that Bush feels the House version is still not strong enough in favor of religious group involvement. House Republican Whip Newt Gingrich accused Democrats of being anti-religious because of their objections to religious group involvement.

One valiant attempt to bar use of federal funds for sectarian worship or instruction and to prohibit religious discrimination in hiring child care workers by sectarian institutions that receive federal funds was proposed by Rep. Don Edwards (D-CA), but the House rejected it 297 to 125.

This defeat for church-state separation was depressing. An analysis of the vote indicates some significant partisan regional and religious differences. Northern Democrats favored the Edwards amendment by 57% but Southern Democrats by only 20%. Republicans gave only 6% support. Support among all Democrats, North and South, was 45%.

Only California and New York delegations narrowly favored Edwards. These states are traditionally strongholds of church-state separation and members from those states have voted against school prayer amendments and other sectarian efforts in the past. Delegates from Rhode Island (both Republicans), Alaska (also a Republican), and Oregon also favored Edwards.

There were 18 states where every House member opposed Edwards. Here the influence of Evangelical and Protestant churches can be seen since many Southern states voted overwhelmingly against Edwards. This includes members from Alabama, Arkansas, Delaware, Kentucky, Louisiana, Mississippi, North Carolina, South Carolina, and West Virginia. Mormon-dominated Utah, Wyoming, and Idaho also unanimously opposed Edwards, as did all members from Kansas, Nevada, New Hampshire, North Dakota, South Dakota, and Vermont.

Religious differences over Edwards are among the most significant in many years. To begin with, the four religiously non-affiliated members of Congress (all Democrats) voted in favor of the anti-discrimination amendment. So did two-thirds of Jews, but only 27% of Protestants and 24% of Catholics.

It was among Democrats that cultural and religious divisions were most intense. Here 76% of Jewish Democrats favored Edwards, showing their historic concern for church-state separation. Protestant Democrats were 46% in favor, and among Protestants the main difference was North and West vs. South. Only about 20% of Southern Democrat Protestants favored the proposal but a majority of Northern Democrat Protestants were supportive. Edwards was strongly supported by congressional Black Caucus members. Most of these are Protestant, but two, Clay (MO) and Rangel (NY), are Catholic.

Unitarians voted 4-3 for Edwards. Unitarian Democrats were 4-1 in favor, but both Unitarian Republicans voted no. Mormons, probably the most conservative religious group in Congress, voted 7-1 against Edwards. All six Mormon Republicans opposed it. Only one Mormon, Mo Udall (D-AZ) voted for it.

Catholic Democrats, who in the past opposed school prayer amendments and were luke-warm on Equal Access and other church-state compromises, this time were apparently influenced by the U.S. Catholic Conference. Catholic Democrats voted 54-25 against Edwards, despite the fact that two Catholic Democrats, Pat Williams (MT) and George Miller (CA) were leaders in the fight for Edwards. Catholic Democrats in states like Illinois, Ohio, Indiana, Pennsylvania, New Jersey and Massachusetts defected from their normal liberal positions in large numbers on this vote. Joseph Kennedy (D-MA), son of Robert Kennedy, and the occupant of President John F. Kennedy's old congressional seat, voted yes, following the Kennedy tradition of support for church-state separation.

Another significant aspect of the vote is the near-total Republican opposition. Only 11 of 171 Republicans voted for it. While 8% of Catholic Republicans and 6% of Protestant Republicans favored it, none of the Jewish Republicans did so. Even Bill Green of Manhattan, a Jewish Republican liberal who usually favors separation, voted no. Two Catholic Republicans who did vote yes were Claudine Schneider (RI, now running for the U.S. Senate) and Connie Morrella (MD), who represents the district where ARL's headquarters is located. Both women can be counted on to vote for separation, including on abortion rights. Not one Southern Republican voted for Edwards, showing again that the South is a bastion of religious conformity and conservatism since most Southern Democrats also voted no.

There was an attempt by Rep. Price (NC), to "permit" rather than require states to apply child care vouchers to church-related schools. It was rejected 243-182, but attracted some Southern Democrats who wanted to vote for a moderate measure. It would not have solved the problem of religious discrimination or the flow of public funds to sectarian education, as Edwards would have.

The fact that Catholic members of Congress were the least likely to favor Edwards is significant. This leads us to look at the role of the U.S. Catholic Conference in this affair.

For the first time since the 1978 tuition tax credit vote, Catholic members have been more conservative and less supportive of church-state separation than Protestants. This is the first time they have been closely in sync with the U.S. Catholic Conference (USCC) on a church-state issue.

Extensive interviews with officials of religious and educational organizations in Washington have made it clear that the USCC, the lobbying arm of the Catholic bishops, is "the number one reason we have such a bad bill." The USCC was the most influential player in pressuring Congress to approve vouchers and grants for church-related day care. They also "shaped the phraseology" and advanced the arguments that weakened the church-state argument. The USCC saw the child care bill as a "wedge to lead eventually to substantial aid to church-related schools." A *Congressional Quarterly* reporter said the USCC "cut a deal but reneged when they initially agreed to accept language limiting vouchers but then demanded a change" months later.

The USCC position was based on three premises: watered-down child care church-state provisions are a step toward tax aid for parochial schools, Catholic schools are declining at a high rate again and everything must be done to stop their decline, and government funding will enable Catholic parishes to expand their now-limited child care programs.

An important Protestant lobbyist labeled the USCC's actions as "tremendously influential" and based solely on "institutional self-interest." He said the bishops were interested in child care only as a pawn in a larger strategy aimed at reversal of U. S. policy against aiding parochial schools. He said bluntly that the USCC "called the shots" in shaping the final legislation that emerged. In his view the USCC institutionalists triumphed over the peace and justice sector, a group which would not have jeopardized good relationships with other religious groups solely to win a controversial decision. He and other critics suggested that USCC would encourage more Catholic parishes to participate in child care if and when the money is forthcoming.

Historic Catholic officialdom's approach to church-state relations continues to favor maximum cooperation with state authorities and public funding.

A nagging problem in researching the child care issues is the lack of good data. According to *Who Cares for America's Children* (National Academy of Sciences, 1990), there are 28.5 million children under 13 whose mothers are in the labor force, including 6.6 million under 3. This reflects rising living costs, declining conditions of the middle class since 1974, high divorce rates, and the number of households headed by women.

Today 56% of all mothers with children under 6 work outside the home, compared to 30% in 1970. (According to the Census Bureau, Americans now work 20% more hours and have 32% fewer hours of leisure time than in 1970.)

In 1988 an estimated five million children were being cared for in licensed and unlicensed (only 27 states require licensing) day care programs. The National Association for the Education of Young Children reported in 1986 that 2.1 million children were being cared for in 62,989 center-based facilities. (A National Academy of Sciences survey found 2,568,000 children in 64,078 facilities.) There are also school-based and Head Start programs, for which reliable data are not available.

The most extensive data—such as it is—available on church-based child care comes from the National Council of Churches' Child Day Care Project. In 1982 detailed questionnaires were mailed to 87,562 parishes representing 15 communions within the NCC, which itself represents 41 million Christians belonging to the mainline Protestant, Eastern Orthodox, and Anglican traditions. Almost 30% of the parishes responded. A study entitled *When Churches Mind the Children,* by Eileen Lindner, Mary Mattis and Jane Rogers, was published in 1983.

According to this study, about 35% of the responding parishes reported that some day care programs were available in their church. Denominationally, the range was from 62% of American Lutheran parishes to less than 1% of black Methodist ones.

In many respects, the authors say, churches are ideally suited for child care. "Many parishes are well equipped to provide facilities for child care." There is "an important financial advantage," the tax-exempt status. "This factor facilitates the development of child care and other community service programs within churches. First, child care programs can simply be operated under the churches' non-profit articles of incorporation, eliminating the need to establish a new corporation. Second, costs are lower because no new taxes are paid, yet churches receive city services: fire and police protection, garbage disposal, and so forth."

There are two basic kinds of programs—*church operated centers* and *independently-operated centers located on church property.* Of the total, 56% are church-operated and 44% are independently operated. (90% of the centers are also nonprofit.)

The key questions—constitutionally speaking—relate to the degree of religiousness or pervasiveness of sectarianism that may exist in these programs. Some significant differences emerge between church-operated and independently-operated programs. Religious belief is "very important" in staff selection in 28% of church-operated centers but only in 6% of the independents. Conversely, religious beliefs are not considered important in staff selection in 61% of independents but only in 22% of church-operated centers. The local parish board is formally involved in setting policy in 41% of church-operated centers but ony in 10% of independents. The church is also far more likely to subsidize building space, utilities, and repairs in church-operated centers and to provide scholarships for low-income families in church-operated centers than in the independents.

The religious factor is much greater, then, in child care centers operated by churches. There is no reason to believe that this would not also be true for Evangelical and Roman Catholic-based centers.

The authors of the NCC study suggest that up to 1,309,000 children participated in church-related or sponsored child care programs in 1982. This figure has surely increased by 1990.

An increasingly rancorous congressional conference committee has made little progress toward a compromise likely to withstand presidential veto. According to one educational official, there is even a possibility that no bill will reach the House and Senate for final approval before the congressional elections.

Still, one has to assume that proponents, the child care lobby and certain church groups, will lobby furiously for some kind of bill, any kind of bill.

Civil libertarians and public education interests have all but agreed to ask for a presidential veto of any bill that emerges, because of the deplorable language in both versions. It is certain that any bill will allow religious institutions to receive public funds and still impose religious standards in hiring and enrollment. This discrimination, coupled with the voucher language and the allowance for religious instruction and worship, will render any bill constitutionally infirm.

One official has warned that these bills "posit a new and unprecedented partnership between the federal government and sectarian institutions, one that goes beyond any relationship that has existed to date." She also stressed the dangers to religious freedom and parental choice: "Many parents will lose what choice they now have. When they find that a child-care program in their neighborhood is teaching a religion they cannot support, they will then have two choices: Either they will have to take their children out of the neighborhood program (or find they can't enroll them there) because the provider is indoctrinating their children in a religious tradition not their own, and next be forced to look for another program (which may or may not exist); or reluctantly send or continue to send their children to this sectarian, government supported, child care center, all the time worrying about their children being indoctrinated and their religion undermined.

"What I am stressing is that government support of sectarian institutions' provision of sectarian child care will *limit,* not expand, parental choice. The government has an obligation to help parents by supporting child care programs that meet their needs. It does not have the obligation, nor should it, to support their religious beliefs."

President Bush, meanwhile, has articulated the typical conservative view that almost any large scale child care legislation is too costly and involves an undesirable expanded role for the federal government in matters that are best handled by state and local interests or by families themselves. In a letter to Republican House members, White House Chief of Staff Sununu reiterated the Administration's view that "a tax credit would be fairer, more efficient, more easily administered, and would provide greater assurance that all needy families will benefit." This is doubtful. The *Washington Post* reported on June 24 that the IRS has said that 40% of those said to be eligible for the earned income credit are in fact *not eligible* under existing regulations.

Sununu also emphasized Bush's support for the sectarian lobbies. "We would view school-based care as an acceptable purpose for which states might use grant funds, *provided that sectarian providers be allowed to compete and participate on an equal basis.*"

This controversy shows the selfishness and parochialism endemic to sectarian special interests. As usual, the people most in need will suffer the most. In many respects, it's the ESEA all over again. The future of a democratic, pluralistic culture is threatened when sectarian interests emerge triumphant.

— *Al Menendez*

The Williamsburg Charter: Fatally Flawed

Too few Americans, unfortunately, understand and appreciate our constitutional heritage of religious liberty. Many people were heartened when the Williamsburg Charter Foundation, founded in late 1986, announced that it was developing a "charter" to "forge a new consensus on the place of religion in public life," and "to celebrate the genius and wisdom of the First Amendment Religious Clauses, to reaffirm religious liberty for citizens of all faiths, to chart the principles and pitfalls of the relationship of religion and public life, to help sustain a constructive understanding of these issues in our time."

After more than a year of drafting and redrafting, the Williamsburg Charter has been completed and is to be signed with great fanfare in Williamsburg, Virginia, on June 25. Among the diverse group of signers are Chief Justice William Rehnquist, former presidents Ford and Carter, several conservative members of Congress, and a number of religious, civic, and business leaders. Absent from the charter are the names of the most prominent church-state separationists.

While the charter, which runs to over 6,000 words, contains some lofty ideas with which nearly everyone could agree, it is also excessively vague and ambiguous, and, upon close examination, is seen to contain some not too subtle attacks on the constitutional principle of separation of church and state and its defenders. This is not surprising, since the principal drafters included a disproportionately large number of people known to be unfriendly to church-state separation, and the leading experts on separation seem to have been excluded

ARL president John M. Swomley and ARL executive director Edd Doerr have analyzed the charter carefully and concur that it is seriously flawed.

It lacks a clear endorsement of the constitutional principle of separation of church and state. The phrase itself was only inserted in the charter at the last minute at the insistence of Swomley, Doerr, and other separationists, and then only rather clumsily and half-heartedly near the end. Indeed, the charter implies that strict separationists are "extremists." (The Foundation's attitude was revealed in an opinion poll it released in February: one question asked, do you think "the ACLU files too many lawsuits regarding religion?" which is analogous to asking if the fire department responds to too many alarms.)

The charter seems to endorse the "moral majoritarian" view that "constitutional jurisprudence has tended... to move toward a *de facto* semi-establishment of a wholly secular understanding of the origin, nature, and destiny of humankind and of the American nation." It then makes the astonishing claim that some undefined "secularist" movement now treats all Christians the way Protestants treated Catholics during the nineteenth century. No evidence for this claim is presented

The charter does not mention public education except for a single reference to "state-supported education," a buzzword used almost exclusively by opponents of public education and advocates of tax support for sectarian private education It ducks the question of tax aid to religious institutions by using the word "preferment," thus shifting the church-state debate away from government aid to church schools, hospitals, charities, and social services, as if such aid had nothing to do with religious liberty.

It gives equal attention to, and therefore validates, government accommodation to religion and church-state separation as though the First Amendment and Supreme Court rulings are up for grabs.

The charter intimates that "naturalistic philosophies" are somehow unfriendly to religious liberty, when in fact persons holding "naturalistic philosophies" have long been the strongest advocates of religious liberty and freedom of conscience. It ignores the fact that some traditional religious forces have been and in some cases still are in varying degrees hostile to religious liberty and church-state separation. It ignores the fact that the Hindu-Muslim riots in India, the Catholic-Protestant mess in Northern Ireland, the Turk-Armenian conflict, anti-Jewish pogroms, and European religious wars did not involve "secularists."

The vaunted Williamsburg Charter, then, is a seriously flawed document. Its signing by a group of largely well meaning but naïve organizational leaders, though not by very many church-state separationists, could well be used as a propaganda tool by people and groups dedicated to undermining separation.

In addition to the charter, the Williamsburg Charter Foundation sponsored a conference in mid-April at the University of Virginia, which revealed a lot about the Foundation's attitudes. While a few of the speakers (Robert S. Alley, William Lee Miller, Samuel Rabinove) supported church-state separation, most of the speakers were either not on point or were hostile to separation.

The first speaker, Canadian political science professor Charles Taylor, showed little understanding of the First Amendment and was critical of the U.S. institution of judicial review. (ARL's Doerr responded that the Canadian Supreme Court has now adopted the principle of judicial review.) Harvard government professor Michael Sandel said that a Supreme Court concerned to avoid social discord" would have decided the 1960s prayer cases differently.

Federal judge John T. Noonan avoided discussing church-state cases, while Emory University law professor Harold Berman showed a disturbing unfamiliarity with public education. Theologian George Weigel took the line of the Catholic bishops and moral majoritarians that since 1947 the Supreme Court has promoted "secularism." Weigel also labelled sectarian schools "public," a propaganda gimmick used to promote tax aid for parochial schools.

Herbert Titus, president of Pat Robertson's CBN University, attacked public education as "anti-Christian" and called for ending government support for schools, research, and the arts.

By far the least civil speaker was theologian Richard John Neuhaus, one of the charter's drafters, who attacked church-state separation, the Supreme Court's rulings against parochiaid, freedom of conscience on abortion, and ARL adviser Leo Pfeffer, the country's most distinguished church-state expert. He echoed the Falwell-Bork view that "moral majorities" should have the right to override constitutional limits on government action.

ARL's Swomley, Doerr, Anne Lindsay, and Edward Ericson attended the University of Virginia conference, and Doerr on several occasions sought to influence the development of the charter, but the church-state "accommodationist" influences were too strong for separationists to have much success.

Whether the Williamsburg Charter Foundation's leaders, headed by British sociologist Os Guinness, are naive about the church-state arrangement in the U.S. or whether they are knowingly working to weaken church-state separation is not clear and not important. What is important is that their well publicized efforts could have the effect of undermining separation and religious liberty. This makes it clear that Americans for Religious Liberty and other defenders of church-state separation have a great deal of work to do.

— Edd Doerr

.ARL Study Reveals Billion Dollar Parochial Subsidy

Over one billion dollars in state and federal tax aid goes annually to parochial and private elementary and secondary schools, according to a study recently completed by Americans for Religious Liberty executive director Edd Doerr. Most people think that little tax aid goes to nonpublic schools because most parochiaid proposals are defeated in the legislative process, parochiaid has lost in every statewide referendum since 1967, and the Supreme Court ruled unconstitutional in the 1970s all major parochiaid plans to come before it—the "purchase of services" from parochial schools, tuition reimbursement grants and tax credits, parochial teacher salary supplements, etc.

However, the Supreme Court has allowed states to provide such "minor and peripheral" forms of parochiaid as bus transportation, textbook "loans," payments for testing and recordkeeping, and certain diagnostic, remedial, and "auxiliary" services. And federal aid for parochial schools, provided since 1965, has yet to have its day before the Supreme Court.

Although the annual *Digest of Educational Statistics* produced by the U.S. Department of Education indicates that no federal or state tax dollars go to support sectarian and other private schools, other surveys have shown that 32 states provide transportation services for nonpublic schools (often under more generous terms than to public schools), that 25 states provide textbook "loans" ("loaning" textbooks for several years is analogous to "lending" someone a stick of gum; it's not really intended to be repaid), that eight states provide various "auxiliary" services, and that nonpublic schools receive federal aid in all states.

Of the five million students in nonpublic schools, 3.1 million are in states which provide full transportation services for their schools. Since 57% of public school students are transported at an average cost of $176 per year (all figures are for the 1980-81 school year, the latest for which data are available), then nonpublic school transportation costs taxpayers at least $311 million annually. However, nonpublic enrollments are more scattered than those of public schools and their attendance areas usually do not coincide with those of public schools, so nonpublic school transportation costs more—44% more in New Jersey, 63% more in New York, and 156% more in the Washington metropolitan area. (In one extreme case in upstate New York, two children are transported to a Christian day school well outside their public school district at an annual cost of almost $10,000 for the pair). Averaging these differentials, ARL estimates $585 million as the probable annual cost to taxpayers of nonpublic school transportation, in the "full service" states.

In addition, partial transportation service in nine other states costs, by conservative estimate, another $22.5 million.

In 25 states textbooks are "loaned" to nonpublic schools enrolling 2.8 million students, at an annual cost of $42.5 million, based on the New York-New Jersey average of about $15 per student per year.

Seven states provide nonpublic schools with about $20.6 million for such "state mandated" services as testing and recordkeeping. Extensive "auxiliary" services, such as diagnostic and remedial programs, are provided by Ohio, Pennsylvania, New Jersey, and New York at an annual cost of about $138 million. Minnesota funnels $3 million per year to nonpublic schools through tuition tax deductions (a plan upheld by the Supreme Court in June ostensibly because public schools also received an insignificant amount of benefit). Until the program was ruled unconstitutional recently, Grand Rapids, Michigan, channeled $5 million per year to nonpublic schools by placing tax-paid teachers in them.

Federal aid to parochial and private schools, at an average of $38 per student (the average reported for New York and New Jersey) amounts to about $190 million per year. That total might be as high as $300 million if the $60 per nonpublic student estimate by some authorities is correct.

Adding these figures, we find that parochial and private schools are receiving at least one billion dollars per year in services and materials paid for out of federal, state, and local taxes. This total does not include federal and state aid for school lunches or health programs; the considerable benefits of tax deductibility of donations (or of tuition payments disguised as donations, a widespread practice known as "tuition laundering") to religious bodies operating private schools; or the benefits of local property tax exemption.

The ARL study also found that, by shifting the billion dollars in federal and state parochiaid from the public to the nonpublic school expenditure columns in the Department of Education statistics, per student nonpublic school spending for the 1980-81 school year reached $2,850 while per student public school spending was only $2,517. It may be noted in passing that the Census Bureau reports that nonpublic school families have average incomes 57 % higher than public school families.

The preceding, of course, are only the monetary costs of parochiaid. The social costs of tuition tax credits or other forms of aid would or do include public subsidy of the religious, class, academic, ideological, ethnic, gender, and other forms of selectivity and discrimination common in nonpublic schools, and the consequent division of children and adults along these lines; public subsidy of religious institutions, in violation of the constitutional right not to be taxed for religion; weakening of support for democratic public education; compulsory support for private institutions not under meaningful public control.

Chapter 2
Trends

Included in this chapter are articles and essays which describe or analyze events which gathered momentum and became trends in the church-state field, such as charter schools, the home schooling movement, and so-called "school choice." International news including the rise of Eastern Orthodoxy and Roman Catholicism as political role players in post-Communist Eastern Europe. The never-ending disputes over religious activities in public schools and the annual Christmas controversies also receive attention. These articles fall under the rubric, "signs of the times."

The Bible Goes to School

Considerable attention has been drawn to a textbook produced by the Bible Literacy Project (BLP) in Fairfax, Virginia, for use in teaching about the Bible in public high schools. *The Bible and Its Influence* (BLP Publishing, 2006, 387 pp.) is a lavishly-illustrated, three-and-a-half pound, 9 x 12 inch page size textbook that the BLP reportedly spent five years and $2 million to develop.

While Americans may be the most religious people in the industrialized world, they are also the most religiously illiterate and ignorant.

Alleviating ignorance would be a good thing. In ruling unconstitutional school- or state-sponsored or mandated devotional Bible reading in public schools in 1963 in *Abingdon v. Schempp*, the US Supreme Court noted that "It might well be said that one's education is not complete without a study of . . . the history of religion and its relationship to the advancement of civilization. . . . Nothing we have said here indicates that such study of the Bible or of religion, when presented objectively as part of a secular program of education, may not be effected consistently with the First Amendment."

As a former teacher I can say without fear of contradiction that this is is far easier said than done. There is no agreement among scholars, educators, or religious leaders as to precisely what should be taught about religion, how much, at which grade levels, whether it should be taught in social studies or language arts courses, whether mandatory or elective, and whether the instruction should be Pollyannishly bland and positive or historically accurate with warts and all. If the kids are going to learn about Dr. Martin Luther King Jr. or antebellum Quaker abolitionists, shouldn't they also learn about clergy who used the Bible to defend slavery and segregation? If the kids learn about the great cathedrals of Europe and the vast amount of religious art, music, and literature, shouldn't they also learn about the religious wars, pogroms, heresy trials, executions of Quakers in colonial Massachusetts?

The Bible and Its Influence appears at first glance to be a good-faith attempt to adhere to the requirement of both the First Amendment and the pluralistic nature of our society that teaching about religion be objective, balanced, and inclusive. The Jewish and Christian scriptures are undeniably significant, one of the most influential sets of writings in Western history, but there is more to alleviating ignorance about religion than simply learning superficially about the Bible.

To its credit the text replaces "BC" (Before Christ) and "AD" (Anno Domini) with the more neutral "BCE" (before the common era) and CE (the common era). The book also contains a comparison of the differences in the ordering of the books of the Hebrew scriptures and those of the Christian "Old Testament," and a list of the Apocrypha in the Catholic and Eastern Orthodox canons but not in the Protestant version, though the text does not attempt to explain why the orderings are different, not an unimportant matter.

Another odd omission: The copyright page indicates that "three translations of the Bible are used in the book," the King James (Protestant) version, the Jewish "Bible" (which Jews prefer to call the Scriptures), and the New Standard Revised Version produced by the National Council of Churches. There is no mention of the Catholic Bible, nor is the Catholic Church represented in the National Council.

The BLP textbook can be read with profit by students and adults of a wide religious spectrum, especially as it dwells largely on the Bible's significant influence on literature, art, rhetoric, and music.

However praiseworthy *The Bible and Its Influence* may be, it has serious shortcomings as a public school text. It does not place the Bible in historical context. It contains no hint that the "earliest" sections of the Hebrew scriptures were written after the "Babylonian captivity"; no reference to the distinction between the Yahwist and Elohist strains in the Hebrew scriptures; no discussion of the contradictions in the Bible or of which parts may be historically more reliable and which are probably myths handed down through oral tradition; virtually no reference to the evolution of Hebrew religious thought or borrowings from other religions and cultures; no attention to "Q" or other sources of the Gospels; no mention of the controversies over what Jesus said or whether things like the utterances in the Sermon on the Mount were delivered in one speech or "assembled" from various sources by the Gospel writers.

Given that all too few students are anywhere near well-grounded in ancient or world history, I must conclude that a student finishing a course using this textbook will have a distorted, truncated, simplistic view of the subject matter. The book makes no reference to the abundant biblical scholarship of the last two centuries.

The Bible does not exist in isolation. The educated person must see how the Bible developed, how the official canon came to be developed, what was going on with real people in the real world during biblical times and during the long centuries after Christianity became the official religion of the Roman Empire, how Christianity won out over its competitors and how it borrowed from them, and what were the effects of the revival of ancient learning transmitted to Europe through Spain by the Arabs, the breakup of the Empire, the Crusades, the Inquisition, the Reformation, the Counter-Reformation, the rise of nation states, colonialism, anti-Semitism, religious wars, the development of religious toleration and freedom and church-state separation.

If public schools cannot present a comprehensive, balanced, fair, inclusive picture of religion in all its complexity, such instruction should not be offered until the student reaches college, though even there few students would likely sign up for an elective course, much less a major or minor. Of course, social studies and language arts as courses cannot avoid dealing with religion at appropriate points, within the restraints imposed by the First Amendment, basic fairness, and our pluralism.

Finally, it is curious that the two "general editors" of the book are a retired publishing executive, Cullen Schippe, and a venture capitalist, Chuck Stetson, whose qualifications to produce this sort of textbook are not to be found. What is to be found, according to one journalist, is that Stetson "has long been active in conservative religious and political causes"; that his father "supported far-right GOP candidates Alan Keyes and Gary Bauer"; that he "is the 'major organizing force' behind the National Bible Association, which . . . promotes the Bible as the path to salvation"; that "Stetson is a disciple of Charles Colson" and that fundamentalist extremist and convicted Watergate conspirator Charles Colson is a strong supporter of the BLP textbook, referring to it "as helping open the door to another 'great awakening' of evangelical religious fervor."

Odd also is the fact that while the book lists two "general editors," nowhere does it name the actual authors, as does every other textbook I've seen. However, the fundamentalist Christian Communications Network revealed last November that among those involved with the BLP are Charles Haynes and Os Guinness, whose 1990 curriculum on religious liberty was analyzed by ARL and found to be seriously deficient as a public school text.

Competing with the BLP textbook is the curriculum produced by the North Carolina-based National Council on Bible Curriculum in Public Schools (NCBCPS), which is claimed to be used in elective courses in over 1,000 high schools in 36 states, though which schools seems to be a carefully guarded secret.

A scathing 42-page analysis of the NCBCPS curriculum by Southern Methodist University biblical scholar Mark A. Chancey, available from the Texas Freedom Network (tfn.org), concludes that "the curriculum advocates a narrow sectarian perspective taught with materials plagued by shoddy research, blatant errors and discredited or poorly cited sources." Chancey concludes that the curriculum is "clearly inappropriate" for public school use. A similar conclusion was reached by Anti-Defamation League director Abraham Foxman, who said that "This wholly inappropriate curriculum crosses the line by teaching fundamentalist Protestant doctrine."

Endorsers of the NCBCPS curriculum include actor Chuck Norris, church-state revisionist David Barton, Phyllis Schlafly's Eagle Forum, Beverley LaHaye's Concerned Women for America, extreme right Rabbi Daniel Lapin, former Senator Jesse Helms, former Representative J.C. Watts, and Pat Robertson's American Center for Law and Justice. Need more be said?

Teaching about religion in public schools, however desirable or well-intentioned, is a very hot potato I have yet to see successfully juggled. Oxford University Press's 17-volume Religion in American Life series is a worthy effort, but its more than 3,000 pages is too much for even four semesters in high school and even then covers only religion in America for the last 500 years and does not deal with the ancient world or the history of Europe, much less the development of religion in the rest of the world.

I believe that the BLP effort's faults outweigh its good points and therefore it should be of higher priority for public schools to improve and expand the teaching of history, science, foreign languages, and world literature, and leave religious education to the university, the home, and the church, synagogue, mosque, or temple, at least until qualified scholars produce properly objective and balanced texts and teachers are adequately trained to deal with this important but extremely complex subject.

—*Edd Doerr*

The Phony War on Christmas

While it may seem preposterous in a world beset by terrorism, political unrest, natural disasters, poverty and medical crises, the use or nonuse of the word "Christmas" became a contentious issue during the 2005 holiday season.

It started when some religious conservatives openly denounced their erstwhile hero George W. Bush for failing to include the word Christmas or any explicit religious message in his annual White House Christmas card sent to 1.4 million Americans (and paid for by the Republican National Committee). The trouble is, these zealots apparently failed to notice that Bush's four previous cards also wished recipients a general happy holidays or season's greetings. So did Bill Clinton on his eight holiday cards. The last president to wish "Merry Christmas" in his end of the year greeting was George H.W. Bush in 1992.

Fox News commentators John Gibson and Bill O'Reilly escalated the controversy by claiming there was a widespread conspiracy or plot to suppress Christmas in the United States. America's right-of-center cable network, joined by the Catholic League and several evangelical pressure groups, denounced retailers and department stores for sending "holiday" catalogues instead of "Christmas" ones.

Researchers at stateline.org surveyed the greeting cards of the 50 governors and found that 37 of them chose the inclusive "Happy Holidays" formula, while nine opted for Christmas greetings and four governors sent no official cards (Minnesota, Nevada, New Mexico, Louisiana). Some of the more generic greetings included Christmas trees as artwork, including California Governor Arnold Schwarzenegger's painting of a tree. Two Southern Baptist Republicans, Governor Bob Riley of Alabama and Governor Mike Huckabee of Arkansas, laid on the religious imagery, mentioning "our savior's birth," "the Messiah," and "the risen Christ" on cards sent to constituents, friends and supporters.

A Pew Research Center poll found that Americans prefer "Merry Christmas" to "Happy Holidays" by 60% to 23%. But 45% also said it didn't really matter. The poll also revealed that more Americans (52%) are disturbed by the "commercialization of Christmas" than are unhappy over (35%) "opposition to religious symbols in public places."

Ironically, evangelical Protestants, many of whose ancestors resolutely refused to even observe Christmas as a religious holy day, were the most likely to favor public Christmas observances.

While some conservatives lambasted the president and the culture generally, several conservative groups themselves sent out generic or secular holiday greetings. The Republican public relations firm Creative Response Concepts wished "Season's Greetings and Best Wishes for a Joyous Holiday" to its supporters, while the conservative Hoover Institution sent secular greetings on a Christmas tree-less card bearing an ink and watercolor painting of a bare conifer tree.

President Bush may have redeemed himself in the eyes of religious conservatives with his "official" Christmas message, a custom dating back to Coolidge and Hoover. Among other things, Bush said, "We rejoice in the knowledge that the god who came to Earth that night in Bethlehem is with us still and will remain with us forever," a remarkably personal statement for the chief executive of a secular democracy.

Not all evangelicals, however, buy the argument that Christmas is threatened. *Christianity Today* editorialized, "Our priority is not to make Christmas recognized in our society, but to make it religiously significant for the people who celebrate it."

To be sure, there was a handful of disputes over religious symbols on public property in such places as Manhasset, New York, Neptune Beach, Florida and Dodgeville, Wisconsin. In Huntington, New York, a lawsuit was filed to remove a crèche and a menorah from the village green.

A Religious Right legal group, the Orlando-based Liberty Counsel, set up a campaign to defend Christmas activities in municipalities and schools, threatening lawsuits if Christmas was not celebrated in some fashion.

But none of these events constituted a national campaign to suppress Christmas. Here are some facts:

• Polls show that over 90% of Americans celebrate Christmas in some fashion – secular, religious, or a combination of the two. That is more than the number of professed Christians (84%) and more than double the percentage who attend church weekly. Nearly 80% of Americans could name a favorite Christmas carol, according to a 1998 survey conducted by Ohio University and Scripps Howard News Service.

• The Christmas season accounted for total retail sales of $439.5 billion, up 6% from last year.

• Publishers routinely issue about 50-75 adult books and 100-150 children's titles devoted to some phase of Christmas, whether music, customs, traditions, or novels and anthologies of short stories with holiday themes. They would hardly publish this many if there were a concerted effort to suppress or downplay Christmas.

But politicians on the right, seeing another opportunity to widen the cultural war, raised tempers. Georgia's legislature saw a number of bills filed that would ban state and local officials from restricting "verbal expressions" of Christmas. Its sponsor, Republican Rep. Sue Burmeister said, "As a group, Christians are feeling more and more persecuted in our country," and then added, "Whether we like it or not, this country was founded by Christian pilgrims."

Even the US House of Representatives saw the introduction of House Resolution 579, which "expressed the sense of the House that the symbols and traditions of Christmas should be protected." Rep. John Dingell (D-MI) wrote a holiday jingle ridiculing the notion.

Hendrik Hertzberg summed up the controversy in a sparkling essay called "Bah Humbug" in *The New Yorker*'s Christmas issue. He observed, "Just as Christmas itself evolved as a way to synthesize a variety of winter festivals, so the War on Christmas fantasy is a way of grouping together a variety of enemies, where they can all be rhetorically machine-gunned at once. . . . In this war, the weapons of Christmas destruction have been found – just a few caches of linguistic over-sensitivity and commercial caution. Christmas remains robust."

In America's deepening culture wars, the phony war on Christmas is an unfortunate but predictable annual event. It should be seen for what it is.

— Al Menendez

Attacks on Independent Judiciary Mount

The Republican leadership in Congress, the White House, and the Religious Right have targeted a basic American institution, an independent judiciary, for extinction. Showing that they are instinctively radical, not conservative in the truest sense of that much maligned word, the American Right today has made the federal court system, and its methods, the primary target in their campaign to restructure American life and culture.

Republican spokespersons have labeled the judiciary "out of control" because most federal courts have sought to uphold basic principles of religious neutrality on the part of government.

Now the latest propaganda thrust by religious and social conservatives (or pseudo-conservatives, as they ought to be called) is to label opponents of President Bush's more extreme judicial choices enemies of "people of faith." This outrageous posturing threatens to poison even more the already miasmic atmosphere between the parties and to up the ante on partisanship and mean spiritedness, and to stoke the flames of religious strife, all to advance their political objectives and to keep this administration in power.

Senate Majority Leader Bill Frist (R-TN) has lent his name to the campaign by addressing a nationally-televised rally from Highview Baptist Church in Louisville, Kentucky, which used evangelical Christians to inundate wavering Republican senators with demands that they support the abolition of the filibuster. The filibuster, which admittedly was used by recalcitrant Southern segregationists to delay the passage of civil rights legislation four decades ago, is still considered an acceptable last-ditch method to derail majoritarian overreach. Republicans themselves used it to stop Abe Fortas's nomination for Chief Justice in the 1960s. Not for nothing is this called the "nuclear option" because it could fracture once and for all any hope of nonpartisanship in the US. Senate.

The rhetoric from the Religious Right has been apocalyptic and threatening to interfaith harmony in a nation already sharply divided on religious and political issues. No wonder an ABC/*Washington Post* poll released April 26 showed Americans opposed to the filibuster's abolition by 66% to 26%. Independents and moderates joined Democrats and liberals in overwhelming opposition, while substantial numbers of rank and file Republicans also opposed the proposal.

The so-called "Justice Sunday" gathering in Louisville brought James Dobson, Charles Colson, and Al Mohler (president of Southern Baptist Theological Seminary) together to accuse Democrats of "a filibuster against people of faith." Dobson denounced the Supreme Court for inaugurating the "greatest Holocaust in history" by "legalizing abortion and killing 44 million Americans." Tony Perkins, president of the Family Research Council and organizer of the televised event, said, "The courts have become the last bastion of the liberal, anti-Christian dogma of the left. Activist courts, aided by liberal interest groups like the ACLU, have been quietly working under the veil of the judiciary, like thieves in the night, to rob us of our Christian heritage and our religious freedoms."

Democrats and many religious leaders were quick to respond. "No party has a monopoly on faith," said Senator Charles E. Schumer (D-NY), adding, "For Senator Frist to participate in this kind of telecast just throws more oil on the partisan flames." Senator Frist's hometown newspaper, *The Nashville Tennessean,* denounced him for injecting religion into a political debate. "Couching this debate in religious terms should be insulting to lawmakers on both sides of the aisle. Personal faith should not be defined by political affiliation... The fray should stay in the political arena. The issue is not about who believes in God and who doesn't," wrote the editors in the April 19 edition.

National Council of Churches General Secretary Bob Edgar denounced the effort to portray opponents of changing the filibuster as enemies of religious faith. The Rev. Clifton Kirkpatrick, a top official of Frist's Presbyterian Church, said, "One of the hallmarks of our denomination is that we are an ecumenical church. Elected officials should not be portraying public policy as being for or against people of faith." Edgar, a Methodist minister and former Pennsylvania congressman, added, "To say that some group of Christians has a monopoly on the ear of God is especially an outrage to Presbyterians."

Other important voices were heard. The Interfaith Alliance delivered a petition to the Senate signed by 406 clergy urging Frist to "defend the nation from efforts utilizing deception and fear-mongering to manipulate Americans of faith." People For the American Way president Ralph Neas said, "It is false and inflammatory to suggest that supporters of the Senate's checks and balances are trying to keep people of faith off the courts or to silence conservative Christians or deny them the right to participate in public life." *New York Times* columnist Frank Rich labeled Justice Sunday "a high tech lynching in prime time." In a hard-hitting editorial, "Bill Frist's Religious War," *The New York Times* said on April 16:

"Right-wing Christian groups and the Republican politicians they bankroll have done much since the last election to impose their particular religious views on all Americans. But nothing comes close to the shameful declaration of religious war by Bill Frist, the Senate majority leader, over the selection of judges for federal courts.

"Senator Frist is to appear on a telecast sponsored by the Family Research Council, which styles itself a religious organization but is really just another Washington lobbying concern. The message is that the Democrats who oppose a tiny handful of President Bush's judicial nominations are conducting an assault 'against people of faith.' By that, Senator Frist and his allies do not mean people of all faiths, only those of their faith.

"It is one thing when private groups foment this kind of intolerance. It is another thing entirely when it's done by the highest-ranking member of the United States Senate, who swore on the Bible to uphold a Constitution that forbids the imposition of religious views on Americans. Unfortunately, Senator Frist and his allies are willing to break down the rules to push through their agenda — in this case, by creating what the senator knows is a false connection between religion and the debate about judges... .

"We fully understand that a powerful branch of the Republican Party believes that the last election was won on 'moral values.' Even if that were true, that's a far cry from voting for one religion to dominate the entire country. President Bush owes it to Americans to stand up and say so."

The injection of a religious issue into what otherwise might be seen as a procedural question relating to checks and balances in the legislative branch has turned bitter. Many evangelicals openly attacked Colorado Senator Ken Salazar, a Hispanic Catholic Democrat, for tolerating and abetting anti-Catholicism because he has opposed some of Bush's federal court nominees who happened to be Catholic. Salazar hit back on April 21, castigating Albert Mohler Jr., president of the Southern Baptist Theological Seminary. Salazar quoted Mohler s statement that "the Roman Church is a false church and teaches a false gospel." Mohler acknowledged having made the statement but called Salazar's statement "absolutely ridiculous." Salazar said that Mohler is the real anti-Catholic.

Another Catholic Democrat, Senator Patrick Leahy of Vermont, told his colleagues on April 22, "Dividing the American people along religious lines is wrong. Smearing political opponents as 'anti-faith' is despicable. Apparently some will stop at nothing and stoop to any level. No scurrilous charge is too coarse. No baseless accusation is too outlandish."

Leahy continued: "I thank the many religious leaders who have come forward this week to uphold America's great traditions of respecting faith, honoring faith and, ensuring that the constitutional prohibition against any religious test for public office be strictly observed. Christian leaders from a variety of denominations, Muslim leaders and Jewish leaders have joined together to reject these disgraceful efforts of a few partisans injecting religion in the discussion of judicial nominations. They have publicly denounced the efforts of the religious demagogues making slanderous charges in a win-at-all-costs bid to rile the passions and further divide Americans from one another. I am grateful for their voices. We need less division, not more. We need to work together more, not less."

He concluded: "This kind of religious smear campaign hurts the whole country. It hurts Christians and non-Christians. It hurts all of us, because the Constitution requires judges to apply the law, not their personal views. Remember that all of us, no matter what our faith — and I am proud of mine—are able to practice our religion as we choose or not to practice a religion. That is a fundamental guarantee of our Constitution. The Constitution's prohibition against a 'religious test' in Article VI is consistent with that fundamental freedom.

"All Americans should understand that the Constitution is there to protect us, and it is the protection of the Constitution that has allowed this country to evolve into a tolerant nation. Those who would try to drag us back into religious intolerance, for short-term political gain, subvert the Constitution, and damage the country."

How "Faith-Based" Works in Rural Pennsylvania

Bradford County, Pennsylvania, is a bucolic, idyllic rural area that borders New York State and is part of Pennsylvania's Northern Tier counties. Settled largely by New Englanders and by the old immigration from England and Germany, Bradford County has supported almost every Republican presidential candidate in the last century and a half. The only modern exception was in 1964, when the GOP's Barry Goldwater lost to Democratic incumbent Lyndon Johnson. The county is mostly Protestant, by about 73% to 27% Catholic among church members, though 55% of residents are not church members, according to the 1990 data from *Churches and Church Membership in the U.S.* Methodists far outnumber other Protestants, with Presbyterians and Baptists coming next.

So Bradford County, which supported Bush over Gore by 63% to 34% in the last election, would seem to be a favorable place for Bush's Faith-Based Initiatives to garner political support. It is not surprising that county commissioners have approved over $200,000 of public monies for Firm Foundation, a faith-based group that provides job training for Bradford County prison inmates.

These funds come from the federal Faith-Based and Community Service programs created by President Bush's Executive Order 13279 in 2001.

An investigation of the Firm Foundation (FF) program by the Bradford County Alliance for Democracy (BCAD) from April to July 2004 reveals widespread violations of the law. BCAD discovered that "FF has violated U.S. law and the grant conditions by engaging in evangelical proselytizing during the program, religiously discriminatory hiring practices, and using government tax monies to work on a building owned by a religious institution." In a letter of June 11, 2004, BCAD urged the Bradford County commissioners to exercise oversight to "ensure that basic fiduciary responsibilities are being carried on in the grant process and in the evaluation oversight."

BCAD concluded that Firm Foundation "violated 26 of its contracted obligations, violated federal and the state regulations intended to protect the religious liberty of Americans. . . . There has been a systemic breakdown in the oversight of Firm Foundation by the individuals and agencies with fiduciary responsibilities to protect the public from program mismanagement, violations of law such as illegal proselytizing, and misuse of local and federal tax monies. We have identified 31 oversight lapses by the agencies responsible for monitoring Firm Foundation's financial and program performance."

Even after the presentation of this devastating report by a committee of local citizens and taxpayers dedicated to preserving separation of church and state, the County Commissioners on July 1 approved an additional $64,562 for Firm Foundation.

Firm Foundation makes no bones about its religious commitments. "This program is based on the belief that lives are changed as hearts become open to faith. The administration, trainers, and staff have committed their lives to this belief and are examples of Jesus Christ the Lord," according to its statement of purpose.

Each day the program begins with prayer, and pressures are placed on inmates to be "born again." Program counselors "share their beliefs" during lunch breaks and transportation. On the last day of the program, an unnamed individual from the Elmira (New York) Police Department asked everyone if they wanted to be born again. Warden Kevin Lonsinger and Counselor Lionel Hyatt said they were aware of the religious activities but saw nothing wrong with them, even though one inmate/trainee Tim Thurston quit the program because of religious pressures. Corrections Counselor Lionel Hyatt said, "Most of the inmates in the Firm Foundation project appeared happy to have found religion."

Job descriptions are vague, except that the Site Manager must "be an example of a believer in Christ and Christian life today, sharing these ideals when opportunity arises," and individuals were paid without indicating what they did to earn their salaries. A grant of $13,000 was given to New Life Church for "acting as fiscal agent" with no supporting documentation.

There was no evidence that "life skills training," "mentoring," "services to inmate families," or "follow-up services for a year after an inmate's release" have ever been implemented, even though they were a part of the grant application. No evaluation of program progress has ever been performed. No project goals were met, nor were required records maintained.

This is the kind of sloppiness and indifference that taxpayers in Bradford County supported.

It appears that FF's only interest was in converting a captive audience of prisoners to evangelical Protestant Christianity, not in helping them readjust to society on the outside or in seriously addressing the recidivism/rehabilitation problems endemic in the U.S. correctional systems.

Yet Bradford County Commissioners ignored a report carried out by concerned taxpayers at their own expense.

Could this be happening elsewhere?

This report, *Performance of the Firm Foundation of Bradford County*, prepared by Laura H. Blain and Clark Moeller for the Bradford County Alliance for Democracy, is available from PO Box 131, Burlington, PA 18814 or online at www.bc-alliance.org.

— Al Menendez

Bush Faith-Based Giveaways Documented

A report by the Roundtable on Religion and Social Welfare Policy concludes that the Bush administration, despite "the absence of new legislative authority" has "used its executive powers to widely implement the Faith-Based Initiative throughout the federal government." The report describes changes in federal regulations that "increase partnership with faith-based groups to provide a vast array of human services." The report, *The Expanding Administrative Presidency: George W. Bush and the Faith-Based Initiative,* finds that, "Religious organizations are now involved in government-encouraged activities ranging from building strip malls for economic improvement to promoting car seats to distributing Medicare prescription cards."

The Roundtable on Religion and Social Welfare Policy is a project of the Rockefeller Institute of Government in Albany, New York, and is supported by the Pew Charitable Trusts. The report was issued in August. Among the report's findings:

- "In the absence of new legislative authority, the President has aggressively advanced the Faith-Based Initiative through executive orders, rule changes, managerial realignment in federal agencies, and other innovative uses of the prerogatives of his office."
- "Among those innovations is the creation of a high-profile special office in the White House, the White House Office of Faith-Based and Community Initiatives, connected to mini-offices in ten government agencies, each with a carefully selected director and staff, empowered to articulate, advance and oversee coordinated efforts to win more financial support for faith-based social services. These ten agencies include: the departments of Agriculture, Commerce, Education, Health and Human Services, Housing and Urban Development, Justice, Labor, and Veterans Affairs, as well as the Agency for International Development and the Small Business Administration. A similar office has also been created within the Corporation for National and Community Service. In addition, the Initiative has been promoted in a myriad of other government offices overseeing programs ranging from homeownership and business development to energy conservation."
- "With assistance from the White House Office, these federal agencies have proposed or finalized a host of new regulations that together mark a major shift in the constitutional separation of church and state."

Examples of these regulatory changes include:

- The federal government now allows federally-funded faith-based groups to consider religion when employing staff.
- The Department of Justice now permits religious organizations to convert government-forfeited property to religious purposes after five years, replacing the previous policy prohibiting such conversions.
- The federal government now allows federally-funded faith-based groups to build and renovate structures used for both social services and religious worship.
- "The Veterans Administration no longer requires faith-based social service providers to certify that they exert 'no religious influence'."
- "The Department of Labor now allows students to use federal job-training vouchers to receive religious training leading to employment at a church, synagogue, or other faith-based organization."

Who pays for this egregious shift in national policy? The "full extent of federal funding for faith-based social services" is not known, say the report's authors. The majority of contracts and grants is awarded by state and local governments, and "few public programs record whether or not contractors are faith-based." Five federal agencies granted $1.17 billion in fiscal year 2003 to faith-based groups, but that may only be the tip of the iceberg.

The report also finds that Bush has "pervasively and methodically implemented" his "personal beliefs" in the implementation of this initiative.

"The Bush Administration has made concerted use of its executive powers and has moved aggressively through new regulation, funding, political appointees and active public outreach efforts to expand the federal government's partnerships with faith-based social service providers in ways that don't require Congressional approval."

Private School Share of U.S. Education

Private schools of all kinds educate only 9.8% of all elementary and secondary students, according to 2002 data compiled by researchers Bert Sperling and Peter Sander. Their compilation, which appears in the just-published *Cities Ranked & Rated* (Wiley Publishing, Inc.), was based on the most recent data available from the National Center for Education Statistics.

The percentage of private school enrollment has remained virtually unchanged for a decade, despite a barrage of pro-voucher propaganda, the passage of voucher programs in several states and favorable court decisions.

Of the 331 Metropolitan Statistical Areas (MSA) defined by the U.S. Office of Management and Budget (OMB), only 45 showed private school enrollments of 15% or higher.

The areas showing the highest private school enrollment reflect historic cultural and religious patterns. Dubuque, Iowa, an old industrial town on the Mississippi River reflecting a predominant German Catholic heritage, has the nation's highest private school enrollment, at nearly 31%. Most of the nonpublic sector attends parochial schools. (Interestingly, Dubuque is a Democratic stronghold and has supported every Democratic presidential nominee since JFK, including George McGovern.)

The second highest percentage, nearly one quarter of all students, attend mostly Catholic schools in New Orleans. Two other Louisiana cities, Baton Rouge and Lafayette, are on the top twenty, reflecting the Pelican State's French Catholic (Cajun) heritage.

Catholic parochial schools are the dominant nonpublic school system in 17 of the top 20 metros. Many reflect the cohesive, European-flavored Catholic culture of such cities as Louisville, Cincinnati, Philadelphia, Erie, Milwaukee, St. Louis, Jersey City, Scranton and Toledo, while New York, San Francisco, and Wilmington (Delaware) have a variety of religious and secular private schools. Lancaster, Pennsylvania is noted for its Mennonite and Amish school systems, while Honolulu has many Protestant schools originating in the 19th century.

— Al Menendez

The Bishops' Dilemma

The Catholic Church sex abuse scandal is likely to have a far ranging effect on law enforcement, criminal justice and financial matters. State legislatures will tighten laws requiring churches to report suspected abusers to local authorities, and states that presently exempt the clergy from this requirement will move to repeal the exemptions. Definitions of sexual abuse or harassment of minors vary from state to state but loopholes allowing perpetrators to escape justice are likely to be closed in light of the widespread publicity This includes extending statute of limitation laws in many states.

The financial costs to the Catholic Church are immense and growing. Estimates range from $600 million to $1.3 billion in pay-off costs to victims and their families, as the various dioceses have tried to settle with outraged victims. Since many of the settlements are sealed by the courts, and recipients of funds are required to remain silent in many instances, the full extent of the financial drain may never be known. The country's 194 dioceses are in reality somewhat autonomous in their relationships to each other, though all are directly controlled by the Vatican. Neighboring dioceses may have different policies regarding sex abuse of minors, and differing standards for reporting claims to authorities or of settling with litigants. Bishops are theoretically equal to each other and are absolute authorities in their dioceses, so there may be little coordination between or among dioceses. The national bishops conferences, which meet twice yearly, have debated these issues since the mid- 1980s, but the present scandals suggest that their policies have not been effective.

Insurance companies are likely to evaluate their policies toward churches and clergy, and rates covering such potential abuses may become so prohibitively high that no religious group can afford them. (This has become a grave problem in the medical profession in relation to medical malpractice insurance.)

All of these financial difficulties lead to another tantalizing question: Will churches seek more public funds for church schools and charities to make up for the financial drain of the lawsuits and for the declining revenue from angry and disillusioned parishioners? Without wanting to seem to be piling on an institution facing its worst U.S. crisis in decades, the question almost has to be asked. Will the U.S. Catholic Church's financial crisis spill over into the public realm, affecting legislative coffers? Or will state legislators and Congress become more wary of giving economic carte blanche to church-run and managed institutions that are increasingly relying on taxpayer support? Who knows? But the fallout could affect American society in many ways that are at present unforeseen and unpredictable.

It should be noted that the clerical sex abuse controversy affects other religious and secular groups, not just the Catholic Church. Two rabbis and cantors in New York and New Jersey face trial on sex abuse charges. A Southern Baptist preacher in South Carolina was sentenced to a lengthy prison sentence for multiple abuses, and a Lutheran pastor in Texas is likely to be arraigned on harassment charges. One of the first cases to establish a precedent in this area of law was settled in 1992 when the Episcopal diocese of Colorado was successfully sued by a woman who was a victim of sexual abuse by a priest at the cathedral in Denver. In that case the diocese was held responsible for the misdoings of one of its clergy. And a forthcoming book from Professor Charol Shakeshaft at Hofstra University claims that 15% of U.S. school children are sexually harassed or abused at some time during their childhood, and that 5% of teachers have been guilty of such offenses. Previous books have exposed widespread sexual shenanigans among Boy Scout leaders.

One difference may be that teachers found guilty of sex abuse of minors are usually removed from their teaching positions and are turned over to the criminal justice system, rather than quietly transferred to another school or district.

The Catholic Church crisis changes daily, and its eventual outcome can not be discerned or predicted at this time. But a new and rather sinister strategy seems to be apparent. Many of the 194 dioceses that face criminal and civil actions from plaintiffs have decided to fight the charges with high-power legal ammunition. The sense of shame and an appeal to public forgiveness, based on the hierarchy's admission of serious errors of judgment, is now being replaced by a hardhitting legal strategy designed to bolster the church's defenses and its finances.

Since the church has already shelled out an estimated $1 billion in claims (some settled out of court, some based on court judgments against the dioceses), a fear of bankruptcy has called forth a kind of circling-the-wagons mentality A desire to protect the church's officials at all costs has begun to supplant the admission of culpability and a sense of contrition that emanated from some clerical sources a few weeks ago.

Some diocesan attorneys are advising Catholic schools and charities to divide assets among shell corporations to protect against claimants. Cardinal Edward Egan of the once-powerful and feared New York Archdiocese has even claimed that priests are "self-employed contractors working for autonomous parishes." (Tell that to the Vatican!) Avoidance of responsibility has created a massive crisis of unparalleled proportions in a church claiming the allegiance of one billion people worldwide.

Every national study shows that top-heavy majorities of American Catholics blame the church leaders for a cover-up of transgressions and for a refusal to face the realities of human sexuality. Support for abolition of mandatory clerical celibacy and for the ordination of married men and women to the priesthood has never been higher. A widespread disillusionment with the way the Vatican relates to national hierarchies and with the way in which hierarchies relate to the men and women who choose to remain in the church is undeniable.

The call for representative democracy in the church and for a massive overhaul of its structures maybe impossible to repel, even by clerical reactionaries and stand-patters. The loss of moral authority by church leaders also calls into question whether Catholics in particular, and all Americans for that matter, will pay much attention to pronouncements on social and political matters by the bishops.

Historian Garry Wills, a practicing Catholic and a severe critic of its hierarchy, writes in a forthcoming book, *Why I Am a Catholic,* "The Church cannot be identified with its leadership, since its leadership has often been morally deficient. In fact, the hierarchy is corrupt, misguided and misguiding."

The effects of this tragedy will have a major impact on church-state relationships throughout the world for years to come.

— Al Menendez

Bush and the Far Right: Cozy Companions

The Bush administration has not only acted as if it won a Reagan era landslide, but it has increasingly governed from the right, not the center, as a bitterly divided electorate and Congress might have expected. Instead, Bush and his top allies have pursued policies that appeal mostly to the extreme right wing of the Republican Party, thereby losing control of the U.S. Senate when Vermont moderate Jim Jeffords broke with the GOP and became an Independent in late May.

Bush's agenda has become clear in these recent developments:

His first eleven nominees for the federal appeals courts show a strong preference for right-wing candidates, especially in areas affecting individual liberty, federal-state relations, and church-state matters. Bush nominated Michael McConnell, professor at the University of Utah Law School, for a place on the Tenth Circuit Court of Appeals. McConnell, an evangelical Presbyterian, has written widely in criticism of almost every major church-state decision since 1947. He advocates limiting the Establishment Clause and allowing a maximum role for institutional religious involvement in politics, government and public policy, and has shown scant concern for religious minorities.

The White House overruled Secretary of State Colin Powell's choice to head the Bureau of Population, Refugees and Migration at the State Department. Instead, it named John M. Klink, who served as Vatican representative to UNICEF from 1988 to 1999 and is presently an "adviser" to the Holy See's diplomatic mission at the United Nations. Klink, who holds dual Irish and American citizenship, also oversees a family investment fund in California and is a member of the Republican National Committee's Catholic Task Force.

Klink, who worked for Catholic Relief Services from 1976 to 1986, was a member of the

Vatican delegation at 17 UN conferences on women and social problems and played an active role in the Holy See's attempt to sabotage family planning efforts at the 1994 Cairo population conference. He was, in fact, the floor manager for the Vatican delegation.

Klink would oversee an annual budget exceeding $800 million that is primarily distributed to the UN High Commissioner for Refugees and the International Committee of the Red Cross. Family planning groups are outraged by the nomination, and Catholics for a Free Choice revealed that Klink was instrumental in withdrawal of Vatican support from UNICEF because a UNICEF manual included information about emergency contraception for refugees. Kenneth W. Bacon, a former Pentagon spokesman and president of Refugees International, warned that Klink's "views on population issues could distort the work of the bureau, could represent a redirection away from refugees towards population issues and could hurt American leadership in refugee issues around the world."

The Bush Justice Department has come under fire because of Attorney General John Ashcroft's daily Bible studies and devotionals which, though voluntary, have added an element of religious division to the nation's 135,000 employee law enforcement agency. Anonymous employees have complained to *The Washington Post* about the feelings of exclusion and separateness that a daily religious session with an evangelical, Pentecostal orientation symbolizes. One department attorney told *The Washington Post's* Dan Eggen, "The purpose of the Department of Justice is to do the business of the government, not to establish a religion. It strikes me and a lot of others as offensive, disrespectful and unconstitutional."

The prayer sessions involve "reading, arguing, memorizing and praying," according to insiders. Ashcroft has been joined at Justice by another ultraconservative, Ted Olson, as Solicitor General, who argues the government's position before the Supreme Court. Olson, a far-right Republican who engaged in a vendetta against President Clinton, was narrowly approved 51-47 in the waning hours of the Republican-dominated Senate.

Bush's White House speechwriting staff is dominated by Michael Gerson, an evangelical graduate of Wheaton College in Illinois, which bars Catholics and Jews from its faculty and board of directors. Gerson, who studied theology, is regarded as a talented speechwriter who adds copious doses of religious rhetoric to the president's addresses.

Bush appointed Jim Nicholson, former Republican National Committee chairman, to the post of U.S. Ambassador to the Vatican. Nicholson, who has no diplomatic experience whatsoever, was regarded as a mean-spirited partisan Republican. But he is called "a devout Catholic," apparently the only qualification now required for the position. The U.S. ambassadorship to the Holy See is increasingly seen as a dumping ground for hack politicians and as an attempt to curry favor with Catholic voters, despite its dubious constitutionality. A decade ago the prestigious Jesuit weekly *America* criticized the apparent use of a religious test for this office and called for the appointment of a well-qualified diplomat, irrespective of religious affiliation.

Bush's appointment of Richard Egan as ambassador to Ireland has provoked widespread disillusion in the Emerald Isle because of Egan's dearth of qualifications. Egan, founder and CEO of EMC Corporation, is one of America's wealthiest men. His only apparent qualification for the post is his membership in the Bush Pioneer Club, a top level coterie of key Bush advisers who contributed more than $100,000 to the presidential campaign.

Egan's "knowledge of Irish politics is rumored to be weak," according to *Irish America*, but his assistant for Irish affairs, Richard Haass, has raised serious questions about U.S. policy. Haass, a fellow at the Brookings Institution, criticized the Clinton administration's 1995 peace efforts in Northern Ireland as "overly concerned with the Catholic minority."

Some observers speculate that these appointments indicate a turning away from the U.S. involvement in the peace process, which has nearly ended more than three decades of strife in Ireland. The new appointments may be seen as an attempt to shift U.S. policy toward Ulster Protestants. This concern was reinforced when Vice President Dick Cheney appeared on the same platform at a conservative political action conference in Washington with David Trimble, the increasingly conservative and intransigent leader of the Northern Ireland Protestant Unionists. The conference failed to invite Catholic leader John Hume, which suggested not only an imbalance but a signal that America's right-wing no longer supports a peaceful settlement to the Northern Ireland problem but favors one side in the centuries-old dispute. America's far right also has elements of isolationism in its makeup, and the Bush administration's disengagement from the Middle East, the Balkans, and Ireland may be an ominous sign that a renewal of isolationism is imminent. The State Department recently announced that 23 of 55 special envoys to the world's trouble spots have been discontinued.

Catholic Bishops' Directive on Politics

The nation's Roman Catholic bishops have issued their most comprehensive statement to date on politics. Issued on October 19 as a document called "Faithful Citizenship: Civic Responsibility for a New Millennium," the statement asserts "a consistent moral framework" by which political "issues, platforms and campaigns" should be assessed.

On balance the document is about 90% liberal, 10% conservative. With the exceptions of abortion and parochial school aid, the bishops urge government to defend the "voiceless" and to support programs fighting poverty, injustice, joblessness, and discrimination. The document singles out "the poor and vulnerable" and criticizes American society for neglecting major segments of the population. "A powerful economy pushes our nation forward, but it widens the gaps between rich and poor in our nation and around the world," they argue; They warn that "Hate and intolerance haunt our nation and turn the diversity we should celebrate into a source of division, bigotry, racism and conflict." "Violence surrounds us," they charge, and "the younger you are, the more likely you are to be poor."

The bishops warn that "scandal, sensationalism and intense partisan combat diminish public life. Too many of our leaders seem to focus more on seeking campaign contributions than the common good." While claiming to be neutral and affirming that "our moral framework does not easily fit the categories of right or left, Democrat or Republican," the U.S. bishops say, "We must challenge all parties and every candidate to defend human life and dignity, to pursue greater justice and peace, to uphold family life and to advance the common good."

Placing abortion first in a list of priorities, however, and claiming that "1.4 million children are destroyed before birth every year" places the bishops, once again, on the conservative side of that issue. They reiterate their support for "constitutional protection for unborn human life," as well as legislative efforts to oppose abortion and euthanasia and "encourage the passage of laws and programs that promote childbirth and adoption." They also oppose assisted suicide laws and "urge our nation to abandon the use of capital punishment."

On foreign policy and immigration questions, the bishops are to the left of both American parties, urging the U.S. to ratify the Comprehensive Test Ban Treaty (recently defeated by Senate Republicans), reduction in nuclear weapons testing, support for landmine treaties, and a reduction in the global arms trade. They also said that "direct and intentional attacks on civilians in war are never morally acceptable," which may have been aimed at U.S. and NATO policies in Yugoslavia.

The bishops stress the need for increasing the minimum wage, affordable housing and "health care that is affordable and accessible to all." They called for "a more serious immigration and refugee policy," and "more consistent financial and diplomatic support for the United Nations." They endorse "gun safety measures and reasonable restrictions on access to assault weapons and handguns."

While the bishops denounced "discrimination based on sex, race, ethnicity or age," they omitted sexual orientation. But they did endorse "judiciously administered affirmative action programs as tools to overcome discrimination and its continuing effects." They also urged increasing foreign aid programs to alleviate global poverty, an issue neither American party wishes to address. (The bishops did add the caveat, "without promoting population control," however.)

Finally, on education, the U.S. bishops took a surprisingly low-key posture, endorsing only the provision of "services that are aimed at improving the educational environment... should be available to students and teachers in private and religious schools as well." They pointedly refrained from endorsing vouchers or tuition tax credits.

The U.S. bishops denied that they "seek the formation of a religious voting bloc" and urged that all voters "examine the position of candidates on the full range of issues, as well as on their personal integrity, philosophy and performance." They endorsed "a consistent ethic of life," a phrase attributed to the late Cardinal Joseph Bernardin.

Home Schoolers Survey: High Marks, Privileged Families

The first-ever independent national survey of 20,760 students who are home-schooled showed that their achievement test scores were in the 70th to 80th percentiles, well above the average for all students in public and private schools. But the same study suggested that the high income and educational levels of the parents played a very significant role in spurring the children to high levels of educational achievement.

The survey was conducted in the spring of 1998 by Dr. Lawrence M. Rudner of the University of Maryland and released on March 23, 1999. It was underwritten by a $35,000 grant from the Home School Legal Defense Association in Purcellville, Virginia. The students took either the Iowa Tests of Basic Skills or the Tests of Achievement and Proficiency, standard exams given widely throughout the U.S.

Home schoolers performed well at every grade level, K-12, and 25% of them are enrolled at one or more grades above their peers in public and private schools. There was no difference in achievement by gender, but students from the wealthiest and best educated families did significantly better than students from less affluent families, a finding replicated in studies of all schools in the U.S.

It is the family profiles that explain most or all of these high test scores, according to Rudner. For example, home schoolers' parents have a median family income of $52,000 compared to $36,000 for all U.S. parents, a 45% difference. A remarkable 54% of home school parents have family incomes exceeding $50,000 compared to 32% of all families. And while

35% of all families have incomes below $25,000, only 8% of home schoolers are at the low end of the income levels.

A similar difference is found in the educational attainment level of parents. Nearly 65% of home school parents are college graduates, compared to 22% of all U.S. adults. Nearly 88% of home school parents have some education beyond high school compared to 48% of all adults. Nearly 77% of home school mothers do not work outside the home, compared to only 30% of all U.S. mothers.

Other differences are stark. Over 97% of home schooled children live with both parents who are married, in contrast to 72% of all families with school-age children. About 94% of home schoolers are non-Hispanic whites, compared to 67% of all American students. And while 29% of all U.S. school pupils are black or Hispanic, just 1% of home schoolers belong to these large minority groups. (Oddly, 5% of home schoolers are Asian American or Native American, compared to 4% nationwide.)

Home schoolers also live in larger families, where 3.1 children are the norm. A surprising number, 24%, of home school parents possess teaching certificates, far above the percentage of all Americans. And home schoolers watch much less television than all U.S. children, with 65% watching one hour or less per day, compared to 25% of all students who watch that little television. Nearly 39% of all students watch more than four hours of television per day, but less than 2% of home schoolers spend that many hours in front of the tube. Interestingly, computer usage is much less common among home schoolers. At grade eleven 41% of home schoolers never use computers compared to 16% of all students, while 31% use computers several times a week or daily, in contrast to half of all students who do so.

One flaw in the survey analysis, admitted by Rudner, is that home schoolers should be compared to comparable samples of public and private school students (upper middle income, white or well educated groups) rather than with all public and private students, but the data are not readily available for that level of sophisticated analysis.

One significant difference between home schoolers, who may total as many as 1.2 million students nationwide, and all students is religion. Nearly half of all home schoolers' religious preference is Baptist or "Independent Fundamentalist," while only one-fourth or less of the U.S. population classifies itself this way (and less than 20% of whites). Almost 15% of home schoolers are Pentecostals or Charismatic Christians, compared to 2 or 3% of all Americans. Only 5% are Catholics, though 28% of all U.S. residents claim to be Catholics. Protestants of all types make up 88% of home schoolers, compared to 58% of all Americans, and the vast majority of home school families who are Protestant are evangelical or fundamentalist Protestants, not mainstream groups like Methodists or Lutherans. (Only about 11% of home schoolers belong to the Methodist, Presbyterian, Lutheran or Reformed Churches.)

The survey also found that students performed better at every grade level if their families spent more than $600 per year on books and educational materials. Ohio, Virginia, and Georgia were the top three states in number of students participating in this survey, followed by Texas, North Carolina, New York, Florida, California, Colorado and Minnesota.

This survey, "Scholastic Achievement and Demographic Characteristics of Home School Students in 1998" is available on the web at www.llepaa.asu.edu.

Charter Schools: Myths and Realities

In his State of the Union address on January 19, President Clinton hailed the increase in the number of charter schools during his presidency, from one when he took office to 1,100 today. Since Clinton is known for forceful advocacy of public education and opposition to vouchers and other schemes to funnel public funds into private and parochial schools, his support for charter schools brings them to the forefront of educational discussion.

What, then, are charter schools? Joe Nathan, director of the University of Minnesota's Humphrey Institute for Public Affairs and an advocate of the movement, defines charter schools as "public nonsectarian schools that operate under a written contract from a local school or other organization."

Minnesota passed the first charter school authorization law in 1991. It was followed by California in 1992. By July 1996, 25 states had passed enabling legislation. As of now, 34 states allow charter schools. Today, 1,128 charter schools now exist nationwide, enrolling about 250,000 students, about one-half of one percent of the nation's student population.

The term "charter school" was coined by a retired public school teacher and administrator, Ray Budde, in a 1988 government-financed report, *Education by Charter,* The idea itself may be traced to a conference of educators at a lakeside lodge near Brainerd, Minnesota, in 1988. Joe Nathan and the late Al Shanker, president of the American Federation of Teachers (AFT), were present. The group talked about establishing alternative public schools that could innovate and choose new methods of reaching at-risk and disadvantaged children. Concerns were immediately expressed, however, by those who feared that groups with partisan ideological agendas might try to establish propaganda mills at public expense. There was also fear that charter schools would not provide the wide range of educational services available in regular public schools and might not attract certified teachers.

Charter schools vary widely, making generalization difficult. Most receive operating money from the public school system, but construction or renovation costs for the buildings are not covered. In some cities, local businesses, philanthropists and even such groups as the YMCA in Boston and the Henry Ford Museum in Dearborn, Michigan, have provided seed money. Some of the schools are even managed by profit-making companies. Some of the schools have failed. About 3% of all charters have been revoked, according to the Center for Education Reform, a charter school and voucher advocacy organization based in Washington, DC.

State laws vary widely. Most limit the number of charter schools that may be established in a given time period. Many require them to be under the control of a local school board. Florida allows state universities to sponsor them, as does Michigan, where charter schools are called public school academies. New Hampshire allows ten or more parents, two or more certified teachers, or nonprofit organizations to set up charter schools.

The discrepancies in state laws and regulations have provoked considerable discussion. In a 1996 book, *Charter School Laws: Do They Measure Up?,* the AFT concluded that "No state laws meet all of AFT's criteria for good charter legislation that is likely to produce quality education and be the basis for widespread reform of public education." A few states, New Jersey, Rhode Island, Louisiana and California, were singled out for having "good" laws that protect students and teachers.

The AFT urged that the following principles be adopted by state legislatures: charter schools must be based on high academic standards; must give students the same tests as other students in the state and district; should be required to hire certified teachers; should recognize employees' right to collective bargaining; should have the approval of local school districts; and should be required to make information available to the public regarding the progress of their students on state standards and assessments.

The AFT has also adopted a strong statement urging that legislation "specifically exclude private schools from receiving charter status." Schools which "promote a religious viewpoint or discriminate against students based on race, ethnicity or gender" should be prohibited under model charter school legislation.

The U.S. Department of Education has also issued *The Charter School Review Process*, a 1998 document based on existing legislation in 29 states, D.C. and Puerto Rico. This "guide for chartering entities" was prepared by the Public Charter Schools Program in the Office of Elementary and Secondary Education.

This report emphatically notes that "all charter laws require that charter schools be nonsectarian," and that "charter schools are prohibited from discriminating on the basis of race, color, national origin, sex, disability and age. Most laws prohibit selection on the basis of race, color, national origin, sex, disability and age. Most laws prohibit selection on the basis of academic or athletic ability." The report continues, "Charter laws prevent schools from charging tuition. Charter schools generally abide by state reporting requirements as well as some charter specific reporting. As holders of public trust, charter schools are generally required to abide by applicable open meetings laws and submit to program and financial audits."

It goes without saying that charter schools must meet state and local standards regarding food safety, child abuse, health standards, transportation safety, and discipline, suspension and expulsion of students.

Federal laws applicable to charter schools include the Age Discrimination Act of 1975, Title 6 of the 1964 Civil Rights Act, the Americans with Disabilities Act of 1990, and the Individuals with Disabilities Education Act.

In theory at least, charter schools are subject to all the regulations that apply to public schools.

Are existing charter schools doing a creditable job of educating their charges? Has any research been done on them? The answer is a qualified yes. But the results are largely inconclusive. A few studies have been carried out in several states, with cautiously optimistic results in some of them. But a word of caution should be applied at the outset: Most of the research and analysis seem to have been organized by relatively sympathetic observers and scholars. As is true with home schooling studies, most of the researchers are sympathetic to the movement, thus skewing the results of the surveys, or at least raising questions about their methodology and premises.

One study by Rebecca Shore in 1997 found that charter school teachers have primary responsibility for governance, experience fewer bureaucratic restrictions and have considerable control over their working environments. A Minnesota legislative study found that charter schools are like new businesses, experiencing start-up costs, cash-flow restraints, and having difficulty recruiting staff and students. Most charter schools are small, averaging about 200 students, but do serve racially and economically diverse student populations. An 18-month evaluation by Cheryl Lange found that the schools were hampered by limited resources and a lack of precedent but did seem flexible and experimental in curriculum content and instructional style. A Colorado legislative study in 1997 found that most of the state's charter schools had met or exceeded their performance goals, were heavily dependent on local school district funding, and spent 82% of their budget on student-specific activities.

A study by Kathleen McGree in 1995 concluded that charter schools provided opportunity for teacher empowerment and greater accountability. A study of 44 California charter schools conducted by the San Diego Chamber of Commerce had mixed results. The California schools used innovative instructional practices, reached out to less advantaged student populations and had a high level of parent and community support. But the schools had inadequate facilities, conflicts with local school districts, and experienced legal challenges. The "Little Hoover Commission" in Sacramento found similar patterns and thought that California's charter school laws limited flexibility and reduced opportunities for innovation.

John Jenkins and Jeffrey Pow concluded that charter schools are not accessible to all students equally, while Louann Bierlein concluded that the movement, while seeming promising, will probably founder due to inadequate financial support, special interest groups, and a lack of entrepreneurial skills among educators. She and a colleague, Lori Mulholland, in a 1995 book (*Understanding Charter Schools*) published by the Phi Delta Kappa Educational Foundation, called charter "a bold reform with great promise." They cited "unique business and community partnerships," "a large percentage of existing funds being focused on instruction," and "numerous at-risk students being served."

A number of right-wing organizations have jumped on the charter school bandwagon. Chester Finn of the Hudson Institute and Diane Ravitch, a long-time critic of public education, are crusaders for charter schools, but they are hardly disinterested observers. The movement has gained some momentum in hard-pressed inner city areas where public schools need the most encouragement and improvement, with crumbling facilities and inadequate funding resulting from years of political neglect. Almost 4,000 students are enrolled in 15 charter schools in the District of Columbia this year.

But there are clearly serious problems with charter schools. In Arizona, which has the largest number of such schools, Republican governor Jane Hull has called for strict monitoring, reversing an earlier position after well publicized reports of many failures involving misuse of the $317 million provided by the state to 271 charter schools. The *Mesa Tribune* found many charter schools collapsing from mismanagement, buying property with state funds, funneling public money to private owners who lacked experience in management. Arizona law allows operators to keep property bought with public funds. The *Tucson Citizen* said, "Charter schools statewide need more rigorous oversight of what they do with the public's money." The paper also opined that charter schools should be subject to open meetings laws, since their deliberations are now closed to the public that finances them.

Another problem in Arizona is the racial makeup of charter schools. The *Arizona Daily Star* found the state's charter schools were racially unbalanced and many were in fact segregated. In Pima County (Tucson) nearly 3,000 students attend 24 charter schools. This 2.3% of all students in charter schools may represent the highest percentage for a county in the nation. The results show how a superficial analysis of statistics can be misleading. In the charter schools 46% of students are white, 35% Hispanic, 9% black, 8% American Indian and 2% Asian. This is similar to the county's population. But a close examination of the data reveals that 13 schools are majority white, 4 are majority Hispanic, 2 are majority American Indian and 1 is majority black. Only 4 of the 24 schools have real racial diversity. One school is 97% American Indian, one is 92% black, one is 90% white, and one is 78% Hispanic. So much for diversity!

The *Daily Star's* Sarah Tully Tapla also discovered that "state taxpayers are picking up the tab for a new group of students — former private and home schoolers who are now trying charter schools." In Pima County alone, $314,226 of public funds is paying to educate former home schoolers and private schoolers.

Arizona has become something of a scandal. Charter school teachers do not have to be certified. Virtually anyone can establish a charter school, with little or no accountability. "Educational diversity is being eroded," says Kim Donohue, a second grade teacher at Edison Elementary School in Mesa. She added, "The Mesa school system spends 12% of its funding on special needs children. Arizona's charter schools spend just 1%. One charter school promises its students a Mormon education, complete with Mormon teachers and tutors."

A similar situation exists in North Carolina. That state's Office of Charter Schools has revealed that 22 of the 60 charter schools violate the diversity clause because their student bodies are more than 85% African American. State legislators require these schools to "reasonably reflect" the demographics of the school districts they serve. Several teachers' organizations and members of the legislature's Black Caucus want the schools to diversify or be closed, but white Republican members are supporting the existing situation. Statewide more than half of all charter school students are black, compared to 30% black in public schools. (Private schools in the Tarheel State are lily white.)

But the most serious problem in charter schools is the church-state angle. While most state charter laws require that these schools be nonsectarian, there are loopholes in many states. In New York the Reverend Floyd Flake of Queens, former Congressman and pastor of the Allen A.M.E. Church, which runs a flourishing parochial school, pushed for loopholes that would allow church-run schools to become charter schools for "secular subjects." He and his supporters maintained that religious and secular studies could be separated in the budgets, a fiction the U.S. Supreme Court rejected in the 1970s.

In Chicago the Reverend Michael Pfleger proposed to turn St. Sabina's School into a charter school, with the support of the public school's top official, Paul Vallas. In Milwaukee charter schools, religious schools and a new entity called contract schools are all eating away at the public education budget, especially since the Wisconsin Supreme Court allowed the use of vouchers at religious schools and the U.S. Supreme Court let the ruling stand. This tragic set of circumstances has already resulted in a loss of $22 million from the Milwaukee school funding programs, all under the dubious rubric of "choice." Ethnic, racial and class divisions are expected to increase in the years ahead.

The church-state collusion problem should be nipped in the bud. All state charter laws should specifically prohibit religious schools from becoming publicly-funded charter schools and should forbid charter schools from becoming quasi-parochial schools. New York State's new law says that "no charter shall be given to a school that would be wholly or in part under the control or direction of any religious denomination or in which any denominational tenet or doctrine would be taught." The charter law also forbids the overt teaching of religion as well as the conversion of existing religious schools into charter schools.

But the *New York Times* charged that church schools "might try to get around the constitutional limits by setting up a secular school on church property and then providing religious instruction during off hours. Others may create a nominally secular school that nonetheless caters mostly to children from a particular religious community. But a school that is largely run by church members — even with a secular program — might well violate the law."

Even the strictest laws, says the *Times,* "may not be enough to prevent charter schools, which are supposed to be alternative public schools, from becoming de facto church schools."

The laws in all states should be tightened to reflect the constitutional principle that church and state must be kept separate. The *Times* editorial of January 17 concluded with an observation that is relevant nationally, "The more prudent course would require that any schools with church-related ties recruit students actively from outside the denomination and that the schools be run by boards dominated by community leaders from outside the church."

Since charter schools seem likely to remain options, at least for now, they should abide by standards applicable to all democratic institutions. States should monitor their educational programs to make certain that high academic standards are maintained. Religious, racial and cultural diversity should be attained and preserved. Teachers should be qualified and certified and not subject to religious or "lifestyle" tests. Those public bodies that fund charter schools should make certain that no harm is done to existing public schools of this nation which, after all, educate 90% of our children. It is the public schools, open to all and serving the needs of a broad community, which should be strengthened and improved as this nation enters the third millennium.

— Al Menendez

Home Schooling: The Facts

In this article ARL's Al Menendez summarizes the findings of his research on a phenomenon that has been receiving increasing attention, home schooling. These findings will be part of a monograph that ARL will publish next year. The article takes no position on whether home schooling is good or bad. We publish it because a number of advocates of tax support for nonpublic education, through tuition vouchers or tax credits, propose including home schooling in those plans.

— Edd Doerr

Home schooling is the new child on the educational block. An estimated half million—some say one million—students are now schooled at home by parents who, for one reason or another, find public and private schools inadequate. The vast majority of home schoolers are religious fundamentalists, according to surveys conducted by the handful of educational researchers who have studied the phenomenon. After two decades of legal conflict, home schoolers have achieved a number of legal victories. All 50 states now accord a degree of legal recognition to those who wish to educate their children at home. Congress has also been increasingly compliant to their demands. Critics see the trend as part of an anti-public school temper which seeks to defund and weaken public education through various choice schemes and voucher plans. Leaders of the home schooling movement have fueled this suspicion with harsh attacks on public education in general and on teachers and teachers' organizations in particular.

Home educators tend to have a higher educational background and socioeconomic status than parents generally and are likely to have much larger families (more than double the national average of children per family). Seventy-five percent attend religious services weekly, almost double the national average. And 90% are of white Anglo-Saxon ancestry.

The home schooling movement has resulted in considerable litigation, since all states have compulsory attendance laws regulating the number of years of education required of children. Furthermore, there are complicated legal relationships involving days of annual attendance, required subjects, certification of teachers and a host of other administrative questions.

Thirty-four states have home school statutes or regulations. Nevada did so in 1956, followed by Utah in 1957. There was a quarter century delay until Arizona and Mississippi passed laws in 1982. Maine, Rhode Island and Utah give school superintendents or school boards authority to approve home schools.

Forty-one states do not require home school parents to have any specific educational qualifications. North Dakota requires passage of a "Teachers Test," while West Virginia allows parents with a GED or high school diploma to teach until the child reaches high school. Seven states (North Carolina, New Mexico, Ohio, Pennsylvania, Georgia, Tennessee, South Carolina) require teachers to have a high school diploma or a GED.

Four states require approval by the local public school district, school board or state commissioner before home schools can exist (Maine, Massachusetts, Rhode Island, Utah).

Seven states (Connecticut, Indiana, Iowa, Kansas, Maine, New Jersey, Nevada) require instruction or amount of time in school to be "equivalent" to public schools. (This requirement was struck down by courts in Minnesota and Missouri.) Maryland, Delaware and Rhode Island require home instruction to be "regular and thorough," while Idaho and Michigan require it to be "comparable" to public education.

California, Kansas, New York, and Ohio require home school teachers to be "competent," "qualified" or "capable of teaching."

Twelve states treat home schools as equivalent to private or parochial schools (Alaska, Alabama, California, Delaware, Illinois, Indiana, Kansas, Kentucky, Michigan, Nebraska, Louisiana, Texas). Five other states (Colorado, Florida, Maine, South Carolina, Utah) allow groups of home schoolers to qualify as private or church schools.

As to standardized testing or evaluation, the pattern varies. Sixteen states require standardized testing: Alaska, Arkansas, Georgia, Hawaii, Minnesota, New York, Nevada, New Mexico, North Carolina, North Dakota, Oregon, Pennsylvania, South Carolina, South Dakota, Tennessee, and Washington. In Georgia and Washington, the results do not have to be transmitted to public school authorities.

Fourteen states require alternatives to testing in order to monitor home schooling progress. They are Arizona, Colorado, Connecticut, Florida, Iowa, Louisiana, Maine, Massachusetts, Ohio, Vermont, Virginia, New Hampshire, Washington, and West Virginia. The remaining twenty states do not require any standardized testing or evaluation of home schooling.

Oklahoma may be the home schoolers' favorite state. It is the only state with a constitutional amendment guaranteeing the right to home schooling.

As a result of litigation by the Home Schooling Legal Defense Association (HSLDA), a number of courts have ruled in favor of home schooling interests. The Michigan supreme court ruled in 1993 that home schoolers opposed to teacher certification because of sincerely held religious beliefs are exempt from this requirement. The HSLDA is run by Michael Farris, an attorney who has worked for Jerry Falwell's Moral Majority and Concerned Women for America and ran unsuccessfully as a Republican for the lieutenant governor of Virginia in 1993)

Eight states now allow home schoolers to participate in public school sports and extracurricular activities.

A number of philosophical premises underlie the home schooling movement. The most prominent is religion. A very significant, indeed dominant, reason for home schooling is a desire by many parents to pass on their religious perspectives without compromise, conflict, or challenge from others who hold different views.

A 1990 study of home schoolers by Western Baptist College in Oregon found that 96.4% of mothers and 93.8% of fathers described themselves as "born-again Christians." As to specific denominational or theological perspectives, about 40% of both parents were "independent charismatic" or "independent fundamentalist evangelical." About 18% were Baptists. Almost 8% belonged to the Assemblies of God denomination and another 3% called themselves "Pentecostal." About 3% were Catholic and just under 3% were members of Presbyterian or Reformed churches. About 1 % were Adventists, Lutherans, or Mennonites. Interestingly, about 16% listed "other" as their religious orientation.

Christopher J. Klicka, senior counsel at HSLDA, wrote a scathing book, *The Right Choice,* attacking public education and extolling home schooling. He says, "Home schoolers must remain committed to prayer for protection and committed to train up the children to think and believe as Christians." Klicka insists that most home schoolers share this religious orientation. "Approximately 90 percent of the estimated 250,000 home schooling families in the United States are Bible-believing Christians. Therefore, the Word of God is recognized as the source of all truth and the standard by which all things are measured. These parents want their children not only to believe as Christians, but to develop minds so they can think as Christians. They want their children to be biblically literate."

Klicka adds, "God will always hold parents responsible for the education their children receive," and "Public schools are teaching the children to be biblically illiterate and to ignore godly, absolute moral values."

Klicka advocates a kind of totalistic religion-controlled education and casts aspersions on those who disagree. "A godly education, therefore, is learning not only to believe as a Christian (for salvation), but to *think* as a Christian. Christian home schooling teaches children to think as Christians. Unfortunately, public schools and some private schools are teaching children who believe as Christians to think as non-Christians. Since Christian parents in the past have neglected their *duty* to follow this comprehensive approach to education, generations of adult Christians now apply ungodly principles in their lives and work places, while simultaneously believing as Christians. In essence, many parents are raising humanistic Christians, many of whom are 'lukewarm' and not thinking God's thoughts after Him."

Home schooling is seen not just as an acceptable alternative to other modes of education but as the only one acceptable to God and "based on God's commands." Klicka says, "Home schooling is truly a biblical form of education. It is clear that God is raising up the home school movement in which properly trained children will one day assume leadership. God is blessing the home schooling movement, not because families are home schooling for home schooling's sake, but because the families are faithfully teaching their children to obey and glorify God."

The Bible, Klicka emphasizes, must undergird the entire educational experience. "Scripture speaks to every area of life. It is clear that education is inescapably religious. Every subject, as a result, needs to be studied through the lens of God's Word."

In an appendix, Klicka recommends a dozen curriculum publishers, including those that have been criticized for religious intolerance, political bias, historical errors, and distortions. Klicka says that "Bob Jones University Press and A Beka Books are the two major Christian school textbook publishers. Both do a very good job."

There is a small Catholic dimension to the home schooling movement, perhaps 3% of the home-educated population. It is vigorous in its belief that traditional Catholic schooling has become as deficient in values and academic formation as public education.

Mary Kay Clark, director of the Seton Home Study School, writes: "Ninety percent of home schooling Catholic parents choose it in order to protect their children from evil influences in the schools, Catholic and otherwise, which are pulling their children away from God, away from the Catholic Church, and away from their own family."

Citing sex education and insufficiently conservative religious instruction in Catholic schools, Clark angrily declares: "Many of the Catholic schools of this nation are the training camps of the enemies of the Catholic Church. No longer do we find in the Catholic schools stalwart and unflinching defense of God's Truth. What we find more often is a tacit acceptance of contraception and other sexual evils, the denial of the existence of absolute truth, the acceptance of secular humanist ideas, along with a general contempt for and neglect of the doctrines of the Faith." She adds, "In our current pagan society, where the Catholic schools have been using secular textbooks since the 1960's, where Catholic parents have trusted the Catholic schools to pass on the Faith and the Culture, many of the Catholic treasures have been lost to millions."

Public education is not an acceptable alternative, however. Clark claims: "The public schools of this nation are the enemy of this nation, and the enemy of each American child. The schools and their promotion of drugs through the drug programs, their promotion of illiteracy through erroneous reading programs, their promotion of contraception, their promotion of homosexuality, their promotion of suicide and abortion, is leading us out of existence as a free nation. No longer a Christian nation, soon we will be no nation at all."

Klicka blames public schools for every imaginable societal problem. "The public schools fail miserably in the area of socialization, with the abundance of crime, drugs, immorality, and gang warfare rampant in the school system." Therefore, "Sending our children to the public school violates nearly every biblical principle. It is tantamount to sending our children to be trained by the enemy. No doubt that if Satan had his choice as to which school system he would want us to send our children to, he would choose the public school system."

As might be expected, the political orientation of the Home School Legal Defense Association is extreme right wing. Its journal, *Home School Court Report,* loathes the Clinton administration and waxed exultant over the 1994 Republican capture of Congress. Two Republican members of Congress, Vernon Enters of Michigan and Donald Manzullo of Illinois, are themselves home schoolers.

The movement continues to grow. It has small liberal, secular, and Muslim segments. But overall it is clearly an ally of the Religious Right's attempt to dismantle and restructure the entire educational enterprise in this country.

— *Al Menendez*

Media Unfair to Catholic Church?

A recently-released study by the Washington, DC-based Center for Media and Public Affairs concludes that the secular news media tend to portray the Roman Catholic Church as authoritarian, oppressive and irrelevant to modern life.

The study, "Media Coverage of the Catholic Church," co-authored by Linda and Robert Lichter and David Amundson, based its findings on coverage of Catholic issues appearing in *Time, The New York Times, The Washington Post,* and CBS Evening News during the years 1964-68,1974-78, and 1984-88.

It admits at the outset, "To analyze media coverage of the Catholic Church is a daunting task, owing to the sheer magnitude and diversity of the material under consideration."

Its conclusions are important, if only because the media involved have taken note of them, and because of the far-ranging implications of the study and of those who would interpret them in such a way as to inhibit future reporting of Catholic Church events.

The report reached several conclusions. Among them: "Opinions in the media were tilted against the Church's teaching on issues involving sexual morality and authority relations within the Church, and its involvement in secular politics (aside from support for Church statements opposing war).... The news was certainly not all bad for the Church. The study found that members of the hierarchy were heavily cited; official teachings were frequently presented, most often without refutation by critics; and on some issues, ranging from abortion and homosexuality to ecumenism and questions of war and peace, the Church's teaching was endorsed by a majority of sources whose opinions were printed or broadcast. Overall, however, the negatives for the Church outweighed the positives. On most controversies involving Catholic teachings, the Church came out on the losing side of the issue debate reported in the media."

The study also found that the media tend to "pit a hide-bound institutional hierarchy against reformers within and without" and to emphasize the church's "conservative ideology, authoritarian forms of control and anachronistic approach to contemporary society." The study also concluded that "long-range trends in the coverage have been less than favorable to the Church" for three reasons: "the sheer volume of coverage has dropped sharply since the 1960s; official church teachings are reported less frequently and are challenged more often when they do appear; and the language used to describe the Church increasingly carries connotations of conservatism, oppressiveness and irrelevance."

In one important area, church-state relations, the study uncovered two trends. One is that "discussions of the Catholic Church's relations with various levels of government in the United

States received the least coverage of any dimension in the study." The news media are simply uninterested in church-state news, which is probably why coverage of the parochiaid issue is often ignored, even during referendum elections. Also, the study found that "virtually every member of the clergy who was quoted (95%) upheld church teaching on issues involving church-state relations, while among the laity five out of six (84%) opposed church activities in the realm of secular politics."

This last finding is encouraging to church-state separationists and should be noted by political correspondents in the secular press.

But what of the study in general? Are its findings relevant or useful? For one thing, the genesis of the project remains suspect because it was sponsored and funded by the Knights of Columbus and the Catholic League for Religious and Civil Rights, which both have private agendas of a right-wing sectarian nature. Both groups frequently label any criticism of church policies or institutions, however valid or fair minded, as bigotry. Both groups lobby for parochiaid and total bans on abortion. Both groups excoriate liberal and progressive Catholics as "not real Catholics" or "anti-Catholic Catholics." In addition, those groups and others which have cited the study seem to have another agenda: the silencing of press criticism of all things Catholic, or the downplaying of events deemed embarrassing to the institutional church and its leaders. This is a disservice to all Americans, including Catholics, who feel that news of internal church activities should be freely reported, in an impartial and fair way, to be sure, but in a way that probes and analyzes events and trends that are important and newsworthy. This is the role of a free press, and in the long run it helps every institution, including religious groups. Cover-ups and suppressions do a disservice to democratic ideals within and without institutions of every kind as well as to society as a whole.

Doesn't criticism help the church by opening up debate and focusing on serious or neglected problems? The eminent liberal Catholic journalist John Cogley wrote around 1975 that Paul Blanshard's searing criticisms of Roman Catholic social policies in the 1940s and 1950s had helped the church face the future, had encouraged updating and democracy within the institution, and had immeasurably improved relations between religious groups in U.S. society. Wouldn't the church benefit from greater discussion about celibacy for the clergy, for example, when the U.S. Church is plagued with sexual discipline problems among the clergy? Pope Paul VI did not help matters when he forbade any public discussion of the issue more than two decades ago. These are issues the Lichter study failed to address.

Finally, the Lichter study is only part of a greater dimension in the reporting of news. One suspects that a similar study of media coverage for evangelical and fundamentalist Protestants, or atheists, would produce similar results. The press today takes its adversarial and critical role seriously. Even conservative Catholic journalist Joseph Sobran found the study unexceptional. He said that journalists see themselves as "activists, advocates and adversaries." He wrote, "By all means let's demand fair treatment for the Church, but let's avoid thinking of Catholics as victims of a media conspiracy. We're not." Everette E. Dennis, director of the Gannett Foundation Media Center at Columbia University, also cautioned, "You can take almost any institution in American life... and find that it is covered more negatively than positively. These are not astounding findings."

Neither the Catholic Right nor the secular media should misrepresent the findings of the Lichter study. The conclusions, such as they are, should not be used to silence or cower the press into inattention or inactivity in reporting religious news, especially as it affects the world's largest and most influential religious body. If anything, the report points up the need for better coverage of church-state news.

— Al Menendez

School Choice: Panacea or Scam?

Choice is a good word, an excellent word. It resonates favorably with nearly everyone. We favor choice when it comes to careers, spouses, friends, elections, religion, entertainment, and brands of cars and toothpaste. Most Americans favor choice of options when women face problem pregnancies.

Choice, however, is now being touted as a cure-all for the ills, real and/or imagined, of our public schools. If families could only choose their children's schools, the argument runs, then bad" schools would dry up and blow away, all children would get better education, and we will march joyfully into Utopia.

The Bush administration, the Catholic bishops, the Brookings Institution (via John Chubb and Terry Moe's 1990 book *Politics, Markets, and America's Schools}*, former Delaware governor Pierre duPont, and a host of propagandists and sectarian special interests have hopped on the school choice bandwagon.

School choice proposals are of concern to all Americans. We the people, we the taxpayers, will have to pay the bills, and the kind of educational arrangement we pay for will profoundly affect our lives, our children's lives, our economy, and the future of our society and our democratic public education system.

School choice can mean many different things. Confined strictly to public schools, it could be positive and manageable, on the one hand, or, on the other, unmanageable, chaotic, and wildly expensive. Extended to include nonpublic schools, choice plans raise fundamental constitutional issues, would surely create far more serious problems than they are supposed to cure, and would raise school costs to unprecedented levels.

As applied to nonpublic schools, tax supported choice is clearly improper. In the 1970s the U.S. Supreme Court ruled unconstitutional all but the most peripheral and "minor" forms of tax aid. Specifically rejected were such schemes as tuition reimbursements via tax credits or vouchers and providing educational services in sectarian schools. The minor and peripheral forms of parochiaid not ruled unconstitutional by the Court, which cost federal and state taxpayers over $1 billion annually, include transportation service (except for field trips), textbooks and equipment "loans," remedial education offered off the private school campus, and diagnostic exams.

Constitutionality aside, tax aid for nonpublic schools means tax support for the denominational instruction or indoctrination found in virtually all sectarian schools. Of the slightly less than 11% of elementary and secondary students in the U.S. who attend nonpublic schools, well over 90% attend pervasively sectarian schools in which sectarian instruction is almost always mandatory, even for students of other faiths.

Women's rights supporters, incidentally, will note that the overwhelming majority of nonpublic students attend schools operated by denominations which refuse to ordain women and which oppose freedom of conscience for women on reproduction.

Because they are pervasively sectarian and generally mandate participation in sectarian instruction, nonpublic schools tend strongly toward denominational homogeneity. In plain English, Catholic schools rarely appeal to Protestants, Jews, or Muslims; fundamentalist schools rarely attract Catholics, mainstream Protestants, or Jews; Jewish schools seldom attract non-Jews;

and Muslim schools almost never attract non-Muslims.

In addition to being religiously rather homogeneous, nonpublic schools tend to practice other types of selectivity and discrimination. They enroll fewer children with handicaps than public schools. A large percentage of private secondary schools discriminate by gender in admissions. Most nonpublic secondary schools enroll mainly college-bound students; they usually require entrance exams and their curricula tend to be college-prep and to ignore vocational subjects. Nonpublic schools seldom retain students with discipline problems, so it is common for expellees from nonpublic schools to turn up in public schools, which are generally required to accept them. Many private schools use religious and other criteria not allowed in public schools in hiring staff. Catholic schools generally do not tolerate teachers who are divorced and remarried or who are known to support freedom of conscience on abortion. A fundamentalist school in southern California once fired its principal because he was "thinking about" hiring a Catholic teacher.

Promoters of school choice plans talk about students and their families choosing schools. But they have the cart before the horse. It is the nonpublic schools which do the choosing. They choose which students to admit and which to reject. Including nonpublic schools in choice plans means that the nonpublic schools, or the religious bodies which run them, choose their students, choose what religion or ideology to teach them, and then choose that the taxpayers will pay for them. Since nonpublic schools, unlike public schools, are not subject to democratic control by those who pay for them, the taxpayer is stuck with "taxation without representation" and is deprived of the choice of which religions he or she will support. Many taxpayers would be funding private schools that would exclude them from their faculties.

Including nonpublic schools in choice plans means increasing the costs of taxes to pay for elementary and secondary education by at least 11%. Most nonpublic schools today may be able to operate at a lower per-student cost than public schools, but that is due to the fact that they pay teachers less, seldom serve severely handicapped children (whose education in public schools can often cost as much as six times that of non-handicapped children), and seldom offer expensive vocational courses. If nonpublic schools had to offer the same levels of programs and teacher salaries as public schools, their per-student costs would at least equal public school costs. And since nonpublic schools tend to be much smaller in enrollment than public schools, their lower economies of scale would make their per student costs even higher.

Transportation costs are another complicating factor. About half of all public students are bussed to school, either because the schools are too far away for walking or because students would have to cross dangerous streets and highways. If students were allowed to go to the public school of their choice within their own school district, obviously a much larger percentage of students would have to be bussed, and bussing costs would increase. If students could attend public schools in other districts, as some choice plans would allow, transportation costs would go still higher. If nonpublic schools are included in choice plans, bussing costs would rise astronomically. Pennsylvania already requires that students be bussed to nonpublic schools miles outside their public school districts and even across state lines into Ohio, Delaware, and New Jersey, at enormous cost to hard-pressed public school districts. Howard County, Maryland, busses students to five church schools within the county (which in Maryland is coterminous with the school district); it costs precisely twice as much to bus a student to a church school as to a public school. In northern Ohio, a school district is required to transport two students *by airplane and taxi* from an island in Lake Erie to a church school on the mainland, even though the island has its own public schools; the transportation alone for the students costs more than Ohio spends per year educating a student.

Who will pay for the transportation to "schools of choice"? If the taxpayers pick up the bill, the costs will be astronomical, and this at a time when states and cities from coast to coast are having to slash school budgets, cut programs, increase class size, lay off teachers, and freeze salaries. If the public does not pay the transportation bills for getting students to schools of choice, then only children whose parents can drive them to school will be served.

Choice plans, whether they include nonpublic schools or not, would surely add to school administrative complexity and costs.

With public school budgets either static or shrinking in most of the country's nearly 16,000 school districts, choice plans, with or without the inclusion of nonpublic schools, can only increase costs or force reduction in already underfunded public school programs.

Even in the extremely unlikely event that choice plans did not increase school costs, most choice plans would be objectionable for other reasons. By further dividing children along creedal, ideological, social class, ethnic, academic ability level, and other lines, they would increase social fragmentation. The great virtue of the American comprehensive school is that it tends to bring all sorts of children and teachers together in a democratic and democracy-enhancing enterprise.

Choice in education can be positive when it functions within a democratically controlled public school system. The comprehensive secondary school offers students many choices in the curriculum and also in extra-curricular activities. A single elementary or secondary school could contain two or more separate public schools. In some cases, two or three public schools could offer differing modes of education. The important thing is that no choice system that is publicly supported should be allowed to promote division and divisiveness among students.

The bottom line is that most of the vocal promoters of educational choice today are less interested in improving public education than in securing tax support for nonpublic, mainly sectarian education. School choice is offered as a cheap, painless panacea for problems both real and imagined. It is being touted as a way to improve education without having to find new sources of revenue.

We know a great deal about what is wrong with American education and what needs to be done about it. For instance, we need to fully fund the proven successful Head Start program for bringing disadvantaged children as close as possible to a level playing field by the time they are ready to start school. We need to fully fund the remedial education programs aimed at keeping as many students as possible up to grade levels. We need to lower class sizes, especially in inner city schools. We need to enrich our school programs in sex and family education, both to better prepare young people for the responsibilities of adulthood and parenthood and to reduce the problem of teens having children. Other educational reforms, such as improving education in reading, writing, science, languages, math, etc., can then follow more easily. Beyond the schools, we must treat the social pathologies associated with poverty, inadequate housing and medical care, drugs, and crime. Our whole society and each of us will benefit from these real reforms.

Doing what needs to be done will obviously cost billions annually. In addition to eliminating government waste, we will surely need to have higher, and hopefully more equitably assessed, taxes. Among the leading 16 industrial nations, the U.S. ranks thirteenth in the level of our effort in supporting elementary and secondary education. The U.S. cannot long remain a world leader at that rate.

Meanwhile, painless panaceas like choice plans that include nonpublic schools must be seen for what they are—devices for distracting our attention from our real problems, scams aimed at wrecking church-state separation, democratic public education, and the fundamental right of citizens not to be forced to support religious institutions.

Eastern Europe: Changes Coming

Recent events in Eastern Europe have been remarkable. Long-entrenched Communist regimes have been toppled without bloodshed in Poland, Hungary, East Germany, Czechoslovakia, and Bulgaria. Only in Rumania was a bloody revolution necessary to overthrow a megalomaniacal dictator.

Furthermore, changes within the Soviet Union, initiated by reformist President Mikhail Gorbachev, are likely to affect nationalist stirrings in the restless republics of Lithuania, Latvia, Estonia, the Ukraine, and Muslim strongholds near Iran and Turkey. It seems unthinkable, but these areas could become independent sometime in the future. This is especially true in the Baltic countries, which were independent republics between the two wars.

While most of the world's press attention has been focused on the political and economic implications of these upheavals, there is a strong religious element present in the situation.

Here is what's happening in each area. A majority of the 74 million practicing Christians in Eastern Europe are Roman Catholics. Their church's present leader is a Pole who lived under a communist regime. Pope John Paul II has played a major role in the events of the past decade, inspiring the Solidarity movement in 95% Catholic Poland. Poland became the first East-bloc country to remove the Communists from power in a free election, and its Prime Minister, Tadeusz Mazowiecki, is the first practicing Christian political leader in the East since World War II. Poland became the first state in the Soviet bloc to enact a law restoring civil rights to churches, and diplomatic relations were established with the Vatican. There is some indication that Polish church authorities want to restore some of their prewar power. Cardinal Glemp, for example, has urged the government to ban abortion, which is widespread in Poland. There is also a residue of anti-Semitism among Polish church people.

Vatican diplomacy is patient and far-seeing. Its *Ostpolitik* appears to have been successful. The Pope dreams of reunion with the Eastern Orthodox Churches, which have millions of followers in the Soviet Union, Bulgaria, Rumania, and Yugoslavia. He also believes that Christianity in general could fill the vacuum that exists when political regimes topple. The Pope's historic meeting with Gorbachev in December highlights his intense interest in the region. On the agenda was a discussion of events in the Ukraine and Lithuania, where there are many Catholics despite decades of repression.

In Lithuania probably 65% of the people are practicing Catholics. The cathedral in Vilnius has been restored for worship after being used as an art museum for decades. Bishops have been appointed. (In nearby Soviet Belorussia a Catholic bishop was appointed for *the* first time since 1926.) The majority of Lithuanians want independence from the USSR

In the Ukraine a serious problem exists concerning four million Catholics of the Uniate Rite. They recognize the Vatican, but their worship and customs resemble Russian Orthodoxy. Their priests are married, for example. In 1948 Stalin, with the connivance of the Russian Orthodox hierarchy, eliminated Uniate Catholicism by abolishing 4,100 churches and imprisoning all the clergy. The Uniate churches were taken over by the Orthodox. Now Gorbachev has promised Catholics freedom to organize and exist once again. Despite persecution a large underground church has existed for 40 years among Catholics who refused to become Orthodox. Catholic enthusiasm, however, has taken an ugly turn. Catholics have seized several churches that originally belonged to them, threatening to reawaken religious conflict between Orthodox and Catholics. Orthodox clergy recently appealed to British Prime Minister Thatcher to intervene on their behalf. (This potential for trouble also exists in Rumania and Slovakia, the eastern region of Czechoslovakia, where Eastern Catholic churches were seized by Communist authorities and given to the Orthodox in 1948.)

Gorbachev has openly proclaimed religious liberty for his people, and 3,000 new churches have opened in the USSR in the past year. Religious services are now broadcast on TV. For the first time since 1918 an Orthodox service was celebrated inside the Kremlin's Assumption Church.

Still, the Supreme Soviet has not given approval for greater religious liberty. Stalin-imposed statutes restricting churches and forbidding religious education have not been repealed. And the Orthodox Church may pressure Gorbachev to refuse freedom to Ukrainian Catholics. (Incidentally, Gorbachev was baptized into the Russian Orthodox Church and his mother is a devout believer.)

A final problem the USSR faces is hatred between the Shiite Muslim majority and the Armenian Christian minority in Azerbaijan, which borders Iran. Reports of pogroms against Armenians have forced Gorbachev to deploy troops to prevent further massacres. (Religious fanatics in Iran may be fomenting the attacks on the Christians.)

In Czechoslovakia repression of the Catholic majority has ceased. Six new bishops are expected to be appointed, and diplomatic relations with the Vatican are probable. The new president, Vaclav Havel, is a playwright, intellectual, and practicing Catholic who was seen crossing himself at his inauguration, which included religious representatives for the first time since World War II. In his inaugural address Havel quoted the 17th century Czech Protestant hero Jan Comenius. Protestantism, especially Lutherans and Calvinists, is also strong in Czechoslovakia.

Hungary, 60% Catholic, plans to establish diplomatic relations with the Holy See. The Office for Church Affairs has been abolished, and laws restricting religious freedom are being abolished. There is a vigorous Protestant presence in Hungary.

East Germany is the most Protestant nation in the East. Evangelical Lutheran churches were centers of organizing mass marches and rallies which overthrew the regime. Lutheran bishops expect to increase their influence on public policy. Religious services are broadcast on radio and TV, and some clergy sit in Parliament.

In Bulgaria the Orthodox Church is coming alive again and will probably play a greater public role than before the Communist takeover. Bulgaria is still torn by antagonisms between Christians and Muslims, a potential threat to future harmony.

The situation in Rumania is uncertain. The least democratic country in the region historically, Rumania's last free election was in 1928. Its one-time monarchy was allied with the Orthodox Church and ruthlessly persecuted minorities, especially Baptists and Jews. When Communism came, all religions were persecuted more or less equally. The bloody overthrow of dictator Ceausescu was welcomed by all religious groups. The dominant Orthodox Church is expected to play a role in the life of the nation. In the western province of Transylvania, the Hungarian Reformed Church is important, and some of its pastors played a role in the revolution. (Many leaders of the church have been accused of collaboration with the Ceausescu regime.) The fate of Byzantine Catholics is also uncertain. Their church was abolished in 1948, though many believers maintained a clandestine existence. The vice-president, whose wife is an active Baptist, is said to be keenly interested in religious liberty.

The smaller Protestant churches—Baptists and Adventists in particular—and the Unitarians are concerned that the reemergence of the historically powerful and once-established churches could threaten their existence. Past persecution is a reason for their trepidation. Optimists hope, however, that the shared suffering of all religious groups under totalitarian regimes for 40 years will bring them together and create harmony and respect for pluralism in a part of the world which has rarely enjoyed either.

Initial enthusiasm for these changes should be tempered somewhat by the possibility that some of the interfaith antagonisms could be reawakened if certain prewar problems are allowed to recur. One needs to remember that every nation in his region at one time experienced established religions, persecution and discrimination against minority faiths.

In Poland, for example, Roman Catholic ties to the state created serious problems for

Protestants, Orthodox, and Jews during the interwar period. There was constant conflict between church authorities who wanted greater influence on and control of education and questions of public morality and those who opposed church political domination. This was true in Roman Catholic and Orthodox countries.

Throughout the region there were sporadic outbreaks of interfaith violence and persecution, some of the worst atrocities of the Reformation and Counter-Reformation were found here. The treatment of large Jewish minorities was atrocious. Pogroms regularly afflicted Jews, particularly in Orthodox-dominated Rumania and Russia. Orthodox persecuted Catholics in some areas, but Catholics in Croatia collaborated with a pro-Nazi regime that ruthlessly persecuted Serbian Orthodox believers. The smaller Protestant and Old Catholic churches still have memories of repression, and whatever new church-state arrangements are developed in Eastern Europe must take these fears into account. (There have been occasional reports, for example, that some Protestant churches have been converted into Catholic churches in Poland, allegedly because of the refusal of authorities to grant permission for building new ones.) Rumania at one time persecuted its non-Orthodox minorities so cruelly that an international commission of observers was sent there in 1925. One hopes that international human rights organizations will maintain vigilance today.

— Al Menendez

December Dilemmas

The U.S. Supreme Court has agreed to review another nativity scene case during the 1988-89 term. This one, from Pittsburgh, gives the High Court another opportunity to set straight the rather murky decisions it has rendered and to offer guidance to communities which must face this now-annual December dilemma.

In 1984, in *Lynch v. Donnelly,* the Court approved the inclusion of religious symbols, like the creche, in publicly-sponsored Christmas ceremonies but only if secular holiday symbols were also included and only if the entire celebration was primarily secular in nature.

This half-victory for the church-state accommodationists has been seized by "moral majoritarian" activists (often the Knights of Columbus) as a wedge toward Court approval of fullscale religious activities by public authorities.

The Reagan White House was the first to move with unseemly haste when it restored the creche to the annual National Pageant of Peace event on the Ellipse in Washington in 1984, just after the Court's ruling in *Lynch v. Donnelly* was announced. Appeals by Jewish, secular, and some Christian groups fell on deaf ears.

This controversy has symbolic significance. Its resolution by the courts and by the court of public opinion may serve as a clue to the strength of the Constitution's Establishment Clause in our times. Admittedly, public opinion seems strongly on the side of publicly sponsored Christmas and/or Hanukkah symbols. The Williamsburg Charter poll in early 1988 revealed that 80% of Americans saw no constitutional problem when public authorities erect symbolic representations peculiar to one's religious tradition. But public opinion is not always right, especially in civil liberties conflicts. Nor is the public well informed on all issues.

Here is what the courts have said during the past decade of controversy:

Government agencies are not required to erect creches at any public site or at the request of any private group. The decision rests on the character of the property. If it is a park which has traditionally been used for various kinds of expression of free speech, a Christmas display is constitutional. But a lawn area in front of the municipal building which has not been a public forum does not fall under this requirement.

It is almost certain that government cannot erect or sponsor a religious Christmas display unless there are also secular symbols of the season included. This makes displays of the Jewish menorah even more complex because Hanukkah is not a secular holiday, nor is it a national holiday as Christmas has become. Some argue that the menorah is equivalent to a Christmas tree rather than a creche but that argument seems specious. Furthermore, *permanent* religious display is clearly unconstitutional.

The context and intent of civil officials are still important considerations. If there is a long history of community conflict or a clearly evident legislative intent to advance a particular religion, the courts may not sustain a Christmas display.

It apparently makes little difference whether private or public land is involved, if there is substantial government involvement. The dispositive issues remain. Religious Christmas carols may be included in public school Christmas programs only if there is a clear educational objective. Schools may not celebrate religious holidays or seek to advance religion or to convince students to accept a particular religious perspective. Religious art and literature may be used as part of the observance of the holiday only in a prudent and objective manner. Religious symbols connected with Christmas or Hannukkah can be displayed in classrooms on a temporary basis as teaching aids. It also appears that students can request dismissal from any of these exercises. "Predominantly religious" activities are not permitted.

Civil libertarians hope that the present Supreme Court will use the Pittsburgh case to strengthen the Establishment Clause rather than weaken it by appeals to "historical memory" or a sentimental fondness for cherished symbols.

But courtroom wrangles won't solve the December dilemma alone. It may be that the ultimate resolution will come from the appeal to reason and conscience which still stands as a vital part of the American experience. The *Washington Post* expressed a reasonable view shortly after the 1984 Pawtucket ruling. Its editors concluded, "The answer lies in the common understanding we have as Americans about our diverse religious views and our respect for each other's beliefs. This tolerance binds us as a people and protects us as individuals. We have agreed that each person may practice his own religion without interference from the state, and we don't want the government to do anything that will promote one religion over another.

"Let crèches appear on every church lawn in Rhode Island. Let the Pawtucket merchant association build one out of marble. But keep the city council and the taxpayers' money on the other side of Thomas Jefferson's wall lest an intrusive government, eager to support the large majority, crowd out, separate and impose on others whose rights are sacred too."

The annual "December dilemmas" might move closer to resolution if more Americans would acquaint themselves with the following facts.

A great many of the early American colonists did not celebrate Christmas. Its celebration was illegal in Puritan New England (too "popish" and profane). By the mid-nineteenth century Christmas was accepted as a holy day by Catholics, Episcopalians, and Lutherans, but not by Presbyterians, Baptists, and Methodists.

Alabama was the first state to declare Christmas a holiday, in 1836. Twenty-eight other states did likewise during the next thirty years, thirteen of them during the Civil War. It was only in 1870 that Congress recognized Christmas as a holiday in the District of Columbia, and it was not until 1890 that all states and territories recognized the holiday.

Public celebration of Christmas has always owed more to commercial than to religious interests in the U.S. Government sponsorship of Christmas observances not only favors Christianity over other religions, but also prefers some branches of Christianity over those which still do not attach religious significance to December 25. Many Christians regard Christmas celebrations as a pagan adoption not based on the Bible.

Americans of many religious traditions believe that they and their religious organizations are quite able to celebrate religious holidays without government sponsorship.

Religion in American Public Schools

Current federal court cases in Tennessee and Alabama could profoundly affect the future of public education and religious liberty in the United States. And adding to the controversy are recently published reports on how public school textbooks deal with religion.

In the Tennessee case, *Mozert v. Hawkins County Public Schools,* seven fundamentalist families are suing a local school board, charging that the reading textbooks teach evolution, witchcraft, situation ethics, idol worship, "secular humanism," "godless, one-world government," that "salvation may be obtained in other ways than by faith in Jesus Christ," and other allegedly "anti-Christian" values in conflict with their own faith. They particularly object to a series of readers published by the old, established firm of Holt, Rinehart, and Winston which include these stories: "The Wizard of Oz," "Rumplestiltskin," "The Emperor's New Clothes," "The Diary of Anne Frank," "The Great Houdini," and "Paul Revere's Ride."

What the fundamentalist plaintiffs want from the federal court is an order giving their public school children the right to use alternative textbooks and the right to be free from exposure to concepts viewed as incompatible with their religious beliefs.

"What is at stake here," points out school board attorney Timothy Dyk, "is whether people who have religious objections to certain ideas can force their public schools to provide their children with a curriculum tailored to their own particular beliefs." If these seven families win their case, then all other families would have the same right, and public education would degenerate into chaos, with different sets of families seeking dozens if not hundreds of alternative textbooks.

In the Alabama case, *Smith v. Wallace* and *Smith v. Board of School Commissioners of Mobile County,* 624 fundamentalist plaintiffs are suing the local school board and the state board, charging the schools with " the unconstitutional advancement of the religion of Humanism" and the "unconstitutional violation of the free exercise of religious rights of teachers and students by the exclusive teaching of Humanism and the systematic exclusion from the curriculum of the existence, history, contributions and role of Christianity in the United States and the world."

Added to this is the stir aroused by release of a Reagan administration study of how public school texts deal with religion by psychologist Paul C. Vitz. Vitz's Department of Education study of 60 elementary social studies textbooks shows that the books contain little mention of religion. Vitz, an ultraconservative ideologue, insists that the relative absence of material on religion in textbooks is due to a conspiracy of "secular humanists" who "have been able to dominate and control education," a charge which echoes the propaganda from such sources as Jerry Falwell's Moral Majority, Pat Robertson's "700 Club," and the writings of Tim LaHaye. By the way, Vitz's proposed remedies for the problem he sees are not only suits to force school districts to adopt new books but also to have government support sectarian and other private schools through vouchers or tuition tax credits.

These are the charges. But the reality is quite different.

Public school textbooks are produced by highly competitive private enterprises. Since the textbook market is so large, publishers spend considerable money and effort developing books that will not only be acceptable to state and local school systems and the tens of millions of parents they represent, but will also beat the competition. Our country's 16,000 local public school districts are almost all controlled by elected boards of local lay people who represent a pretty good cross section of the American public If anything, school boards tend to be more conservative than liberal. It is quite unlikely that more than an insignificant few of them could have a "liberal bias" or collaborate with a "secular humanist conspiracy" which exists only in the minds of paranoid Falwellians. While textbooks are never perfect, they do generally represent what the vast majority of people in a state or local district want. The annual Phi Delta Kappa polls of public attitudes toward public education have never registered the kind of dissatisfaction with textbooks voiced by the Tennessee and Alabama plaintiffs.

It is true that textbooks say very little about religion. But there are good reasons for this. There is wide disagreement among experts, scholars, and educators as to what facts or generalizations about religion should be taught, how they should be taught, and at what grade levels. There is even more disagreement among school administrators, school board members, and the lay public, very few of whom have any sort of clear picture of how the schools might teach about religion, which the Supreme Court has said may be done if the instruction is objective and neutral. When materials about religion have been included in texts or curricula, there are quite often objections that they are not balanced or objective, or are offensive to some people. Some people even object to teaching facts: several years ago a Catholic bishop in New York objected to a sentence in a history textbook which referred to the massacre of Huguenots in France. School districts, teachers, and textbook publishers seem to have tacitly concluded that the less said about religion in the classroom the better.

In any event, there is no great demand for the kind of academic, neutral, objective teaching about religion which the Supreme Court has said is both constitutional and desirable. Parents and religious bodies are free, of course, to provide any sort of religious instruction they wish to their children. Children spend only a quarter of each day on only half the days of the year in school, so there is ample time for parents and churches to expose children to as narrow or as broad a religious education as they please.

What about the charge that public schools teach "secular humanism" or that they are controlled by Humanists? It is nonsense. Our public schools are run by elected lay people who are broadly representative of their communities. Some may indeed be Humanists, but far, far more are mainstream Protestants, Catholics, and Jews. Just because John Dewey was a Humanist does not mean that the public schools whose teaching methods he influenced to a degree teach Humanism, any more than that people who use electric lights are atheists because Thomas Edison was an atheist.

There is a sense in which a generally agreed upon set of humane, civilized values, shared by mainstream Christians and Jews—humanistic with a lower case "h"—are included in school curricula, but the schools would be rather worthless, sterile, ugly places without them. But the naturalistic philosophy or lifestance (or religion, if you will) of Humanism with an upper case "H" is not and may not constitutionally be taught in public schools.

Finally, it should be noted that the shrill charges of "secular humanism" and complaints about textbooks saying too little about religion really serve, and may even be intended to serve, the purpose of masking the massive intrusions of fundamentalism into public schools. A number of school districts, especially in the South, continue to ignore the Supreme Court rulings against government sponsored prayer and religious instruction in public schools. Fundamentalist pressures have led to widespread downgrading of evolution in textbooks and classes. And, as we have reported in this newsletter, there are at least 4,500 fundamentalist missionaries operating in and through public schools to proselytize students.

Ours is a pluralistic society. Our common schools must be religiously neutral and sensitive to the wide religious and philosophical diversity of our students. The First Amendment requires religious neutrality in public education and the Supreme Court has consistently reinforced that principle. Parents, educators, lawmakers, and religious leaders need to work hard to defend that neutrality.

Chapter 3
Polls, Politics and Votes

Since its inception, VOR has devoted extensive coverage to the presidential election campaigns, the party platforms and primaries. But the heart of our coverage has been a detailed analysis of the election returns, particularly focusing on the impact of religion.

Albert Menendez, who served as a consultant to ABC News during the 1980 presidential race and to NBC News in 1988, wrote the 1988, 1992, 1996, 2000, 2004, and 2008 analyses. Menendez is also author of *Religion at the Polls* (Westminster), a groundbreaking 1977 book published during the beginning of the Carter presidency, as well as two 1996 titles: *The Perot Voters and the Future of American Politics* (Prometheus) and *Evangelicals at the Ballot Box* (Prometheus). His most recent political book is *The Geography of Presidential Elections in the United States, 1868-2004*, published by McFarland in 2005.

Included in this chapter are reports of changes in religious affiliations in Congress, religious influences on voting in Congress, and analyses of recent referendum elections that concern social and religious issues.

The Geography of the 2008 Election

These are some of the major trends:

1. Obama did best in cities (with incredible margins of 94% in Washington, DC, 85% in Chicago, San Francisco and Manhattan), suburbs (capturing long-time GOP bastions around Chicago and Philadelphia) and improving the Democratic vote in some exurbs and rural areas. Obama topped 60% in every New England state but New Hampshire and carried every county in the region except for rural and sparsely populated Piscataquis County, Maine. A sentimental vote of 72% in his home state of Hawaii pushed the Aloha State to Obama's top state, followed by once-Republican Vermont. The entire Northeast and Great Lakes region backed the Illinois Senator, and he put a crack in the once solid Republican South, carrying Virginia, North Carolina and Florida.

The Mountain West joins the Democratic map, with a sweeping Obama victory in Nevada, which now may be the new bellwether state since it has supported the presidential winner in every election since 1912 (except for 1976 when it backed Gerald Ford). Obama also won easily in Colorado and New Mexico.

Another impressive Obama win came in Indiana, which had not supported a Democrat since Lyndon Johnson in 1964 and, before that, Franklin D. Roosevelt in 1936. Neighboring Ohio, a key swing state since 1964, returned to the Democratic column.

2. McCain still carried 8 of 11 Southern states, and the Southern-flavored border states of Kentucky, West Virginia, Missouri (by a hair) and Oklahoma (his number one state, where he

received 66% of the vote and carried every county). An election with dramatic regional and/or county-level shifts may qualify as what some political scientists call a "realigning" election. We will not know whether this is true for 2008 until subsequent elections are held, but Obama's 53% to 46% victory, the most impressive Democratic showing since LBJ, may end up being one.

3. Realigning elections usually involve some voters and regions moving in an opposite direction from the winner, creating an "anti-trend" effect. John McCain ran stronger than President Bush in Arkansas, Tennessee, Louisiana and about even in Kentucky and West Virginia. The rural white South, in counties from north and east Texas all the way to West Virginia and spilling over into western Pennsylvania represent a sub-regional backlash, possibly based on race or some subliminal cultural factors. A *New York Times* study found that white rural counties characterized by low levels of education and income shifted three percentage points towards McCain. Many of the anti-Obama counties were anti-Kennedy in 1960, when voters in these heavily Baptist rural areas moved toward Nixon for religious reasons. Nearly 100 counties, mostly in Kentucky, Tennessee, Arkansas, Oklahoma and Missouri, switched from Adlai Stevenson in 1956 to Richard Nixon in 1960. Many of these same counties gave Barack Obama a lower level of support than they had given John Kerry or Al Gore. These are clearly some of the voters, Obama said, "whose support I have yet to earn."

But even in the pro-McCain areas, Obama did well in some cities, winning Nashville, Memphis, Louisville, Lexington, Little Rock, New Orleans and Baton Rouge, for example.

4. The outpouring of African American, Latino, young white, and college-educated white voters made the difference, swelling the Democratic vote totals in unlikely areas. "Breakthrough counties," a phrase I coined for my book, *The Geography of Presidential Elections in the United States, 1868-2004* (McFarland, 2005), tells us a lot about changing voting patterns, especially at the county level. The ability of one party or the other to break long-established voting habits, carrying counties that were once thought impossible, is one key to rewriting political history and to redrawing the map of political success. First, let's look at the Obama winning coalition breakthroughs.

Obama's popularity in the Chicago area led to the first Democratic victory since the Republican Party was founded in Du Page County, Illinois. Obama picked up 55% and a 44,000-vote plurality in this rock-ribbed Republican suburb west of Chicago. Even Barry Goldwater carried Du Page by 60-40 in 1964. (Just for the record, Du Page did go for Martin Van Buren in 1840, when the Whigs were the Democrats' opposition, but that was a long time ago!)

Chester County, Pennsylvania, the last Republican holdout in suburban Philadelphia, joined the other suburban counties, giving Obama 55% and a thumping margin of 23,000 votes.

Jefferson County, Alabama, which includes the state's largest city, Birmingham, went Democratic for the first time since Adlai Stevenson carried it in 1952. Obama won 52-47% and built up a 16,000 vote margin.

More Warning Signs

If this tour of the breakthrough counties isn't depressing enough for Republicans, consider this:

In **Sarasota County**, Florida, Obama came within 177 votes, out of 205,000 cast, of winning a county that has gone for the GOP since Tom Dewey in 1948. This is a "moderate" Republican area of prosperous Midwestern retirees, and very low church membership (just 36% of county residents belong to any congregation). The hard-right persona of the Republican Party has just about lost it another stronghold. **Salt Lake City**, Utah, came within 2,000 votes out of 382,000 cast of going Democratic. The Utah capital is fast becoming a non-

Mormon bastion in the shadows of the Mormon Tabernacle.

Region – McCain won only in the South, carrying eight of the 11 states, in addition to four of the six culturally Southern Border States. Therefore, 12 of the 22 states that backed McCain are in the Cultural South (though Maryland and Delaware have changed so much in recent decades that they probably should be classified as Northeast). The South is the only region that sent more Republicans than Democrats to Congress, and three of the four House seats that switched from Democrat to Republican were in this region. This is hardly the prescription for future success. (The GOP also held the Upper Plains area by reduced margins.)

The Democrats swept every state in the Northeast and Great Lakes region, the Pacific Coast, and carried New Mexico, Nevada and Colorado in the Mountain West, and came within three points of winning Montana.

The Republican Dilemma – Republicans continue to receive their greatest level of support nationally from white evangelicals and Mormons, with slim majorities from white Catholics and mainline Protestants in a few states. The attempted Democratic breakthrough and heavy campaign effort among white evangelicals was not successful, since the 25% vote for Obama is not much of an improvement over Kerry's 22%. Within one segment, however, Obama was successful: young evangelicals, aged 18-29, gave him 36%, nearly double the Kerry vote. But his 22% vote among those 45 and over was the same as Kerry's, and his vote actually declined from 32% to 26% among evangelicals over 65, many of whom live in the rural South.

— Al Menendez

Democrats Gain Across the Board

The Democratic victory this year was wide and broad. Barack Obama won the presidency 53% to 46% in nearly complete returns, a gain of nearly five points over John Kerry's showing four years ago. His electoral vote majority was 365 to 173, a 113-vote gain. He won 28 states, up from Kerry's 19. Nine states switched from Bush to Obama: Colorado, Florida, Indiana, Iowa, Nevada, New Mexico, North Carolina, Ohio and Virginia. Obama carried 320 counties, spread over 42 states that had supported Bush in 2004. McCain carried 44 counties in nine states (mostly in Tennessee and Arkansas) that had backed Kerry in 2004.

Obama won many normally Republican suburbs and cities, including Cincinnati, Reno, the Denver suburbs (Arapahoe and Jefferson Counties) and Kent County, Michigan (Grand Rapids, a Dutch-flavored Republican town and home of President Gerald Ford).

High-tech and scientific professional areas, such as Olmsted County, Minnesota (home of the Mayo Clinic), Somerset County, New Jersey (home base of many pharmaceutical companies), and Los Alamos, New Mexico, went Democratic for the first time since 1964.

Republican-leaning exurbs around Washington, DC, (Loudon and Prince William Counties, Virginia), Richmond (Henrico County) and Atlanta (Douglas and Rockdale Counties) supported Obama. So did Chicago-area exurbs (Kane, Kendall, McHenry Counties). Even in the South, Obama carried Winston Salem (Forsyth County), North Carolina, and Charleston, South Carolina – the first Democrat since Jimmy Carter in 1976 to do so.

He also won such long-time Republican areas as the counties containing Fargo and Grand Forks, North Dakota, Reading and Harrisburg, Pennsylvania, the Pocono Mountains resort and retirement area (Monroe County) and Tippecanoe County, Indiana, home to Purdue University.

The Obama triumph in the suburbs reflects several realities. Obama won 60% to 39% among self-designated "moderates" and 52% to 44% among those who call themselves Independents. Both groups are strong in suburban areas, as are college graduates, who gave Obama 54% to 45%, the highest level of support for any Democratic candidate, including Lyndon Johnson.

In academic counties, where college students, faculty and administrators are a major portion of the electorate, Obama's majorities reached landslide proportions, reflecting his 68% to 30% win among voters 18 to 29, 69% to 30% among first-time voters, and 58% to 40% among voters with postgraduate university degrees.

In the Senate, at press time, the Democrats lead 56 to 40, with two seats still undecided in Minnesota and Georgia. Two seats are held by Independents: Bernard Sanders of Vermont, a true Independent who caucuses with the Democrats, and Joe Lieberman of Connecticut, an "Independent Democrat," who campaigned for John McCain and spoke at the Republican National Convention. Lieberman caucuses with Democrats and retained his committee chairmanship.

The House will probably end up 259-176 for the Democrats, according to *Congressional Quarterly*, though there are recounts in California, Ohio, and Virginia, runoff elections in December in Louisiana, and a vacancy in Illinois, where Rep. Rahm Emanuel has resigned to become Obama's White House chief of staff. (The Senate seats held by Obama and Biden are also vacant but will be filled by Democratic governors). Emanuel's seat is a safe Democratic one in Chicago.

Democrats hold 29 governorships to the Republicans' 21, a gain of one, and picked up a number of state legislative seats. Democrats now control 27 state legislatures, compared to 14 for the Republicans, while eight are split, with each party controlling one house. (Nebraska has a nonpartisan legislature). Democrats gained in several states, including New York, Nevada, Ohio, Wisconsin and Delaware. Republicans gained only in Tennessee and Oklahoma, which gave the GOP control of their state legislatures for the first time.

Religion a Key Factor in 2004 Vote

A survey released on February 3 by the Pew Forum on Religion and Public Life showed major differences among religious groups in the 2004 presidential election. The new poll's findings are similar to exit polls and previous studies at the University of Akron, but are more refined in their breakdown of religious positions.

What the poll calls "Traditional Evangelical Protestants" gave 88% of their votes to Bush, followed by 80% of "Other Christians," which includes Mormons, a key Republican voting block. Bush received the support of 72% of "traditionalist Catholics" and 68% of "traditional mainline Protestants," a group that includes Methodists, Presbyterians and Lutherans of a conservative stripe. Bush also won the backing of 64% of "centrist evangelical Protestants," a

Religious Group	% for Bush	% for Kerry	% of All Voters	% Turnout
Traditional Evangelical Protestant	88	12	15	69
Other Christians	80	20	3	60
Traditionalist Catholic	72	28	6	77
Traditional Mainline Protestant	68	32	6	78
Centrist Evangelical Protestant	64	36	9	52
Hispanic Protestant	63	37	2	49
Centrist Mainline Protestant	58	42	8	68
Centrist Catholic	55	45	7	58
Modernist Evangelical Protestant	48	52	2	65
Unaffiliated Believers	37	63	3	39
Modernist Catholic	31	69	6	70
Hispanic Catholic	31	69	3	43
Secular	30	70	7	55
Jewish	27	73	3	87
Other Faiths	23	77	2	62
Modernist Mainline Protestant	22	78	6	71
Atheist, Agnostic	18	82	4	61
Black Protestant	17	83	8	50

new term for more moderate religious believers. The Catholic equivalent was 55% for Bush, and the centrist mainline Protestant equivalent was 58% for Bush.

A somewhat surprising finding was that 63% of Hispanic Protestants supported Bush's reelection, while a narrow majority of the same group supported Democrat Al Gore in 2000. Bush's Hispanic gains came from the Protestant sector of the Latino community, which is primarily Pentecostal and evangelical in orientation. Only 31% of Hispanic Catholics backed Bush, a figure virtually unchanged from 2000.

Senator John Kerry received the support of 83% of black Protestants, 77% of those who belong to "other faiths" (Muslim, Hindu, Buddhist, New Age, Native American), 73% of Jews and 70% of secular voters.

The Massachusetts senator was backed by 78% of "modernist mainline Protestants," 69% of "modernist Catholics," 63% of "unaffiliated believers," a category of Christians who rarely attend church and are not members of a local congregation, and 82% of atheists and agnostics.

Within every category, voters who defined themselves as traditionalists were more supportive of the Republican ticket than were the middle of the road centrists and the modernists, who called themselves liberals and progressives. Even among evangelicals, for example, Kerry won 52% of the modernists. Centrist evangelicals went 64% for Bush.

In a comparison to the 2000 election, Bush made his largest gains among Hispanic Protestants, traditional Catholics who rejected the first Catholic nominee in 44 years, black Protestants and "other" Christians. Moderate gains for Bush came from Jewish voters and centrist Catholics. Kerry, on the other hand, ran stronger than Gore, and Bush's support declined, among modernist Catholics, mainline Protestants of all kinds, and atheists and agnostics.

John Green, director of the Bliss Institute of Applied Politics at the University of Akron, which conducted the survey of 2,730 adults just after the election, said, "There was strong polarization not only between different religions as was common in the past, but also within the major religious traditions—a relatively new phenomenon."

Overall, 47% of respondents said that religion was an important influence on their presidential vote. Social issues, such as abortion and gay marriage, were strong vote-getting issues among Bush's top four constituencies. Among all voters, foreign policy and economic issues took top billing, though the culture issues were also important.

Bush Wins Again, With Big Assist from Religious Conservatives

Religious factors loomed large in the 51% to 48% reelection of President George W. Bush over his Democratic challenger, Senator John Kerry of Massachusetts. While other issues such as the economy and foreign policy and the war in Iraq were major factors in the vote, the religious makeup of the nation and how its components responded to the issues and personalities of this election are important.

Bush clearly owes his victory to the 23% of the electorate who call themselves "born again" or "evangelical" Christians, the white Protestants who shape the political landscape of the American South and much of the rural North and Midwest. Bush won 78% of their vote, and this support did not vary much regionally. The entire South with its 153 electoral votes, and the states of Missouri, Oklahoma, Kentucky, West Virginia, Kansas and Indiana, with 48 additional electoral votes, gave the president an almost insurmountable electoral vote lead that would have required Kerry to win three-fourths of the remainder of the nation to offset it. Bush received 201 of the required 270 electoral votes in the heartland of evangelical America.

Related factors are the 22% of voters who cited "moral values" as the primary issue determining their presidential vote. They cast 80% of their ballots for Bush. This category overlaps with some other religious groups, of course, but tends to isolate the social issue voter into a cohesive unit that can be studied. Then there was the tiny 8% who said the candidate's religious faith was a major factor in their vote. They gave more than 90% to Bush. This small segment was entirely evangelical and could have reflected some anti-Catholic sentiment, though it was probably more of an endorsement of Bush's intense public image of religiosity. (This sliver of the electorate favored Democrat Jimmy Carter in 1976 and 1980.)

Church attendance was a factor in voting, though a bit less so than in 2000. Bush won a bit over 60% among weekly churchgoers and less than 40% among voters who said they never attend religious services. The vote was closet among occasional or rare attenders. The more important factor is where people attended church, or how they defined themselves religiously. Bush, for example, received the votes of 36% of those who never attended religious services, but only 31 % of those who said they had no religious affiliation. Bush gained 7% over his 2000 vote among the non-churchgoers, which might raise an eyebrow or two. The 10% who reported no religion (up from 9% four years ago), favored Kerry 67% to 31%, up slightly over Gore.

Kerry ran much stronger than Gore among the 7% (up from 5% in 2000) who defined themselves as "other religions," a category that includes Muslims, Buddhists, New Agers, and Eastern Orthodox Christians. Bush's close ties to the Protestant-dominated Religious Right may have cost him votes among these diverse communities, though it will take some digging at the precinct level to discover the cost, if any, since exit polls are rather vague. The "other" vote was 74% to 23% for Kerry, compared to 54% for Gore, 33% for Bush and 9% for Nader in 2000. Precinct and township level data are always helpful in fleshing out the larger picture of voting.

The Catholic vote proved to be a great mystery. It was, once again, the closest to the national divide, showing that Catholics (27% of the electorate) are the classic swing voters. The Catholic vote was near 50-50, and it may have been 52-48% for Bush, according to the final exit poll results. (In this election, however, the exit polls came under fire for serious flaws of sampling, over-sampling and other problems that raise questions about their accuracy and validity.) What the results suggest is that there are several Catholic votes, not a monolithic one. Perhaps that is to be expected of such a large and diverse community.

If the national Catholic vote was narrowly for Bush — a big if — it had little impact on the results. Kerry's two strongest states in popular vote, Rhode Island and Massachusetts, are the two most Catholic states. States where Catholics are 40-50% of the vote, New York, Connecticut, and New Jersey, also went for Kerry. The 30%-40% Catholic states, Pennsylvania, Illinois, Wisconsin, Vermont and New Hampshire, also went for Kerry. States with 25%-30% Catholic went mostly for Kerry. They include California, Michigan, Minnesota and Maine. The only strongly Catholic states to go for Bush were Louisiana and New Mexico.

None of this tracks well with the exit poll findings. If the poll is accurate, Bush must have received the bulk of Catholic voter support in states where Catholics are a minority, such as the South and the nation's interior regions, where they have become like their Protestant Republican neighbors. It is true that Bush gained 5-7% among Hispanic Catholics, a factor in his New Mexico victory perhaps, and did win a majority of Hispanics in Florida, though not in California, Texas, Arizona, Colorado, New York or Illinois.

Catholics who reside in predominantly Catholic areas still voted for Kerry. In Dubuque, Iowa, for example, Kerry received 57%, an increase of 2% over Gore's 2000 vote. In St. Paul, Minnesota (Ramsey County), Kerry piled up a 75,000 vote margin and won 63%, 6% more than Gore. Kerry carried Jersey City 2-1, won easily in Buffalo and Albany. In tiny French Canadian Berlin, New Hampshire, Kerry received 64% compared to Gore's 59%.

In Pennsylvania Kerry carried predominantly Catholic Scranton and Erie and the Catholic neighborhoods of Philadelphia and Pittsburgh. Bush carried the rural Catholic areas of Elk, Cambria and Schuylkill Counties, suggesting that the rural/urban divide is strong among the same category of voters in the same state.

Bush won narrowly (1%) in the strongly Catholic towns of Manchester, New Hampshire, and Waterbury, Connecticut, and won big in the Italian Catholic bailiwick of Staten Island, New York. (Bush gained 5% in New York City and the surrounding counties, where there must have been some political fallout from the events of 9/11.)

Bush carried most of the rural Midwestern German Catholic vote, which has favored the GOP since the days of Wendell Wilkie. And he did win in the Detroit and Pittsburgh Catholic suburbs of Macomb County, Michigan, and Westmoreland County, Pennsylvania, and squeaked ahead in South Bend, Indiana (St. Joseph County). (But Kerry won easily in substantially Catholic Baltimore County, Maryland, and St. Louis County, Missouri.) Bush was victorious in the Catholic Cajun country of southern Louisiana, which has had an uncanny ability to support the winning presidential candidate in 12 of the last 13 presidential elections.

The Catholic community was the most divided of any religious community in this election, and the most unexpected development was Kerry's failure to win a higher percentage of it. As the first Catholic presidential candidate in 44 years, he was expected to do better and should have, since Catholics remain somewhat more liberal than Protestants on most issues. The impact of the attacks on Kerry by many Catholic bishops and by conservative Catholic organizations will need to be studied by political scientists.

Was there any anti-Catholic voting by evangelicals in 2004? It is difficult to say, since Kerry

Exit Poll Results, 2004 and 2000

| | 2004 | | 2000 | | |
	Bush	Kerry	Bush	Gore	Nader
Religion					
All White Protestants	67	32	61	35	2
White Evangelical					
Protestants	78	21	79	19	1
Catholic	52	47	47	50	2
Jewish	25	74	17	81	1
Other Religions	23	74	33	54	9
No Religion	31	67	28	61	9
Church Attendance					
More Than Weekly	64	35	62	36	1
Weekly	58	41	56	41	2
A Few Times a Month	50	49	45	51	2
A Few Times a Year	45	54	41	55	3
Never	36	62	29	62	6
Issue Related					
Strongly Pro-Abortion Rights	25	73	24	71	5
Strongly Anti-Abortion Rights	73	26	73	23	1
Favor Gay Marriage	22	77	-	-	-
Favor Gay Civil Unions	52	47	-	-	-
Against Gay Marriage/Unions	70	29	-	-	-

was also attacked by Catholic conservatives. But it may be significant that Bush's largest gains over his 2000 vote came in Alabama, Oklahoma and Tennessee, three of the most anti-Catholic states in 1960. And of the 97 U.S. counties that bolted against John F. Kennedy in 1960 after having supported Adlai Stevenson in 1956, Bush carried 92 of them, including five of the ten that voted for Al Gore. (Four of the five that supported Kerry were predominantly African American, where blacks could not vote in 1960, or Native American, where tribal Indians were discouraged from voting in 1960). In heavily Baptist and anti-Kennedy Lea County, New Mexico, Bush beat Kerry 80% to 20%. In nearby Roosevelt County, New Mexico, Kennedy and Kerry both received 29%, a lower vote than Stevenson or Gore. And in Dunklin County, Missouri, usually a Democratic area, Bush defeated Kerry 58% to 42%. Whether it was due to his Catholicism or his liberalism, Kerry ran poorly in those rural areas where JFK had also faced considerable opposition more than four decades ago.

African Americans of all religious persuasions gave Kerry about 90% of their votes. Native Americans voted heavily for Kerry (85% in Shannon County, South Dakota). Kerry carried all of the Indian Reservation areas in Montana, North Dakota, South Dakota, Arizona, New Mexico, Wisconsin, Maine, Minnesota and Massachusetts, and generally ran ahead of the Gore vote. Native Americans belong to several religious traditions, Roman Catholic and Episcopalian primarily, but Native non-Christian religions, Mormons, Lutherans and Presbyterians also have a following. In Alaska, the Native or Indigenous population is mostly Russian Orthodox.

Mormons were overwhelmingly supportive of Bush, solidifying his victory in Utah and Idaho, two of his strongest states. In Utah County, where Brigham Young University is located in Provo, Bush piled up an 86% to 11% margin. In Madison County, Idaho, where Ricks College, the only other Mormon College in the mainland U.S. is located, Bush was victorious by the stunning margin of 92% to 7%.

In Dutch-American counties, where the two branches of the Reformed Church are dominant and where many students attend faith-based schools maintained by the Christian Reformed Church, Bush won handily. In Sioux County, Iowa, Bush defeated Kerry 86% to 14%. Rural Dutch communities in Iowa, Minnesota, Wisconsin and Michigan provided similar margins for the GOP nominee.

Lutheran voters, a major voting bloc in Minnesota, Wisconsin, Iowa and the Dakotas (and a smaller but still significant vote in Nebraska, Montana, Illinois, Ohio and Pennsylvania), are almost as divided as Catholics. But the Republicans maintain an overall edge among Lutherans as a result of the German ancestry segment of this eight million member community. (Lutherans of Scandinavian ancestry are somewhat more Democratic, but Swedes and Danes are more Republican than Norwegians and Finns.) Bush won easily in counties where the Lutheran Church-Missouri Synod (LCMS) is influential. The LCMS is one of America's most conservative religious groups and maintains a large network of faith-based schools. In the last two elections, Lutherans in rural Minnesota have moved in a Republican direction and voted twice for Bush.

Methodists are strong in a string of states stretching from the Eastern Shore of Maryland to Kansas and Nebraska. They lean Republican, particularly in the small towns and rural communities where they are most numerous. The other mainline Protestant churches, including Presbyterians, have long supported the Republican Party, despite holding fairly moderate to liberal theological views and occasionally progressive stances on social issues. They still went 55% to 44% for Bush, making them an unshakably GOP-leaning segment of the national electorate.

Jewish voters were tied with "other religions" voters as the strongest group for the Democrats, giving Kerry 74% to 25% for Bush. This reflects a 6% to 8% Bush gain, however. The Jewish vote impact appears slight on a state level, and only 3% of the national electorate is Jewish. The Jewish gain for Bush, however, shows up in Rockland County, New York, which has a large Orthodox Jewish community. Bush narrowly carried this New York City suburb by 1,000 votes, while Gore had carried it by 16,000 votes four years before.

It appears, all in all, that the Bush campaign made modest gains among Jewish, Catholic and Hispanic voters, and precipitated a surge of evangelical votes for the president, while losing ground among voters of other or no religious traditions (which may also reflect Kerry's gains among younger voters and among voters with advanced college degrees).

The basic contours of American religious voting were reaffirmed by the 2004 election but several minor shifts could point to major changes in the future.

— Al Menendez

The Curious Case of the Congressman's Koran

The voters in Minnesota's 5th Congressional District, which includes the city of Minneapolis, elected a new Democratic congressman in 2006, Keith Ellison. Ellison is a Muslim, the first member of that faith to win election to the U.S. House of Representatives. Ellison won a tough Democratic primary, then easily defeated a Republican and an Independent in November.

Instead of celebrating Ellison's election as a validation – long overdue perhaps – of America's religious diversity, some Religious Right and Republican Party leaders pronounced themselves horrified by the election. This criticism escalated when Ellison announced that he would use the Koran during the private swearing-in that takes place after the public ceremony.

The attack began when Dennis Prager, a Los Angeles conservative talk radio host, wrote on *TownHall.com*, "America is interested in only one book, the Bible. If you are incapable of taking an oath on that book, don't serve in Congress." In an interview with Religion News Service, he added, "This has nothing to do with the Koran. It has to do with the first break of the tradition of having a Bible present at a ceremony of installation of a public official since George Washington inaugurated the tradition."

Prager's comments produced both support and outrage. An Islamic civil rights group, The Council on American-Islamic Relations (CAIR), urged that Prager be removed from the U.S. Holocaust Memorial Council, to which he was appointed by President Bush in August. CAIR executive director Nihad Awad said, "No one who holds such bigoted, intolerant and divisive views should be in a policymaking position at a taxpayer-funded institution that seeks to educate Americans about the destructive impact hatred has had, and continues to have, on every society."

The Anti-Defamation League said Prager's views were "intolerant, misinformed and downright un-American." Former New York City Mayor Edward Koch, a member of the U.S. Holocaust Memorial Council, said he would ask the group's advisory board to remove Prager as one of its 55 members. The Holocaust Museum issued a statement that said, "Talk show host Dennis Prager speaks solely for himself. His statements do not reflect the position of the U.S. Holocaust Memorial Museum, whose board is not self-appointed."

Prager received support from one shrill outpost of the Religious Right, the American Family Association (AFA), based in Tupelo, Mississippi. The group sent out an "action alert" to its members, urging them to lobby Congress "to pass a law making the Bible the book used in the swearing-in ceremony of representatives and senators." Ignoring both Article VI and the First Amendment guarantees of religious neutrality by government, AFA's email said bluntly that Ellison "should not be allowed to take his oath of office on the Koran because the act undermines American civilization and is an act of hubris that perfectly exemplifies multiculturalist activism."

The controversy soon proved to be an educational experience. Historians noted that there is nothing in the Constitution requiring the use of any holy book in the ceremony of taking of oaths of office for members of Congress or the presidency. It has been a custom for some to swear on the Bible but it is not required. Even conservative legal scholars agree. Kevin Hasson, head of the Becket Fund, told *The Christian Science Monitor*, "A congressman having to swear an oath on a scripture that he doesn't believe in was unconstitutional from the very moment the Constitution was signed. It would be beyond irony to violate the Constitution in the very act of requiring a congressman to swear his loyalty to uphold the Constitution."

Library of Congress researchers and congressional historians pointed out that John Quincy Adams took the presidential oath in 1825 on a law volume, and that Theodore Roosevelt used no Bible in 1901. Franklin Pierce in 1853 and Herbert Hoover in 1929 "affirmed" rather than "swore" allegiance to the Constitution.

According to Omar Sacirbey of Religion News Service, "But Ellison would not be the first member of Congress to forgo a Bible at the swearing-in ceremony. Congresswoman Debbie Wasserman Schultz (D-Fla.) took her oath in 2005 on a Tanakh, the Hebrew Bible, which she borrowed from Representative Gary Ackerman (D-N.Y.) after learning a few hours earlier that the Speaker of the House didn't have any Jewish holy books."

The conflict seemed to have died down when an obscure Virginia congressman, Republican Virgil Goode, reignited it. In a December 5 letter sent to hundreds of his constituents, Goode warned that the country was in danger of being taken over by Muslims unless Americans "wake up," he said, or else there would "likely be many more Muslims elected to office and demanding the use of the Koran."

In a strange brew of ignorance, bigotry, and Nativism, Goode added, "I fear that in the next century we will have many more Muslims in the United States if we do not adopt the strict immigration policies that I believe are necessary to preserve the values and beliefs traditional to the United States of America and to prevent our resources from being swamped."

Representative-elect Ellison generally ignored the attacks, though he noted that Rep. Goode seemed ill-informed about the Constitution. He added, "I'm not an immigrant. I'm an African-American." Ellison, whose American ancestors date back to 1742, was a college-age convert to Islam. Ellison told *The New York Times*, "I'm looking forward to making friends with Representative Goode, or at least getting to know him. I want to let him know that there's nothing to fear. The fact that there are many different faiths, many different colors and many different cultures in America is a great strength."

Goode's remarks, and his adamant refusal to apologize, did not go down well with many members of Congress and the media. Incoming House Speaker Nancy Pelosi called his comments "offensive." Rep. William Pascrell (D-NJ), whose congressional district has a large Muslim community, said he found the Goode statement "personally offensive." *The Washington Post* was outraged. In a December 22 editorial, "A Bigot in Congress," the capital's leading newspaper commented, "Mr. Goode, evidently in a state of xenophobic delirium, went on a semipublic tirade against the looming peril and corrupting threat posed by Muslim immigration to the United States." The paper continued, "This country's history is rife with instances of uncivil, hateful and violent behavior toward newcomers, be they Jewish, Irish, Italian or plenty of others whose ethnicities did not jibe with some pinched view of what it means to be American. Mr. Goode's dimwitted outburst of nativism is nothing new.

"No, the real worry for the nation is that the rest of the world might take Mr. Goode seriously, interpreting his biased remarks about Muslims as proof that America really has embarked on a civilizational war against Islam. With 535 members, you'd think that Congress would welcome the presence of a single Muslim representative. Whether it can afford a lawmaker of Mr. Goode's caliber is another question."

Ellison had the last word on this bizarre and completely unnecessary imbroglio. When taking his private ceremonial oath, he used a Koran that once belonged to Thomas Jefferson. The Jefferson Koran was provided by Mark Dimunation, chief of the rare book and special collections division of the Library of Congress. The English translation was published in the 1750s and survived the 1851 fire that destroyed most of Jefferson's collection that formed the nucleus of the Library of Congress. Goode was unmoved. In an irony of history, Goode represents Jefferson's birthplace of Albemarle County. But he has adopted none of Jefferson's tolerance. "I believe that the overwhelming majority of voters in my district would prefer the use of the Bible," he told Fox News.

Stem Cell Research Wins House Endorsement

The U.S. House of Representatives voted 253 to 174 on January 11 to broaden federal financial support for stem cell research, using stem cells derived from excess embryos that fertility clinics might otherwise discard. Democrats voted 216-16 (93.1% yes), in favor of HR3, the Stem Cell Research Enhancement Act, while Republicans opposed it 158-37 (19% yes). The overall support (59.3%) was the highest of several recorded votes in recent years. The bill, expected to pass the Senate easily, still faces a probable presidential veto. Its sponsors in the House were Diana DeGette, a Colorado Democrat and a Presbyterian, and Michael Castle, a Delaware Republican and a Roman Catholic.

Besides the expected partisan divide, there were the usual regional differences. The Northeast and Pacific Coast states were overwhelmingly supportive, while the Midwest, the Border South and the Interior West were split. The South was opposed (see chart 1).

Every New England member supported stem cell research, as did more than 75% in the Pacific Coast and Mid-Atlantic regions. The vote was divided in the Border states, the Midwest and Plains States, and in the Interior or Mountain West. Half the representatives, including a number of Republicans, voted in the affirmative in the Mountain States. The South was the least sympathetic region, with the naysayers winning 57% to 43%.

Democrats were overwhelmingly supportive, except in West Virginia where both voted no, and the lone Republican voted yes, making the Mountaineer State the odd man out. In Minnesota and Indiana 40% of Democrats were opposed. Republicans were opposed, especially in the South, where the vote was 68-6 against. But a majority of Republicans backed the measure in Alaska, Connecticut, Delaware, Nevada, Oregon and West Virginia.

About half of GOP members in California and New Mexico voted yes. In a number of states, party-line differences were paramount. All Democrats voted yes, and all Republicans voted no, in Alabama, Arizona, Arkansas, Colorado, Iowa, Kansas, Kentucky, Louisiana, Oklahoma, South Carolina, Utah, and Wisconsin.

Religious differences were also significant on the vote, which was expected since religious bodies have taken different positions on the stem-cell issue. The religiously nonaffiliated, Jews,

Chart 1 – Vote by Region

Region	Yes	No %	Yes %
New England	22	0	100.0
Pacific Coast	57	12	82.6
Mid Atlantic	46	15	75.4
Border South	16	15	51.6
Mountain West	14	14	50.0
Midwest	43	45	48.9
South	55	73	43.0
All	253	174	59.3

Eastern Orthodox Christians, non-denominational Protestants, Roman Catholics, Methodists and Christian Scientists all gave 60% or greater support to stem cell research (See Chart 2). Lutherans and Episcopalians gave majority support. Presbyterians, Baptists, Mormons, non-denominational Christians, and members of smaller evangelical groups gave a majority against the measure, but there were many supporters in all religious traditions.

Religious affiliation shows up as a factor among dissenters, i.e., Democrats opposed to SCR and Republicans in favor of it. Ten of the 16 Democrats who voted no were Catholics, while 6 were conservative Protestants. (However, 77 Catholic Democrats voted yes, as did 6 Catholic Republicans, making the overall Catholic support 83-46, or 64.3%, which was higher than the overall Protestant support (51.4%). (see chart 2) Among Republicans (see chart 3), Christian Scientists, non-denominational Protestants, and members of the United Church of Christ were most likely to support SCR. Episcopalians, Methodists, Mormons and Presbyterians also gave disproportionate support for the measure.

Baptist and evangelical Republicans were nearly unanimous in their opposition. Six of 42 Catholic Republicans also voted yes. Only 8 House members did not vote on this important bill (three Methodist Republicans, two Protestant Republicans, one Catholic Republican, one Baptist Democrat and one Baptist Republican).

The fact that this was the third bill voted on by the 110th Congress indicates its importance in the eyes of legislators.

Chart 2 – Vote by Religion (All Members)
Stem Cell Research Enhancement Act – HR3, January 11, 2007

Religion	% Yes
No Affiliation	100.0
Jewish	96.7
Eastern Orthodox	75.0
Protestant (non-denominational)	70.0
Roman Catholic	64.3
Methodist	63.0
Christian Science	60.0
Lutheran	57.1
Episcopalian	51.9
United Church of Christ	50.0
Presbyterian	47.1
Baptist	44.8
Mormon	40.0
Christian (non-denominational)	37.5
Assembly of God	0
All Others	50.0

For: Unitarian Universalist, Quaker, Buddhist, Muslim, Disciples of Christ
Against: Christian Reformed, Evangelicals

Buddhists, Muslims Win U.S. Congressional Seats

For the first time in U.S. history, members of the Buddhist and Muslim faiths will join Christians and Jews in the U.S. Congress. In November, two Buddhists, Hank Johnson (D-GA) and Mazie K. Hirono (D-HA), and one Muslim, Keith Ellison (D-MN), were elected to the House of Representatives. These dramatic firsts suggest that U.S. politics is beginning to catch up with the increasing religious diversity of the country.

The only previous representative from a religion other than Christian or Jewish was D.S. Saund, a Sikh who was elected as a Democrat from California in 1956. Saund, who represented Imperial and Riverside Counties, was reelected in 1958 and 1960 and defeated in 1962.

Hank Johnson, who ousted Rep. Cynthia McKinney in the Democratic primary in August, won easily in November in his 54% African American district in Georgia. Johnson is a "practicing Buddhist" but believes that religion "is a personal matter," according to *Congressional Quarterly*.

Mazie Hirono, a former lieutenant governor of Hawaii who was born in Japan, is the first Buddhist elected to Congress from the nation's most heavily Buddhist state. Hirono told CQ reporter Laura Blinkhorn that she is "a strong proponent of the separation of church and state" who respects "the right of the individual to practice his or her beliefs."

Keith Ellison is noted for two firsts. He is the first African American elected to Congress from Minnesota and the first Muslim ever elected to the U.S. Congress. Ellison's victory symbolizes the demographic changes in Minneapolis, the location of the Minnesota 5th District. Minneapolis was once a Scandinavian city, and its former congressman for the last 28 years was Martin Olav Sabo, a Democrat from a Norwegian Lutheran family. Minneapolis is increasingly diverse in culture and religion and is a Democratic stronghold, giving 72% of its vote to John Kerry.

Ellison told CQ that he did not stress his religion during the campaign and did not try to "make a political statement." But he observed that his fellow Muslims should know they are "welcome to the table of American politics." Ellison was particularly popular among the large community of Somali immigrants. He noted that "a lot of Muslims feel highly vulnerable and feel that they are under a tremendous amount of scrutiny."

While Ellison chose to downplay his religion, emphasizing instead his support for universal health care and withdrawal of U.S. forces from Iraq, Muslim Americans were naturally elated, as were Muslims overseas. *The New York Times* reported, "Attacks on Mr. Ellison's religion helped galvanize Muslim Americans nationally, with supporters raising money from Florida to Michigan to California. ...Mr. Ellison's victory was widely noted in the larger Muslim world."

All three of the Buddhist and Muslim members are Democrats, which points up a central difference between the two parties. Historically, the Democratic Party has been more welcoming of religious minorities than Republicans. The Democrats have nominated eight members of religious minorities for president and vice president since 1928. Three Catholics (Alfred E. Smith—1928, John F. Kennedy—1960 and John Kerry—2004) were presidential nominees while three Catholics were vice presidential candidates (Ed Muskie— 1968, Sargent Shriver—1972, and Geraldine Ferraro—1984). The 1988 presidential nominee, Michael Dukakis, was Greek Orthodox, and the 2000 vice presidential aspirant was Joe Lieberman, who is Jewish. In contrast, only one Republican candidate since 1856, Rep. William Miller of New York, a Catholic who was Sen. Barry Goldwater's running mate in 1964, belonged to a religious minority.

In the present Congress a majority of Catholics, Jews, and Eastern Orthodox Christians, as well as African Americans, Asian Americans and Hispanics belong to the Democratic Party. The Republicans are the majority among Mormons and Arab Americans. A large majority of secular, or religiously nonaffiliated, voters and Congress members also favor the Democrats.

Roman Catholics remain in first place, as they have since the early 1960s, with 154 members in the 110th Congress. They are followed by 66 Baptists, 61 United Methodists, 44 Presbyterians and 43 Jews. There are also 37 Episcopalians, 26 nondenominational Protestants, 18 nondenominational Christians, 17 Lutherans and 15 Mormons.

Other groups with at least 4 members include 7 members of the United Church of Christ, 6 religiously nonaffiliated, 5 Eastern Orthodox Christians, 5 Christian Scientists and 4 members of the Assemblies of God. Seventeen other groups also are represented.

A larger than usual number of members list their religion as "Protestant" or "Christian" without any additional definition. This may symbolize the post-denominational society that 21st Century America has increasingly become. Many Americans attend megachurches or community churches that are unattached to any historic branch of Christianity.

While the number of Catholics remained about the same since the 109th Congress, the number of Catholic Democrats increased and Catholic Republicans decreased. This may be due to the strong Democratic gains in the Northeast and Midwest. Baptists, Presbyterians and Episcopalians declined. The 37-member Episcopalian contingent is the smallest recorded since religious membership data for Congress have been compiled, suggesting a long-term decline among this influential religious group. Episcopalians now rank sixth in membership. They were second in 1980, when Ronald Reagan was elected president. A factor in the Episcopalian decline may have been the rout of moderate Republicans in the 2006 elections. Both New Hampshire Republican Episcopalians lost their seats. So did Jim Leach of Iowa, a moderate Republican who was first elected in 1976. The Episcopal Church was often the religion of choice for moderate and liberal Republicans, who are now nearly extinct in the U.S. political system.

The Jewish contingent increased by six, and Jewish Democrats won seats in places like Louisville, Kentucky, Tucson, Arizona, and even in Memphis, Tennessee, where Stephen Cohen won Harold Ford's old seat in a 60% African American district.

Editor's note: This tabulation is based on 533 seats where winners were declared or certified at press time. Two seats in Louisiana and Texas will be decided in December runoffs. We will issue an update in our next issue, when tight races have been officially decided. Our website, www.arlinc.org, will be updated with the final information.

A Report on the Referenda

Bans on same-sex marriage were approved by voters in seven of the eight states where the issue was on the ballot. Only Arizona rejected a ban, by a 51% - 49% margin, making it the only state so far to oppose the anti-gay marriage movement in recent years.

Exit Polls

Arizona

The national exit poll examined voter reaction to this issue in Arizona, Virginia, Tennessee and Wisconsin. Unfortunately, the geniuses who devise these often valuable polls failed to include a religious question in Arizona, apparently believing that religious affiliation was irrelevant. This is disappointing, since Arizona has large Mormon, Catholic, Baptist and secular communities that might have shed light on why Arizona, surely a more conservative state than Oregon, which approved a ban in 2004, and Wisconsin, which did so this year, rejected a ban.

County data offer some clues. Graham County, the most heavily Mormon, was the most in favor of the ban (69%). Latino-Catholic majority San Juan County voted 55% No, while opposition was 57% in the Tucson area (Pima County), which is also significantly Hispanic and Catholic. Apache County, which has an American Indian majority, voted No 51% to 49%, while Coconino County, home to Northern Arizona University and many religiously nonaffiliated voters, cast a solid 59% to 41% No vote. Conservative Phoenix (Maricopa County) surprisingly opposed the ban (Proposition 107) by a narrow margin, but its suburbs (Mohave, Pinal and Yavapai) favored it. The measure lost by 48,000 votes in Phoenix and Tucson but won rural Arizona by 16,000 votes.

Virginia

Virginia, where a ban on same-sex marriage and civil unions passed by 57% to 43%, revealed sharp religious differences in the vote. White Catholics voted 53% to 47% against Amendment One, while all white Protestants favored it 67% to 33%, a 20-point difference. White evangelicals voted 88% to 12% in favor of Amendment One. Voters of "other" religions voted 65% No, while those who are not affiliated with any religion voted 80% against the ban. Catholics defied their church leaders. The Virginia Catholic Conference and the state's bishops urged a Yes vote.

Church attendance frequency, a major defining difference in political attitudes during the past decade or so, showed up in the Virginia referendum. The more frequently voters attend religious services, the more likely they were to support the same-sex marriage ban.

In Virginia 85% of Republicans, 47% of Independents and 32% of Democrats voted for the ban. Support for the ban was much higher among those who never attended college (73%) than among college graduates (49%). Among those with two or more college degrees, only 44% were in favor. Voters over age 65 were 13 points more favorable than voters under age 30.

Income was a factor. Lower income voters were more supportive of a ban (70% for those under $15,000) than higher income (48% for voters whose income topped $100,000). Men were 6 points more in favor (60% to 54% for women), but race was irrelevant. The ban won the support of 58% of whites and 56% of African Americans.

Tennessee

The Volunteer State, where 53% of voters were white evangelicals, voted 81% in favor of Amendment 1, the ban on same-sex marriage. Evangelicals, mostly Southern Baptists and Church of Christ members, supported the ban by 90% to 10%. All white Protestants were 85% in favor, as were 85% of African Americans. The small Catholic community only gave 67% support. Many rural counties approached or exceeded 90%, and the ban carried every county and every region of this conservative state. Only the tiny secular community (7% said they had no religion and 9% said they never attended church) voted No by 55% and 60%. Weekly church attendees gave 89% support.

Same-Sex Marriage Bans		
State	*% Yes*	*% No*
Arizona	49	51
Colorado	56	44
Idaho	63	37
South Carolina	78	22
South Dakota	52	48
Tennessee	81	19
Virginia	57	43
Wisconsin	59	41
Average	62.6	37.4
Total Vote	6,598,502	3,944,517

Wisconsin

The "bellwether" state of Wisconsin, where recent presidential elections have been cliffhangers (though Democrats have managed to win since 1988), went 59% to 41% for Referendum 1. Protestants (47% of the vote and mostly Lutherans) backed the ban 64% to 36% while Catholics (31% of voters) supported it 60% to 40%. Religious differences were much smaller in Wisconsin than in other states. But party affiliation, ideology, and church attendance were central factors. Those who attend church more than weekly voted 88% yes, while those who never go gave only 25% yes. More frequent church attendance led to higher support for the ban. Also, those who classified themselves as "other" religion or "no religion" voted over 70% against the ban. The proposal received the support of 84% of Republicans, 50% of Independents and 35% of Democrats. Similar results were registered for conservatives (87%), moderates (54%) and liberals (26%). There was little difference by region or size of community. Opposition was strongest in liberal Madison (Dane County) where the measure was rejected 2-1, and in other counties with large college student populations. Support topped 70% in the Milwaukee exurbs and in rural German Lutheran counties.

Idaho

Conservative, Mormon Idaho passed the same-sex marriage ban by 63% to 37%, but that was actually *lower* than President Bush's 68% to 30% drubbing of John Kerry two years ago. Some Republicans must have opposed the ban, since Boise, the state's only large city (Ada County) backed the ban narrowly 52% to 48% after giving 61% to Bush. The largest No vote (66%) came from Blaine County, the Sun Valley ski resort area and the only county to go for Kerry. Latah County, home to the University of Idaho, also voted No 55% to 45%. But ultra-conservative Mormons in the state's far East counties were the strongest supporters of the ban. Madison County, which gave Bush 92% of its vote, returned 88% for the ban, the highest support in the state. Two other rural Mormon bailiwicks, Franklin and Jefferson Counties, voted 85% and 80% respectively for the ban.

Colorado

Sharp divisions typified the Colorado electorate, which is often liberal on social issues like abortion and vouchers. The state that is seen as moving leftward, giving Democrats a good shot at majority status, pulled back a bit on the same-sex marriage question, as the ban, embodied in Amendment 43, passed 56% to 44%. (A similar question allowing domestic partnerships also failed 53% to 47%). The evangelical stronghold of Colorado Springs (El Paso County), home to Focus on the Family and other parachurch groups, voted unsurprisingly 66% yes.

Douglas County, a wealthy Denver exurb and Republican bastion, voted 62% yes. Support was even higher in rural evangelical, farming and ranching counties in the eastern part of the state. But support also exceeded 60% in the rural Hispanic areas of the Sangre de Christo Mountains (Conejos, Costilla, Huerfano, Las Animas and Pueblo Counties).

The opposition won 62% in Denver, 65% in Boulder, home of the University of Colorado, and in the liberal ski resort areas around Aspen (Pitkin County voted 70% No). Unlike Idaho, Colorado backed the same-sex marriage ban by a bigger margin than it gave George Bush. For example, German Catholic Lake County went for Kerry 55% to 43% but supported the ban 52% to 48%. Hispanic Pueblo voted 65% to 35% for the ban after supporting Kerry 53% to 46%. The ban also carried in the high-population growth areas in the Denver suburbs.

South Carolina

The conservative, Republican, and evangelical/Baptist Palmetto State gave a whopping 78% Yes vote for Amendment 1. It carried every county, though the margin was higher in rural areas and in the fundamentalist Up Country than in the Low Country and resort areas from Myrtle Beach to Hilton Head. The support level reached 90% in Cherokee County, the most

Same-Sex Marriage Bans – Sample Counties

County, State	% Yes	Description
Chesterfield, South Carolina	90	rural Baptist
Buchanan, Virginia	90	coal mining area
Grainger, Tennessee	90	rural Baptist
Madison, Idaho	88	rural conservative Mormon
Washington, Colorado	77	rural Republican evangelical
Dodge, Wisconsin	73	small town German Lutheran
Douglas, South Dakota	71	rural Dutch, German Protestant
Graham, Arizona	69	rural Mormon
Shannon, South Dakota	35	Pine Ridge American Indian Reservation
Blaine, Idaho	34	ski resort (Sun Valley)
Pitkin, Colorado	30	ski resort (Aspen)
Arlington, Virginia	26	liberal professionals – upper income
Charlottesville, Virginia	23	University of Virginia

heavily Southern Baptist county. But it also won 83% in Newberry County, a Lutheran stronghold, and in Marlboro County, a Methodist area. In Greenville County, where Bob Jones University is located and where Republicans have been dominant since Eisenhower, the ban received 79% support. Only in more cosmopolitan and religiously diverse Charleston did support dip to 65%. (The liberal state capital and University of South Carolina area in Richland County gave 67% support). Allendale, a predominantly African American rural area, which gave Kerry 71%, backed the ban with 84% support. This is one cultural issue on which there is virtual unanimity in the Deep South.

South Dakota

Red-state South Dakota is becoming a positively liberal area. Voters turned down a sweeping ban on abortion and only gave 52% for a same-sex marriage prohibition, the lowest level of support in any of the 27 states which have thus far

How the Cities Voted – Same-Sex Marriage Bans	
City	*% Yes*
Memphis, Tennessee	80
Greenville, South Carolina	79
Nashville, Tennessee	68
Colorado Springs, Colorado	66
Charleston, South Carolina	65
Virginia Beach, Virginia	57
Milwaukee, Wisconsin	55
Boise, Idaho	52
Sioux Falls, South Dakota	51
Phoenix, Arizona	49
Norfolk, Virginia	46
Tucson, Arizona	43
Denver, Colorado	38
Boulder, Colorado	35
Madison, Wisconsin	33
Richmond, Virginia	31
Alexandria, Virginia	30

approved these measures. The vote was close (51% Yes) in the two metropolitan counties, Minnehaha (Sioux Falls) and Pennington (Rapid City). Pennington has a large military vote (Air Force) and gave Bush 67% in 2004. But on social issues it is moderate. The highest support for the ban (71%) was recorded in Douglas County, a Dutch-German area that was noticeably anti-Catholic in the 1960 presidential race. (Kennedy dropped 11 points behind Stevenson).

Some Republican rural areas showed a considerable No vote. Harding County (86% for Bush) only gave a 59% Yes vote, while Haakon County (81% for Bush) only favored the marriage ban by 52%. Two counties voted 65% No. One was Shannon County, the Pine Ridge Indian Reservation, which was John Kerry's strongest county in the entire U.S. (Kerry 85%, Bush 13%). The other was Clay County, where the University of South Dakota is located. Brookings County, where South Dakota State University is located, voted 55% to 45% No.

The Religious Right Remains a Force in GOP State Parties

The Religious Right (organized Christian conservatives who take partisan politics seriously) is not going away. The Christian Right is stronger in 15 state Republican parties and weaker in only eight, according to a state-by-state report published in *Campaigns & Elections* magazine in February.

Eight years ago this journal of political professionals, campaign managers and public relations people involved in elections reported on the extent of Religious Right influence in the Republican Party apparatus in each state. The report was widely circulated and revealed a pervasive penetration in many states and at least a moderate influence in most states.

The 2002 survey reveals that the Religious Right is spreading out across the states, especially in the South, Midwest and West, according to the report's authors, Kimberly H. Conger and John C. Green. Thus, they add, Christian conservatives have become a staple of politics nearly everywhere. On the other hand, its national impact is still limited. Conger and Green write, "However, the Christian right did not become more strongly implanted within the state Republican parties between 1994 and 2000. Indeed, it lost ground in key Southern states and in the far West. In some conservative areas, such as Kansas, it has gained and then lost ground in a short period of time. Meanwhile, its success in other states may be only temporary, tied to the fortunes of particular candidates and causes."

The authors note that Christian rightists have helped produce successful candidates and big wins at the polls, but have also proven disastrous for all concerned in some cases. Because the Religious Right has become so cozy with the GOP establishment, the influence of Christian conservatives within the GOP has made them less visible, distinctive and independent, but it has also made them a critical component of the Republican coalition.

The report was based on an assessment of Christian right political influence in the Republican state committees from 395 key informants and well-placed political observers in all 50 states and the District of Columbia.

The Religious Right holds a strong position in 18 states today, the same as in 1994. It has a moderate influence in 26 states, up from 13 eight years sago. And it is weak in only seven states compared to 20. In the evangelical Protestant South, the Religious Right is digging in and becoming a commonplace part of the Republican coalition. It made its biggest gains, from weak in 1994 to strong in 2000, in Tennessee and West Virginia, two culturally conservative, Baptist/Methodist states with a historic Democratic bias and Democratic registration majority. Both states unexpectedly rejected Al Gore in 2000 and became major players in the outcome of that tightly contested race. But the Christian Right influence declined in Florida, Georgia, Louisiana and North Carolina.

In the Midwest Christian conservatives remain most influential in Iowa and Minnesota, though both states stuck narrowly with Gore. They have increased their influence in Missouri, South Dakota, Michigan and North Dakota. These gains appear to be limited to pro-life activism and reflect the pockets of evangelical Protestants and traditional mainline Protestants and Catholics in the region.

In the West activist Christian conservatives remain strong in Alaska, Idaho and Oregon, even though the West's secular and libertarian tendencies make it somewhat difficult for the Religious Right to dominate the culture. The biggest increase in influence and power came in Colorado, which moved from weak to strong in the survey's assessment of influence. "The Colorado change may reflect the arrival in Colorado Springs of Focus on the Family, a major evangelical ministry," say the authors, who add, "In most of these states, Latter-Day Saints have been an important force as well." The Christian right was perceived to have lost ground in California, Arizona, Hawaii and Washington, which are significantly Asian and Hispanic and Catholic.

In the Catholic, Jewish and liberal Protestant Northeast, the Religious Right is weakest in influence and remains weak, except perhaps in New Hampshire, the only state in the region to support Bush in 2000. The authors explain, "Christian conservatives have always had the least influence in the Northeast. The small number of evangelicals plus the strength of moderate and liberal religious groups in the major metropolitan areas has sharply limited the impact of the Christian right, even in Republican circles." In fact, all seven cases in the weak category are in the Northeast: Connecticut, the District of Columbia, Massachusetts, New Jersey, New York, Rhode Island and Vermont. These include the four most heavily Catholic states in the nation. At the other extreme, nine of the 18 strongholds of the Religious Right are states with a significant Baptist influence.

Finally, 14 of the 18 states where the Christian conservatives are strongest supported George W. Bush in the last election, while all seven states (including D.C.) where they are weakest went for Gore. Bush carried 16 of the 26 states where Religious Right influence is in the moderate range. Bush also carried 11 of the 15 states where the Religious Right has increased its influence since 1994.

Congressional Religious Affiliations Change Little

A count of the religious affiliations claimed by the 535 members of the 105th Congress show relatively little change since 1994. Roman Catholics remain in first place as they have been since 1964, with 151 members. Baptists, who captured second place from Methodists in 1994, easily held second position with 67 members, while the United Methodists are in third place with 59. Presbyterians (55), Episcopalians (42) and Jews (35) hold the fourth, fifth and sixth positions respectively. They are followed by nondenominational Protestants (28), Lutherans (21) and Mormons (14).

There will also be 10 members of the United Church of Christ, 10 who call themselves "Christians," six Eastern Orthodox Christians and seven who have no religious affiliation. Thirty members belong to a variety of other religious communities.

Several trends are discernible in these results, and all of them may relate to the increasing influence of conservative religion in the United States today. Among these trends:

• Episcopalians have dropped to their lowest representation in 50 years. The 42 Episcopalian members are nearly half of the number elected when Ronald Reagan first won the presidency in 1980. Only two of the 100 freshmen class belong to this historically influential community, which has given the U.S. its largest number of presidents and Supreme Court justices. On social and church-state issues, Episcopalians have been liberal. During the Reagan prayer amendment vote in the Senate in 1984, Episcopalian Republicans were the most likely members of the president's party to defect and oppose the prayer amendment. This decline harms the pro-separation forces in Congress.

• Other liberal groups continue to decline. The 59 United Methodists, 10 members of the United Church of Christ and three Unitarian Universalists represent the lowest point in their memberships in Congress in a half century. (Not all Methodists are pro-separation by any means — a number of the newly elected freshmen from the South are staunch social-issue conservatives.) There are now more members of the fundamentalist Assemblies of God serving in Congress than Unitarians. Congressional members from five mainline denominations (Methodist, Presbyterian, Episcopal, United Church of Christ, and Unitarian-Universalist) have declined from 237 members after the 1976 election to 169 members today. Most of these losses have come during the 1990s.

• A growing number of members call themselves Protestant or Christian, vague terms that are theologically and sociologically rather meaningless. Fully 38 members of Congress — 29 of them Republican — prefer this designation. It may represent the increasing trend toward what some sociologists describe as a post-denominational society. Or it may represent the rise of conservative, evangelical religious groups which have no historic ties to any denominational family. More than one out of ten Republicans — most of them conservatives — now define themselves in these categories. Those from the West are most likely to use the term Protestant; only four of the 28 "Protestants" are from the South, since most Southerners seem to know which denomination they belong to.

One small religious group appears for the first time in many years with one representative: the Reorganized Church of Jesus Christ of Latter-day Saints, who are completely separate from the Utah-based Mormons. Leonard L. Boswell, a Democrat from Iowa's Third District and the party's only Iowa House member, belongs to this small church. He graduated from one of the group's two colleges, Graceland College in Lamoni, Iowa. The Reorganized Mormons, who claim to be the continuation of the original church founded by Joseph Smith in 1830, have 238,000 members and are headquartered in Harry Truman's hometown of Independence, Missouri.

While "Protestants" and "Christians" gained ten members since the 1994 election, the "Establishment" churches, Episcopalians and Presbyterians, declined the most. There are seven fewer Episcopalians and four fewer Presbyterians in the new Congress. Methodists declined by four, and the United Church of Christ and Unitarians each lost two.

Party affiliations within the religious groups generally remained constant (Jews and the religiously unaffiliated are Democrats, while Mormons, "Protestants," Episcopalians and Presbyterians are largely Republican). But an interesting shift among Lutherans from 12-9 Republican to 12-9 Democrat may indicate a growing Lutheran distaste for the Republican Party of the 1990s. Three of the four freshmen Lutherans are Democrats, and strongly Lutheran counties in the Midwest went for Clinton over Dole by a larger margin than Clinton's victory over Bush.

Among Catholics the Democratic margin also increased from 83-65 to 91-60, a significant shift probably related to a 10-point Democratic margin in Catholic voting for Congress and a 16-point edge for President Clinton. Methodists moved toward the Republicans, and 13 of the 14 Mormon members belong to the GOP. Baptists are the most ideologically divided, between a large number of conservative Southern Baptist Republicans and a sizable contingent of Congressional Black Caucus members, who have the most liberal voting record in Congress.

Congressional religious affiliation patterns generally reflect the geography of American religion. Catholics are strongest in the Northeast, the Great Lakes region and in California. Baptists, Methodists and Presbyterians have a distinct Southern coloration, since 51% of Baptists, 49% of Methodists and 45% of Presbyterians hail from the eleven states of the Old Confederacy. Including the Border South the figures rise to 72% of Baptists, 53% of Methodists and 58% of Presbyterians. The Presbyterians have an unusual strength in the North Carolina delegation, where they hold seven of the 14 seats.

Episcopalians are strongest in Florida (six members) and California (four members). Not surprisingly, 40% of Jewish members come from California or New York. A majority of the "Protestant" members represent Western or Midwestern states. Thirteen of the 21 Lutheran members are from the Midwest, the citadel of Lutheranism. The entire Utah five-person delegation is Mormon, as are four California Republicans (a state with 675,000 Mormon residents). Three members from Idaho, Arizona and Nevada, which have considerable Mormon communities, belong to the L.D.S. Church. All 14 Mormon members represent states west of the Mississippi River. All of the religiously unaffiliated members come from the West or from Massachusetts.

Slowly but surely, the changing religious configuration in Congress represents the changing landscape of American religious experience. One summary finding shows how different are the appeals of America's two great political parties. In the present Congress, over seven out of ten Republicans (71%) are Protestants of one kind or another. But fewer than half of Democrats (48%) are Protestants. The Democrats remain a far more religiously and culturally pluralistic party than the Republicans.

— Al Menendez

Chapter 4
Church and State in the Courts

As Leo Pfeffer, dean of church-state scholars and attorneys, observed decades ago, the U.S. Supreme Court has become the chief referee in resolving church-state disputes. More rulings affecting the Religion Clauses of the First Amendment have been issued during the lifetime of ARL than at any comparable period of U.S. history. This journal has reported on these rulings for a quarter century. Here is a selection.

ARL Goes to Court: A Special Report

In its quarter century of activism in defense of church-state separation and freedom of conscience, Americans for Religious Liberty has been involved in over 60 actions in the courts. Following is a concise summary of that work.

This action has generally involved participating in or originating *amicus curiae* (friend of the court) briefs to the U.S. Supreme Court and lower courts. Usually, in the interest of economy and because the Court prefers not to have to deal with duplicative briefs, where possible ARL has worked with other organizations in coalition briefs.

Americans for Religious Liberty is grateful to all of the mostly *pro bono* attorneys and organizations with which we have collaborated for so many years.

These briefs are divided into several types of cases (e.g., government aid to religious institutions, reproductive rights, etc.) The dates of the briefs refer to the Supreme Court's terms, which begin in October of every year.

One of our most important cases, in which ARL played an important role, *Lamont v. Woods,* did not reach the Supreme Court but was settled in the U.S. Second Circuit Court of Appeals in New York on September 26, 1991. Unfortunately, the case received almost no media attention. It involved a challenge to U.S. government aid to faith-based schools in other countries. Between 1983 and 1989 the U.S. Agency for International Development (USAID) distributed more than $14 million to faith-based schools in the Philippines, Egypt, Israel, Jamaica, South Korea, and Micronesia.

The suit was a cooperative effort with the American Civil Liberties Union. ACLU provided the attorney, Professor Herman Schwartz of American University, while ARL provided the plaintiffs in New York: philosopher Corliss Lamont, writer Isaac Asimov, Rabbi Balfour Brickner, the Rev. Bruce Southworth, and church-state separation activists Florence Flast and Nina Untermyer.

Second Circuit Chief Judge James L. Oakes wrote in his opinion that, "Where the expenditure of federal tax money is concerned, there can be no distinction between foreign religious institutions and domestic religious institutions – particularly when the former are sponsored and supported by the latter. Religions such as Catholicism and Judaism know no national boundaries, and are strengthened domestically when promoted abroad. Given the primacy of the tax factor in the minds of the Framers, we cannot but conclude that Madison, Jefferson, or any of the supporters of the Establishment Clause would have abhorred – as much as a tax for the support of Christian teachers – the use of federal tax money for the support of foreign sectarian schools."

The ruling added that "recent history supports the view that the religion clauses do have extraterritorial application." Further, "The expenditure of tax dollars for the support of religious institutions or activities offends the 'no taxation' principle regardless of the physical situs of those institutions or activities. Likewise, the message communicated by direct government funding of religious institutions remains the same whether those institutions are located in the United States or abroad."

In rejecting a central argument put forth by the George H.W. Bush administration, that foreign policy matters are beyond constitutional scrutiny, the court held that "While we recognize the importance of foreign aid programs in promoting United States foreign policy, we do not believe that this warrants freeing all foreign aid programs from all constitutional constraints."

In a concurring opinion, Judge John M. Walker, Jr., observed that "The text of the First Amendment's limitation on Congress' competency to act in regard to religion bears no construction that confines its operation to the United States."

Lamont v. Woods never reached the Supreme Court because the Bush administration decided not to appeal. Nonetheless, the ruling stands as an important but little noticed precedent.

(Note: Before ARL was founded in 1982, ARL's Doerr and Menendez were involved in a number of important church-state cases while working for another organization. Among those cases were *Lemon v. Kurtzman*, the first successful Supreme Court challenge to tax aid to faith-based schools (1971); *Malnak v. Yogi*, a successful challenge to the promotion of Transcendental Meditation, with its hidden religious content, in New Jersey public schools; and a challenge to forced "deprogramming" of adults in Maryland.)

Free Exercise of Religion

2005. *Gonzalez v. O Centro Espirita Beneficente Uniao Do Vegetal.* ("May the Government satisfy the 'compelling interest/least restrictive alternative' standard that Congress enacted in the Religious Freedom Restoration Act simply by asserting, without case-specific evidentiary support, a compelling interest in the uniform enforcement of the law, and then arguing, tautologically, that a policy of denying any religious exemptions is the least restrictive means of furthering that interest?")

2005. *Cutter v. Wilkinson.* (Free exercise rights of prisoners.)

Physician-Assisted Suicide

2005. *Gonzalez v. State of Oregon.* (Defense of Oregon's physician-assisted suicide law.)

1996. *Vacco v. Quill* ("The right of a competent, terminally ill individual to end his or her life with the aid of a physician. . . .")

Religion in Public Schools

1997. *Bauchman v. West High School.* (Challenge to religious proselytizing in public school.)

1996. *Chauduri v. State of Tennessee.* (Graduation prayers at Tennessee State University.)

1994. *Ingebretsen v. Jackson Public School District.* (Prayer at school events.)

1990. *Lee v. Weisman.* (Challenge to religious exercises in public school.)

1989. *Board of Education of the Westside Community Schools v. Mergens.* (Challenge to the "Equal Access Act . . . requiring Westside High School to recognize and sponsor a Christian prayer club.")

1988. *Barry v. Slaughter.* (Challenge to graduation prayers at University of Maryland.)

1988. *Virgil v. School Board of Columbia County, Florida.* (Textbook censorship.)

1987. *Smith v. Commissioners of Mobile County.* (Prayer in public schools.)

1987. *Mozert v. Hawkins County Public Schools.* (Religious opposition to certain textbooks.)

1986. *Edwards v. Aguillard.* (Challenge to Louisiana law promoting "creationism" in science classes.)

1986. *Edwards v. Aguillard.* (Brief of 72 Nobel laureates and other scientists. Although ARL's name is not on the brief, it was ARL's idea to have Nobel laureates sign a brief challenging the Louisiana "creationism" law.)

1985. *Bender v. Williamsport.* (Challenge to "equal access law.")

Religious Displays in Government Buildings

2004. *Van Orden v. Perry.* (Challenge to Ten Commandments display at Texas state capitol building.)

2002. *Freethought Society v. Chester County.* (Ten Commandments display in courthouse.)

1994. *Capitol Square Review and Advisory Board v. Pinette.* (Challenge to placement of religious displays on Ohio State House grounds.)

1987. *American Jewish Congress v. City of Chicago.* (Challenge to city hall Nativity display.)

Reproductive Rights

2005. *Scheidler v. National Organization for Women.* ("Whether the Hobbs Act prohibits acts or threats of physical violence that obstruct, delay or affect interstate commerce; Whether RICO authorizes the district courts to grant injunctive relief in private lawsuits.")

2005. *Ayotte v. Planned Parenthood of Northern New England.* (Challenging lack of health exception in a New Hampshire law restricting reproductive rights.)

2001. *Bost v. Low Income Women of Texas.* (Challenge to Texas restrictions on Medicaid funding for abortions.)

2000. *Stenberg v. Carhart.* (Challenge to Nebraska's so-called "partial-birth" abortion ban.)

1993. *Madsen v. Women's Health Center.* ("Whether, in the context of a pattern of illegal conduct and violations of previous injunctions, a court may constitutionally impose specific time, place and manner restrictions on individuals and organizations and those acting in concert with them to prohibit blocking access to a medical facility, harassing the facility's patients and staff, engaging in activities that threaten patients' health, and harassing and picketing staff members at their homes.")

1990. *Rust v. Sullivan.* (Challenge to gag rule on discussing abortion in federally aided family planning facilities.)

1990. *In re: AC.* (Are fetal rights superior to those of persons already born?)

1989. *Turnock v. Ragsdale.* (Defense of rights of clinics and doctors.)

1989. *Hodgson v. Minnesota.* (Challenge to abortion rights restrictions.)

1989. *Ohio v. Akron Center for Reproductive Health.* (Challenge to abortion rights restrictions.)

1988. *Webster v. Reproductive Health Services.* (Though not formally listed on this brief, ARL originated the brief representing twelve Nobel laureates and 155 other distinguished scientists in defense of reproductive choice. The brief challenges the anti-choice position that human personhood begins as early as conception. NOW said that this brief might well be "the most powerful brief" submitted in this case.)

1988. *Webster v. Reproductive Health Services.* (Coalition brief challenging Missouri restrictions on abortion rights.)

1988. *Massachusetts v. Bowen.* (Challenge to federal restrictions on reproductive rights.)

1988. *Northeast Women's Center v. McMonagle.* (Defense of women's clinics for RICO Act violation.)

1985. *Thornburgh v. American College of Obstetricians and Gynecologists.* (Reproductive rights in Pennsylvania.)

1985. *Diamond v. Charles.* (Abortion rights in Illinois.)

Tax Aid to Faith-Based Schools

2004-2005. *Bush v. Holmes.* (Successful challenge to Florida school voucher plan. Florida Supreme Court ruled the plan unconstitutional on January 5, 2006.)

2001. *Zelman v. Simmons-Harris.* (Challenge to Ohio school voucher plan.)

1999. *Mitchell v. Helms.* (Challenge to tax aid to religious schools in Louisiana.)

1996. *Agostini v. Felton.* (Challenge to tax aid to faith-based schools in New York.)

1994. *Lipscomb University v. Steele; Americans for Religious Liberty.* (Challenge to municipal bonds to aid a pervasively sectarian university.)

1993. *Board of Education of the Kiryas Joel Village School District v. Grumet.* (Challenge to "the constitutionality of vesting the power to operate a public school district in a municipality that functions as a religious establishment.")

1992. *Zobrest v. Catalina Foot Hills School District.* ("Whether [Federal Regulation] C.F.R. § 76.532(a) prohibits the government from paying for the sign language interpreter requested by the Petitioners. ")

1990. *Pulido v. Cavazos.* (Challenge to tax-paid services to faith-based schools.)

1990. *Southside Fair Housing Commission v. New York.* (Challenge to New York turning over city land to a faith-based school.)

1990. *Helms v. Cody.* (Challenge to public school teachers working in faith-based schools in Louisiana.)

1984. *Aguilar v. Felton.* (Challenge to tax aid to sectarian schools.)

1984. *Witters v. Washington Department of Services for the Blind.* (Defense of Washington State constitution prohibition of tax aid to a faith-based school.)

1983. *Grand Rapids v. Ball.* (Challenge to school district's operating an extensive program of classes on the premises of faith-based schools.)

1983. *Mueller v. Allen.* (Challenge to tax deductions for faith-based schools.)

Miscellaneous

2004. *Elk Grove United School District v. Newdow.* (Challenge to Congress' inclusion of the phrase "under God" in the Pledge of Allegiance in 1954.)

2002. *Kong v. Min de Parle.* (Challenge to government support of Christian Science sanatoria.)

1999. *Children's Health is a Legal Duty v. Vladek.* (Do the 1997 Medicare and Medicaid Amendments violate the First Amendment by creating and defining "religious non-medical health care institutions"?)

1997. *Coles v. Cleveland Board of Education.* (Challenge to prayers at school board meetings.)

1990. *Welsh v. Boy Scouts of America.* (Challenge to religious discrimination by BSA.)

1987. *Bowen v. Kendrick.* ("Does the Establishment Clause permit the Government to pay religious organizations to promote government policies that such organizations teach as articles of religious faith?")

1986. *American Baptist Churches in the U.S.A. v. Reagan.* (Challenge to establishment of U.S. diplomatic relations with the Holy See.)

1986. *Karcher v. May.* ("Whether a state legislature may enact a statute requiring state school employees, principals and teachers, to direct group meditation in their public school classrooms.")

State Court Cases

1993. *American Academy of Pediatrics v. Lundgren.* (California abortion law restrictions.)

1990. *Davis v. Davis.* (Treatment of frozen embryos in Tennessee.)

1988. *In re: Unborn Child.* (Challenge to father's veto of a woman's abortion decision.)

Supreme Court Forbids Some Commandments Monuments

On June 27, the last day of its 2005 rulings, the U.S. Supreme Court held 5 to 4 that county commissioners in McCreary and Pulaski Counties in Kentucky ran afoul of the Establishment Clause by erecting Ten Commandments plaques in the courthouse six years ago. The High Court ruled that erecting religious insignia on government property constituted an improper and unconstitutional promotion of religion. But at the same time and by the same 5-4 margin, the Court upheld a Commandments monument at the Texas Capitol because it was older (44 years), was mixed with other secular historical material, and was seen as less controversial and less visible. (ARL had joined an *amicus* brief to the Court in the Texas case.) This somewhat contradictory decision came about because of the single vote of Justice Stephen Breyer, who cast the deciding vote in both cases.

In announcing the Kentucky ruling *(McCreary County v. ACLU of Kentucky,* No. 03-1693), Justice David Souter said, "The divisiveness of religion in current public life is inescapable. This is no time to deny the prudence of understanding the establishment clause [of the First Amendment] to require the government to stay neutral on religious belief, which is reserved for the conscience of the individual." Souter added, "Context matters."

Justice Sandra Day O'Connor issued a concurring opinion with an eloquence that will stand the test of time. "Those who would renegotiate the boundaries between church and state must therefore answer a difficult question: Why would we trade a system that has served us so well for one that has served others so poorly?" O'Connor reiterated another long-standing principle when she observed, "Allowing the government to be a potential mouthpiece for competing religious ideas risks the sort of division that the Constitution sought to avoid."

The Court held that the Kentucky authorities, in specifying that the Protestant King James version be used in its gold-framed copies of the Commandments in their courthouses, showed "a predominant religious purpose." The county supervisors and other Kentucky lawmakers clearly intended to promote Christianity when they also endorsed Alabama Chief Justice Roy Moore's attempts to keep a similar religious display in the rotunda of the Alabama Supreme Court.

Souter argued, "The touchstone for our analysis is the principle that the First Amendment mandates government neutrality between religion and religion, and between religion and nonreligion."

The majority opinion, written by Souter and joined by Stevens, O'Connor, Ginsburg and Breyer, took careful pains to show that the Ten Commandments is "a sacred text." Attempts to deny or soften that, in order to pass muster constitutionally, are dishonest. "This is not to deny that the Commandments have had influence on civil or secular law; a major text of a majority religion is bound to be felt. The point is simply that the original text viewed in its entirety is an unmistakably religious statement dealing with religious obligations and with morality subject to religious sanction. When the government initiates an effort to place this statement alone in public view, a religious object is unmistakable."

The Kentucky context was politically significant and constitutionally suspect. "At the ceremony for posting the framed Commandments in Pulaski County, the county executive was accompanied by his pastor, who testified to the certainty of the existence of God. The reasonable observer could only think that the Counties meant to emphasize and celebrate the Commandments' religious message.... [T]he display's unstinting focus was on religious passages, showing that the Counties were posting the Commandments precisely because of their sectarian content. That demonstration of the Government's objective was enhanced by several religious references and the accompanying resolution's claim about the embodiment of this in Christ. Together, the display and resolution presented an indisputable, and undisputed, showing of an impermissible purpose."

In his dissent, Justice Antonin Scalia, joined by Chief Justice William Rehnquist and Justices Clarence Thomas and Anthony Kennedy, issued another scathing attack on his colleagues. He charged that it is "false that the government cannot favor religious practice" and said the Kentucky decision "extends the scope of that falsehood even beyond prior cases." Attacking once again the *Lemon* test of 1971, which requires a secular purpose in legislative actions, Scalia said the *McCreary* ruling "modifies *Lemon* to ratchet up the Courts hostility to religion." Scalia argued that government acknowledgment or invocation of a Creator is not an establishment of religion. "Governmental invocation of God is not an establishment."

Scalia's harsh rhetoric, which caused Souter to issue a multi-page rejoinder in his majority opinion, suggests that future church-state cases will be pervaded by rancor and incivility. (Scalia even suggested that this case "does not rest upon consistently applied principle" and therefore may represent "the dictatorship of a shifting Supreme Court majority" rather than "the rule of law").

There was one Scalia sentence in a footnote to his dissent that does raise hopes that he is not totally impervious to religious liberty. Scalia wrote, "The Establishment Clause would prohibit governmental endorsement of a particular version of the Decalogue as authoritative."

Scalia also invoked the personal religious views embodied in several presidential inaugural addresses, but that argument seems largely irrelevant to the case at hand.

The justices reached a different conclusion in *Van Orden v. Perry* (No. 03-1500). A 5-4 majority upheld district court and Fifth Circuit Court of Appeals rulings that a Texas Commandments monument was so embedded with other historical memorabilia that it had a valid secular purpose.

Chief Justice Rehnquist wrote for the majority and was joined by Justices Scalia, Kennedy and Thomas. Scalia and Thomas also submitted separate concurring opinions. Justice Breyer filed an opinion concurring in the judgment, which resulted in the overall favorable verdict. Justice Stevens filed a dissenting opinion, which Justice Ginsburg joined. Justice O'Connor filed her own dissenting opinion. Justice Souter filed a dissenting opinion and was joined by Stevens and Ginsburg. This paper flood caused the Chief Justice to quip that he never knew there were so many members of the Court!

Rehnquist's opinion concluded that the Commandments monument, a six-foot-high monolith erected by the Fraternal Order of Eagles in 1961, was "passive" and did not constitute direct government endorsement of religion. He argued that there has been an unbroken history of official acknowledgement of religion's role in American life by all three branches of government since at least 1789.

The majority admitted that "the Ten Commandments are religious - they were so viewed at their inception and so remain. The monument, therefore, has religious significance,... But Moses was a lawgiver as well as a religious leader and the Commandments have an undeniable historical meaning,..."

In conclusion, the majority held, "Texas has treated her Capitol grounds monument as representing the several strands in the state's political and legal history. The inclusion of the Ten Commandments monument in this group has a dual significance, partaking of both religion and government. We cannot say that Texas' display of this monument violates the Establishment Clause of the First Amendment."

It was hardly a ringing endorsement.

Justice Breyer decided the case even though he admitted that it was "a borderline case." Seemingly reaching for evidence to buttress his conclusion that the monument was constitutional, he argued, "In certain contexts, a display of the tablets of the Ten Commandments can convey a religious message but also a secular moral message (about proper standards of social conduct). And in certain contexts, a display of the tablets can also convey a historical message (about a historic relation between those standards and the law)... Here the tablets have been used as part of a display that communicates not simply a religious message, but a secular message as well. The circumstances surrounding the display's placement on the Capitol grounds and its physical setting suggest that the state itself intended the latter, nonreligious aspects of the tablets' message to predominate."

Breyer was also swayed by the fact that no opposition was expressed for the first 40 years. "As far as I can tell, 40 years passed in which the presence of this monument, legally speaking, went unchallenged." Breyer also praised the Eagles for trying to "find a nonsectarian text," as if such a thing actually exists.

Even Breyer, in casting the decisive vote, admitted that "these factors provide a strong, but not conclusive, indication that the Commandments' text on this monument conveys a predominantly secular message."

Justice Scalia's concurrence said, "There is nothing unconstitutional in a state's favoring religion generally, honoring God through public prayer and acknowledgement, or, in a nonproselytizing manner, venerating the Ten Commandments." Justice Thomas used his concurrence to advocate "a more fundamental rethinking of our Establishment Clause jurisprudence" and allowing almost every public support for religion that falls short of "coercion."

Justice Stevens' dissent emphasized that "the Establishment Clause has created a strong presumption against display of religious symbols on public property." Texas has violated that principle. "The message transmitted by Texas' chosen display is quite plain: This state endorses the divine code of the 'Judeo-Christian' God."

Stevens clearly expressed concern that decisions breaking down or weakening the wall of separation between church and state "is plainly not worthy of a society whose enviable hallmark over the course of two centuries has been the continuing expansion of religious pluralism and tolerance."

Stevens added that the text used in Texas was "the expurgated text of the King James version of the Ten Commandments that is unlikely to be accepted by Catholic parishes, Jewish synagogues, or even some Protestant denominations." He concluded, "The judgment of the Court in this case stands for the proposition that the Constitution permits governmental displays of sacred religious texts. This makes a mockery of the constitutional idea that government must remain neutral between religion and irreligion."

In dissent Justice Souter observed, "The Ten Commandments constitute a religious statement, their message is inherently religious, and the purpose of singling them out in a display is clearly the same."

Reaction to the two decisions varied widely. Activists on both the separationist and accommodationist sides of church-state issues cited a victory, though no one thought the results would add clarity to the debate over religious symbolism on public property. *The Washington Post* opined that the decisions "were not a model of clarity or judicial consensus . . . but in practical terms [they] were not a bad way to evaluate public religious monuments." *The New York Times* said, "They are an important reaffirmation of the nation's commitment to separation of church and state."

University of Texas law professor Douglas Laycock warned that the decisions "mean we will be litigating these cases one at a time for decades." Dr. C. Welton Gaddy, president of the Interfaith Alliance, observed, "Today's Supreme Court split decision will, for now, keep the wall of separation between religion and government intact but greatly weakened. The venerable wall remains seriously threatened as intense assaults on religious liberty continue from many different parts of the nation. First Amendment guarantees of a free exercise of religion without entanglement between the institutions of religion and government are no longer secure in the present environment."

New York Times legal correspondent Linda Greenhouse predicted that the ruling in the Texas case "will immunize from constitutional challenge hundreds of granite Ten Commandments monuments that were erected in public places around the country by the Fraternal Order of Eagles, a national civic organization, in the 1950s and 1960s." She added, "Outside the court, the split decisions enabled each side in the larger debate over the role of religion in the public square to claim a measure of victory. It may take further litigation, not in these particular cases but in others that raise related questions, before the import of the decisions becomes clear."

Reaction from the Religious Right and from conservative Republicans was swift and predictable. Rev. Patrick Mahoney, director of the Washington, D.C.-based Christian Defense Coalition, announced a campaign on the steps of the Boise, Idaho, city hall to install Commandments displays in at least 10 cities and towns during the coming year. Mahoney, a minister in the very conservative Reformed Presbyterian Church, said a coalition of evangelical Christian organizations would lead the effort. Idaho religious conservatives want the city of Boise to restore a Commandments monument in a public park that was removed last year by the Boise City Council. Brandi Swindell, director of the Keep the Commandments Coalition of Idaho, said the monument is now constitutional. But Boise Mayor David Bieter said he preferred that it stay in front of an Episcopal church, where it had rested for the past year. Bieter said, "It's very difficult to tell what kind of display would be constitutional." He noted that the Texas monument was one of 38 historical markers around the state capitol complex, something not present in Boise.

U.S. House Republicans were quick to enter the fray. Rep. Ernest Istook (R-OK) introduced a constitutional amendment with 107 co-sponsors on June 30 to reverse the Supreme Court's Kentucky ruling. Istook's so-called Religious Freedom Amendment, defeated back in 1998, would have allowed prayers and religious displays on public property, including schools. Rep. Trent Frank (R-AZ) said, "The Supreme Court seems determined to continue its arrogant and inexorable march to strip the American people of their constitutional rights." Rep. Spencer Bachus (R-AL) claimed, "Our forefathers clearly based our legal system on biblical moral law, and to prohibit the displaying of that law contradicts their intent. The usurpation of this collective wisdom by five members of the Supreme Court continues and is simply disgraceful and baseless."

The present Court apparently thought it has solved the controversy, and on June 29 denied review of cases regarding the Commandments in Harlan County, Kentucky, and Adams County, Ohio. (In both cases lower courts declared such displays in public schools unconstitutional.)

Some communities are trying to apply the Court's dual rulings in local circumstances. Authorities in Montgomery County, Maryland, have decided that a Commandments plaque in the county judicial center in Rockville is constitutional because it is part of a larger secular exhibit. The Commandments have been displayed at the Montgomery County Circuit Court since 1940 and are part of an exhibit including the Magna Charta, the U.S. Constitution, the Declaration of Independence and the Maryland Toleration Act. In Arizona it is likely that a stone monument of the Commandments in a park across from the state capitol will remain despite an ACLU lawsuit. Attorneys in Baltimore are undecided which ruling applies in Frederick, Maryland, where a federal judge recently allowed a privately owned display in a Frederick city park. Robert Percival, a constitutional law professor at the University of Maryland, said the issue turns on the motivation behind the decision to erect a Commandments monument. Did the city intend to promote religion or to recognize religious documents as part of a legal or historical display? "It really turns on the difficult decision of how you go about discerning what the motive is behind a decision that allows something religious in nature to be on public property," Percival told the Associated Press.

Supreme Court Upholds State Ban on Funding Religious Education

By a resounding 7 to 2 margin, the U.S. Supreme Court ruled that states do not have to make taxpayer-funded scholarship programs available to students preparing for the ministry.

The February 25 decision in *Locke* v. *Davey,* No. 02-1315, held that Washington State was correct in refusing its Promise Scholarship aid to a student majoring in pastoral studies in preparation for a ministerial career.

Writing for the majority, Chief Justice Rehnquist said, "Washington's program imposes neither criminal nor civil sanctions on any type of religious service or rite.... The State has merely chosen not to fund a distinct category of instruction."

Rehnquist added, "Since this country's founding, there have been popular uprisings against procuring taxpayer funds to support church leaders, which was one of the hallmarks of an 'established' religion. Most States that sought to avoid such an establishment around the time of the founding placed in their constitutions formal prohibitions against using tax funds to support the ministry. That early state constitutions saw no problem in explicitly excluding only the ministry from receiving state dollars reinforces the conclusion that religious instruction is of a different ilk from other professions. Moreover, the entirety of the Promise Scholarship Program goes a long way toward including religion in its benefits, since it permits students to attend pervasively religious schools so long as they are accredited, and students are still eligible to take devotional theology courses under the programs current guidelines. Nothing in the Washington Constitution's history or text or in the program's operation suggests animus towards religion. Given the historic and substantial state interest at issue, it cannot be concluded that the denial of funding for vocational religious instruction alone is inherently constitutionally suspect. Without a presumption of unconstitutionality, Davey's claim must fail. The State's interest in not funding the pursuit of devotional degrees is substantial, and the exclusion of such funding places a relatively minor burden on Promise Scholars."

The only dissenters, Antonin Scalia and Clarence Thomas, issued two separate dissents. Scalia engaged in a labored argument that the neutrality principle required the government to aid any kind of education, religious or secular. The acerbic Scalia said the case " is about discrimination against a religious minority" and represents "modern popular culture's trendy disdain for deep religious conviction." He warned that the Court's ruling could "deny priests and nuns their prescription drug benefits," a comment so off the wall as to be embarrassing. Justice Thomas rather meekly argued that "the study of theology does not necessarily implicate religious devotion or faith." Some may wonder, what else is it?

Temple University constitutional law professor Burton Caine, who is also chair of the ARL board, called the ruling "a significant victory for the constitutional separation of church and state" and added, "In rejecting the government's argument that the state's choice discriminates against religion, the Court's decision repudiates the entire basis for the Bush administration's faith-based initiative program. The ruling is a welcome development in the battle to preserve the separation of religion and government."

The Pew Forum on Religion and Public Life said the opinion "effectively upholds laws in 37 states that prohibit state funding of religious education in colleges and universities." (For background, see *VOR* 86, pages 2,4.)

Supreme Court Upholds Pledge - For Now

On June 14, Flag Day, the U.S. Supreme Court unanimously held that the phrase "under God" may remain in the Pledge of Allegiance because its challenger, Michael A. Newdow, lacked legal standing to sue. While all eight justices who participated in the case voted to overturn the Ninth Circuit's decision that held the practice unconstitutional, five did so on procedural grounds.

Justice John Paul Stevens wrote for the majority: "In our view, it is improper for the federal courts to entertain a claim by a plaintiff whose standing to sue is founded on family law rights that are in dispute when prosecution of the lawsuit may have an adverse effect on the person who is the source of the plaintiff's claimed standing."

Stevens was joined by Anthony Kennedy, David Souter, Ruth Bader Ginsburg and Stephen Breyer.

Three other justices, Sandra Day O'Connor, Clarence Thomas and Chief Justice William Rehnquist, wanted to rule on the merits of the case, and in their separate concurrences, supported the concept that including the phrase was constitutional. (Justice Antonin Scalia had recused himself from the case.)

While there was some disappointment that the Court had failed to address the constitutional issues, many observers saw the ruling in *Elk Grove Unified School District v. Newdow,* No. 02-1624, as a wise attempt to defuse a potentially explosive political issue in a presidential election year. The *Washington Post* editorialized that "passivity was a virtue," and argued, "Resolving a case on grounds of the legal standing of a litigant always has the feel of a cop-out. But the doctrine actually serves a vital function in the U.S. judicial system, particularly in constitutional challenges to laws and government policies. It prevents the courts from considering complaints unnecessarily. The pledge case is an excellent example. The pledge, after all, has been around in its current form for a half-century, and it has existed with relatively little political or legal controversy. Even as public school prayers were banned, and people began suing over religious symbols such as the Ten Commandments in public buildings, people haven't been flooding the courts with complaints that they or their children are unconstitutionally oppressed by the Pledge of Allegiance. Insisting that the courts refrain from considering such matters unless someone with a clear stake in them objects is one of the central checks against overly broad judicial power."

Similar views were expressed by Americans for Religious Liberty: "Today's Supreme court ruling dismissing a challenge to the inclusion of the phrase 'under God' in the Pledge of Allegiance is the optimal outcome of this controversial case," according to Burton Caine, professor of constitutional law at Temple University School of Law and board chair of Americans for Religious Liberty. "A decision striking down the 'under God' phrase would have provoked a disruptive firestorm of protest and probably led to the unstoppable passage of a constitutional amendment that could seriously weaken the constitutional protections of religious freedom."

ARL president Edd Doerr added: "This outcome was one included in the 'friend of the court' brief to the Supreme Court filed by Americans for Religious Liberty, the American Civil Liberties Union, and Americans United for Separation of Church and State. We believe that Congress' inclusion of the phrase in the Pledge in 1954 violated the First Amendment, but that the matter is neither ripe for consideration by the Supreme Court nor of high priority compared to such other threats to religious freedom and church-state separation as coerced tax support for faith-based schools and charities or faith-based attacks on women's rights."

The case arrived at the nations highest court after a 2-1 ruling in June 2002 from the Ninth U.S. Circuit Court of Appeals saying that the phrase was unconstitutional. The appeals court stayed its decision until the High Court ruled, thus allowing children in nine Western states to continue to recite the Pledge in its present, 1954 format. (The phrase was added by a unanimous vote of Congress in that year and signed by President Eisenhower.) Courts in several jurisdictions have held that students are not required to recite the Pledge, but as a practical matter it has become almost obligatory and coercive in many communities.

The plaintiff in the case, a California physician and outspoken atheist, Dr. Michael A. Newdow, argued his own case before the Coutt on March 24. By most accounts, Newdow, who also has a law degree, acquitted himself well and engaged in a spirited defense of his position. He argued, "Government needs to stay out of this business altogether," because requiring a statement of religious belief violates the Constitution's mandate for neutrality in religious matters by governmental authorities.

As an advocate, Newdow was impressive. Linda Greenhouse, the legal affairs reporter for *The New York Times,* called his performance "spellbinding," even if it "bore a closer resemblance to dinner-table conversation than to formal court-room discourse."

Newdow closed with a compelling argument: "There's a principle here, and I'm hoping the court will uphold this principle so that we can finally go back and have every American want to stand up, face the flag, place their hand over their heart and pledge to one nation, indivisible, not divided by religion, with liberty and justice for all."

Attorneys for the U.S. Government and the Elk Grove Unified School District near

Sacramento, California, where Newdow's daughter attends school, urged the Court to overrule the appellate decision and allow the Pledge to remain as it was amended. The California school district attorney, Terence Cassidy, emphasized that Newdow's daughter remains in the primary custody of her mother, Sandra Banning, who never married Newdow. Both Banning and daughter are Christians who favor the retention of "under God" in the Pledge, and the girl's mother makes the educational decisions for the child.

Several justices noted that students can opt out of saying some or all of the Pledge, and schools have an obligation to permit those options under a 1943 decision involving the Jehovah's Witnesses. Justice O'Connor asked Newdow if his daughter did not have the "right not to participate," and he replied that any participation is coercive. When O'Connor and Rehnquist suggested that the Pledge is not a prayer, Newdow argued that it is "an affirmation of belief."

The Bush administration's Solicitor General, Theodore B. Olson, claimed that the Pledge is not really religious but is a patriotic and historical statement. He said the Pledge "is not a religious exercise" but was merely a "civic and ceremonial acknowledgment of indisputable historical facts." Justice David H. Souter chided Olson, responding that "the reference to 'under God' means something more than a mere description of how somebody else once thought." But Souter also suggested that the phrase had become so "tepid and diluted" that "whatever is distinctively religious as an affirmation is simply lost."

Dozens of briefs were filed in the case by supporters and opponents of the Pledge. Some normally liberal groups, including the National Education Association, the National School Boards Association, and the American Jewish Congress, filed briefs in support of the Pledge (and thus in favor of overturning the Ninth Circuit ruling). They joined conservative religious groups and the American Legion.

Americans for Religious Liberty joined Americans United for Separation of Church and State and the American Civil Liberties Union in a brief affirming the Ninth Circuit decision. This brief argued that "children are uniquely susceptible to coercive pressure in school settings" and that "ritual classroom recitation of the Pledge coerces children to affirm religious beliefs, including monotheism." The brief cited the historical record of the 1952-1954 congressional debates, which showed that Congress added " 'under God' so that schoolchildren would daily declare religious belief and affirm religion." In signing the bill, which became Public Law No. 83-396, 68 Stat. 249, President Dwight D. Eisenhower proclaimed that students would "daily proclaim the dedication of our nation and our people to the Almighty." Senator Alexander Wiley of Wisconsin said that students "would reassert their belief in the all-present, all-knowing, all-seeing, all-powerful Creator." President Eisenhower also admitted the political aspects of the new legislation when he said the new phrase would "strengthen those spiritual weapons which forever will be our country's most powerful resource in peace or in war." Of course, the U.S. was victorious in two world wars without these words being a part of the Pledge of Allegiance.

One interesting brief came from 32 Christian and Jewish clergy who said that including "under God" in the Pledge "invites a troubling kind of civic blasphemy. If children are supposed to utter the phrase without meaning it as an affirmation of personal faith, then every day government asks millions of schoolchildren to take the name of the Lord in vain," the brief observed.

Many observers thought the justices were trying desperately to find some way to keep the Pledge as it is, if only to restrain the political consequences in an election year when ties between Christian Right activists and the Republican-dominated national government have reached new levels. This brings to mind Finley Peter Dunne's lovable Irish bartender character Mr. Dooley, who observed that the Supreme Court follows election returns. This is in fact what happened.

High Court Gives Nod to Vouchers

As many had long feared, the US. Supreme Court blithely ignored a half century of jurisprudence limiting public aid to religious private schools and gave its seal of approval to the long controversial Cleveland voucher program.

By a 5-4 margin on June 27, the same justices who gave the presidency to George W. Bush have now advanced one of his primary political objectives, tax aid to sectarian schools.

To be sure, the majority decision, written by Chief Justice William Rehnquist, took pains in its labored language to say that it was merely following precedents established in such cases as *Mueller v. Allen* and *Aguilar v. Felton* — which are borderline cases at best— while ignoring the *PEARL v. Nyquist* ruling in 1973 which was more directly on target.

Basically the court's conservatives concluded that the Ohio voucher program (officially the Ohio Pilot Project Scholarship Program) was not unconstitutional because "it is neutral with respect to religion and provides assistance directly to a broad class of citizens who, in turn, direct government aid to religious schools wholly as a result of their own genuine and independent private choice."

Rehnquist took pains to claim that the recipients were offered a wide variety of educational options and the fact that 96% of them ended up in parochial schools had no constitutional consequence. In so doing, Rehnquist ignored the discriminatory nature of church school hiring and admissions practices, as well as the longstanding principle that no taxpayers should be compelled to support religious education—their own or anyone else's. To claim, as Rehnquist did, that the ruling in *Zelman v. Simmons-Harris*, No. 00-1751, was "in keeping with an unbroken line of decisions rejecting challenges to similar programs," is simply untrue.

Justice Sandra Day O'Connor, the crucial swing vote, filed a concurring opinion which suggested that she must have read and digested the now classic fifty-year-old book called *How to Lie with Statistics*. She denied that 96% of participating students were enrolled in religious schools by ingeniously including public community schools and public magnet schools as "reasonable educational alternatives to religious schools" and—presto!—the percentage of voucher students attending parochial schools drops to 16.5%. By using this novel statistical method, O'Connor denied that this decision "marks a dramatic break from the past." She added insult to injury when saying that even though "most of $8.2 million in public funds flowed to religious schools under the voucher program... it pales in comparison to the amount of funds that federal, state and local governments already provide religious institutions." This odd argument seems to say that because American religious groups are feeding generously from government coffers, they might as well be given a little additional largesse at the voucher trough.

Ignoring all available evidence about tuition costs and availability of alternatives, O'Connor insisted that "genuine non-religious options" were available to "parents of eligible children" and that "non-religious schools were able to compete effectively with Catholic and other religious schools."

Justice Clarence Thomas filed a separate concurring opinion which inexplicably quoted the 19th century black patriot Frederick Douglass and then claimed that "many of our inner-city public schools deny emancipation to urban minority students." Without citing credible evidence, Thomas wrote, "Religious schools, like other private schools, achieve far better educational results than their public counterparts." There is a wide body of evidence refuting this finding, especially when parental income and educational level are considered as explanatory influences.

There were three eloquent dissenting opinions. Justice John Paul Stevens said the majority decision "is profoundly misguided" and rests on the shaky argument that "the mere fact that a family that cannot afford a private education wants its children educated in a parochial school is a sufficient justification for this use of public funds." Stevens said that the "voluntary character of private choice to prefer a parochial school education" is "quite irrelevant to the question whether the government's choice to pay for religious indoctrination is constitutionally permissible." Stevens warned, "Whenever we remove a brick from the wall that was designed to separate religion and government, we increase the risk of religious strife and weaken the foundation of our democracy."

Justice David Souter frankly accused his colleagues in the majority of repudiating the classic *Everson* decision of 1947 which held, "No tax in any amount, large or small, can be levied to support any religious activities or institutions, whatever they may be called or whatever form they may adopt to teach or practice religion." *(Everson v. Board of Education,* 330 US. 1 at 16.) "How," Souter asked, "can a Court consistently leave *Everson* on the books and approve the Ohio vouchers? The answer is that it cannot. It is only by ignoring *Everson* that the majority can claim to rest on traditional law in its invocation of neutral aid provisions and private choice to sanction the Ohio law It is, moreover, only by ignoring the meaning of neutrality and private choice themselves that the majority can even pretend to rest today's decision on those criteria."

Souter pointed out that the program was carefully designed and limited so that in practice only parochial schools were affordable to potential users of the voucher scheme. Furthermore, he noted, "At each level, the religious schools have a comparative cost advantage due to church subsidies, donations of the faithful, and the like." Souter analyzed two flaws inherent in the program: The value of the vouchers limits availability almost solely to Catholic religious schools, since most private nonreligious and other religious schools are far more expensive; and any increase in the program to expand availability "would be even more egregiously unconstitutional than the current scheme due to the substantial amount of aid to religious teaching that would be required."

Souter angrily observed, "The scale of the aid to religious schools approved today is unprecedented, both in the number of dollars and in the proportion of systemic school expenditure supported."

Souter said that "every objective underlying the prohibition of religious establishment is betrayed by this scheme." Souter argued that "respect for freedom of conscience" and a desire "to save religion from its own corruption" were the two primary objectives of the Establishment Clause, both of which will suffer irreparable damage from this decision. He chided the majority, saying, "The majority makes no pretense that substantial amounts of tax money are not systematically underwriting religious practice and indoctrination."

Souter warned that "the third concern behind the ban on establishment, its inextricable link with social conflict," is also compromised because " as appropriations for religious subsidy rise, competition for the money will tap sectarian religion's capacity for discord." He added, "With the arrival of vouchers in religious schools,... will go confidence that religious disagreements will stay moderate."

Souter's dissent, joined by Justices Stevens, Breyer, and Ginsburg, was one of the most spirited rejoinders ever issued at the High Court. The fact that all four dissenters read their opinion from the bench underscored the intensity of the feeling.

In a highly unusual epilogue, Justice Souter urged the "political branches," i.e. the legislatures, to "save us from the consequences of the majority's decision." He added sadly, "In the matter of educational aid the Establishment Clause has been largely read away" Now, " a federal court will not save them from it," he said in referring to the political thrust for parochial school aid. "I hope," he concluded, "that a future Court will reconsider today's dramatic departure from basic Establishment Clause principle."

In a separate dissent Justice Stephen Breyer pointedly warned of "the risk that publicly financed voucher programs pose in terms of religiously based social conflict." Breyer said Ohio's voucher plan allowed "direct financing to a core function of the church: the teaching of religious truths to young children," and involved "a considerable shift in taxpayer dollars from public secular schools to provide religious schools."

Breyer accused the Court of "turning the clock back" on fundamental constitutional principles and adopting "an interpretation of the Establishment Clause that the Court rejected more than half a century ago." He added, "In a society composed of many different religious creeds, I fear that this present departure from the Court's earlier understanding risks creating a form of religiously based conflict potentially harmful to the nation's social fabric."

This case is surely one of the most important church-state decisions in many decades and sets the stage for years of intense conflict.

Supreme Court Allows Religious Clubs in Grade Schools

By a 6-3 vote the U.S. Supreme Court in June gave the green light to religious clubs that meet on elementary school grounds. Ignoring church-state separation requirements, the Court majority saw the issue more as a free speech issue, believing that religious clubs should be able to meet on school campuses if nonreligious clubs are allowed to meet. The decision clearly widens the opportunities for off-campus evangelistic groups to use the lower grades to press their religious convictions in what has been regarded as a religiously neutral setting.

Writing for the majority, Justice Clarence Thomas held that letting a Good News Club, an evangelical Christian organization that targets children, use a room in an upstate New York school on the same basis as other groups "would ensure neutrality, not threaten it." The decision overturned a federal appeals court ruling that held that excluding the religious group was a reasonable policy of not permitting "quintessentially religious" subjects from being taught on school property.

Thomas' opinion concluded that the "school has no valid Establishment Clause interest." He was joined by the usual ultra-conservative Antonin Scalia and William Rehnquist, the two moderate swing votes Sandra Day O'Connor and Anthony Kennedy and, surprisingly, by the usually liberal Stephen Breyer, who filed a concurring opinion. Justice David Souter, who is becoming the court's leading defender of church-state separation, criticized the majority for "ignoring reality." Souter, whose dissent was joined by John Paul Stephens and Ruth Bader Ginsberg, observed, "Good News's exercises blur the line between public classroom instruction and private religious indoctrination, leaving a reasonable elementary school pupil unable to appreciate that the former instruction is the business of the school while the latter, evangelism, is not."

Souter reiterated this point, writing, "It is beyond question that Good News intends to use the public school premises not for the mere discussion of a subject from a particular Christian point of view, but for an evangelical service of worship calling children to commit themselves in an act of Christian conversion."

Justice Breyer's concurrence was conditional. He supported the Club's asking for equal treatment and nondiscrimination by the school, but he worried openly that a reasonable child might see the Club's presence on school property as an endorsement of religion.

The case, *Good News Club v. Milford Central School,* No. 99-2036, was accepted by the Supreme Court in part because two appeals courts had reached different conclusions about the issue in recent years.

The Religious Right immediately hailed the ruling. One Religious Right group, the Rutherford Institute, was involved directly in the suit. Another, Religious Liberty Advocates, filed a friend of the court brief on behalf of the Good News Club's parent organization, Child Evangelism Fellowship, a group headquartered in Warrenton, Missouri. Of the 4,622 Good News Club chapters around the country, 527 meet in public school buildings. The evangelical group admits that its purpose is "to evangelize boys and girls with the Gospel of the Lord Jesus Christ and to establish them in the Word of God and in a local church for Christian living." This stark admission suggests that the group could convert students of one faith and try to place them in a congregation different from the one attended by parents. This potential for religious acrimony was noted by Edwin Darden, attorney for the National School Boards Association, who warned that the decision placed local school boards in an untenable position by "setting up a competition between different religious groups trying to gain the religious fidelity of children."

Many Jewish and civil liberties groups expressed dismay at the ruling, fearing that it opens the door to religious proselytizing and enhances the likelihood of religious strife in public elementary schools. Commented *The New York Times,* "Now that the Supreme Court has allowed this beachhead, it would not be surprising to see a rapid proliferation of frankly religious after-school programming in public school classrooms across the country, blurring the line between regular classroom instruction and religious indoctrination — exactly the meld of government and religion that the Establishment Clause is supposed to prevent."

Abortion Rights Upheld

The nation's highest tribunal strengthened abortion access and availability in two closely-watched rulings. By a narrow 5-4 margin, the Supreme Court invalidated three state laws banning a rarely-used third trimester abortion procedure labeled "partial birth" abortion by opponents.

Justice Stephen G. Breyer wrote the majority opinion in *Stenberg v. Carhart,* which originated in Nebraska. Breyer said the state's ban—similar in content to those of 30 other states—"lacked any exception for the preservation of the health of the mother" and "imposes an undue burden on a woman's ability to choose." The Nebraska ban was so vaguely worded that it could have been construed to forbid even the most common second trimester abortions, thus contravening *Roe v. Wade* and *Planned Parenthood v. Casey.*

Breyer was also critical of the punitive nature of the Nebraska statute. "All those who perform abortion procedures... must fear prosecution, conviction and imprisonment. The result is an undue burden upon a woman's right to make an abortion decision." Breyer was joined by

O'Connor, Stevens, Souter and Ginsburg in constructing the majority ruling.

Justice Antonin Scalia wrote a scathing dissent, filled with inflammatory rhetoric referring to physicians as "abortionists" and calling the disputed procedure "live-birth abortion" and a "visibly brutal means of eliminating our half-born posterity." In a separate dissent Justice Clarence Thomas was only slightly milder in his rhetoric, referring to "profound respect for fetal life" and abortion that "borders on infanticide." Justice Anthony Kennedy, in still another dissent, denied that the Nebraska law placed an undue burden on the right to choose and said states had the right to enact such determinations. Chief Justice William Rehnquist joined the Thomas and Kennedy dissents.

The thirty-one states affected by the decision are mostly in the South and Midwest. Every Southern state except North Carolina and George W. Bush's Texas had enacted the ban as had most of the evangelical and Baptist-oriented Border states. In the Midwest and Plains every state but liberal Minnesota had such a ban as did the Mormon-dominated Rocky Mountain states. However, only two of the eleven Northeastern states (New Jersey and Rhode Island) are affected. Most of the Far West had no such statutes, except for conservative Alaska. The more libertarian but Republican states of Colorado and Wyoming also refused to enact the ban.

Some states are already contemplating ways to get around the ruling by drafting new legislation and looking for loopholes. Virginia Attorney General Mark Earley, an ally of the Religious Right, is spearheading this effort.

Dr. LeRoy Carhart, the Omaha surgeon who challenged the Nebraska law, said he was pleased but warned, "This shows *Roe* is hanging by a very fragile thread. It's a true wake-up call to the American people. If they want to keep abortion for their children and themselves, they need to go out and vote for choice." Carhart has survived death threats and economic pressures in recent years and is the only physician in Nebraska who performs late-term abortions.

Anti-abortion activists have vowed to fight again until all abortions are eliminated. Republican presidential candidate George W. Bush said he was "disappointed" by the ruling and would work to overturn it.

In a companion ruling, the Court upheld a Colorado law that requires anti-abortion demonstrators to stay at least eight feet away from people entering health care facilities. The restriction applies within a 100-foot radius around any clinic entrance. The vote in this case was 6-3, with the chief justice joining the majority. Justice John Paul Stevens, writing for the majority, said the Colorado law was "content neutral" and was based on "the right to be left alone." He wrote, "Private citizens have always retained the power to decide for themselves what they wish to read, and within limits, what oral messages they want to consider." The Colorado Supreme Court had originally upheld the law and expressed concerns about tension and violence around clinics.

Supreme Court Upholds Parochiaid in a Big Way

In a decision that is nothing short of devastating to advocates of strict church-state separation at the money line in education, the Supreme Court invented some new doctrines to uphold public aid to parochial schools. In a 6-3 ruling in *Mitchell v. Helms,* the court majority opinion, written by Clarence Thomas, held that the provision of computers and other educational materials to private and parochial schools in Jefferson Parish (county), Louisiana, does not violate the federal constitutional ban on establishment of religion. Thomas was joined by Chief Justice Rehnquist, and Justices Antonin Scalia and Anthony Kennedy.

To reach this decision Thomas and his allies (joined more narrowly in a concurring opinion by Justices O'Connor and Breyer) invoked "the principle of private choice" and neutral-based legislation that includes all kinds of schools as a broad class of recipients. Thomas wrote, "Where the aid would be suitable for use in a public school, it is also suitable for use in any private school."

Shockingly, Thomas has succeeded in overruling and apparently obliterating a quarter-century rule prohibiting aid to "pervasively sectarian schools." Thomas proclaimed, "Nothing in the Establishment Clause requires the exclusion of pervasively sectarian schools from otherwise permissible aid programs, and other doctrines of this Court bar it. This doctrine, born of bigotry, should be buried now." Thomas went out of his way to attack a straw man, namely the history surrounding the Blaine amendment controversy in the U.S. Congress nearly 130 years ago, when Congress came close to passing a constitutional amendment permanently banning all forms of public aid to religious schools. Thomas wrote angrily, "Hostility to aid to pervasively sectarian schools has a shameful pedigree that we do not hesitate to disavow. . . . Consideration of the Blaine amendment arose at a time of pervasive hostility to the Catholic Church and to Catholics in general, and it was an open secret that 'sectarian' was code for 'Catholic'."

The Thomas opinion also rejects the inquiry regarding who will benefit from legislation of this nature. It matters not a whit if 99% of the aid goes to religious schools as long as the legislation is neutral on its face. "The religious nature of a recipient should not matter to the Constitutional analysis, so long as the recipient adequately furthers the government's secular purpose," wrote Thomas. (The last phrase, however, may cause some concerns among very conservative private school administrators.)

Even if religious indoctrination is clearly a purpose of certain schools, aid to them is still constitutional unless "such indoctrination could be attributed to the government." The new doctrine allowing parochiaid rests on the twin pillars of "private choice and the absence of government-provided sectarian content."

Clearly, the Court has been moving in this direction for years. Thomas based his ruling in part on the previous cases, *Agostini* and *Zobrest,* which overruled the earlier anti-parochiaid decision *Aguilar* in full and *Ball* in part. Thomas went out of his way to note that this ruling also overrules *Meek* and *Wolman,* two classic defeats for parochiaid at the Supreme Court in the 1970s.

The ruling flies in the face of common sense and reason at one point, by denying that "reducing the cost of securing a religious education creates an incentive for parents to choose such an education for their children."

Justices Sandra Day O'Connor and Stephen Breyer concurred in this result but said they were "troubled" by the "expansive" nature of the Thomas opinion. Some of the sharply-focused criticisms of the "plurality" opinion (Thomas and his allies) by O'Connor still strongly suggest that future parochiaid programs, or tuition voucher schemes, might be struck down.

O'Connor chose to uphold the Chapter 2 programs in this case by invoking two concepts embedded in the three-year-old *Agostini* decision. They are (1) whether the aid results in governmental indoctrination and (2) whether the aid program defines its recipients by reference to religion. Using these narrow criteria, in addition to the question of whether the aid creates an excessive entanglement between government and religion, O'Connor held the Louisiana implementation constitutional. She was convinced that "Chapter 2 aid is allocated on the basis of neutral, secular criteria" and that "No Chapter 2 funds ever reach the coffers of religious schools."

Still, O'Connor is unlikely to support any school aid program that allows "direct monetary subsidies" to church schools or to any "participating religious organizations (including churches) that could use that aid to support religious indoctrination." O'Connor also reiterated her personal doctrine of "endorsement" and "public perception," a view that would invalidate programs that could be conceived by the general public as endorsing religion.

Justice David Souter wrote a blistering and powerful dissent which chided the Court for going too far in accommodating religion in the question of church school aid, thus transgressing the Establishment Clause. Joined by John Paul Stevens and Ruth Bader Ginsburg, Souter wrote bluntly that the First Amendment's Establishment Clause "bars the use of public funds for religious aid."

In a succinct argument which could be used in future cases, Souter summarized the historic view of the Establishment provision: "The Establishment prohibition of government religious funding serves more than one end. It is meant to guarantee the right of individual conscience against compulsion, to protect the integrity of religion against the corrosion of secular support, and to preserve the unity of political society against the implied exclusion of the less-favored and the antagonism of controversy over public support for religious causes."

Souter angrily accused the majority justices (actually a plurality, since it took the two concurring judges to agree to this ruling) of ignoring long-established precedent. He said, "The plurality opinion espouses a new conception of neutrality as a practically sufficient test of constitutionality that would, if adopted by the court, eliminate enquiry into a law's effects. The plurality opinion breaks fundamentally with Establishment Clause principles, and with the methodology painstakingly worked out in support of it."

Souter reminded the Court that "compelling an individual to support religion violates the fundamental principle of freedom of conscience." Pointing out that neutrality in a law's language is only "one, nondispositive pointer toward intent," Souter accused the Court of ignoring "the religious mission and education level of benefited schools and their pupils, the pathway by which a benefit travels from public treasury to educational effect, the form of content of the aid, its adaptability to religious ends and its effects on school budgets."

Souter noted that the factual record from Louisiana, noted in the two lower court decisions, suggested that the aid had been diverted to religious textbooks and possibly used for religious ends, especially since local authorities were initially less than careful in monitoring the program. Souter noted, for example, that "religious education in Roman Catholic schools is defined as part of required practice; aiding it is thus akin to aiding a church service."

Souter bluntly asserted that the Thomas opinion was "unequaled in the history of Establishment Clause interpretation" because of its "break with consistent doctrine" and "its manifold errors." Rarely has a dissent been more eloquent or hard-hitting than this one. Warning about future cases that might be influenced by the new Thomas-era doctrine, Souter concluded, "The plurality's mistaken assumptions explain and underscore its sharp break with the Framers' understanding of establishment and this Court's consistent interpretative course. Under the plurality's regime, little would be left of the right of conscience against compelled support for religion; the more massive the aid the more potent would be the influence of the government on the teaching mission; the more generous the support, the more divisive would be the resentments of those resisting religious support, and those religions without school systems ready to claim their fair share."

Souter said that "government can in fact operate with neutrality in its relation to religion," primarily by not aiding it financially.

This Supreme Court judgment overrules two lower federal district and appellate court rulings, which had held such aid unconstitutional. The case arose in 1985 when two Louisiana taxpayers with children in public schools filed suit to stop the distribution of federal Chapter 2 funds at area private and religious schools. In their county (Jefferson Parish, a New Orleans suburb), 41 of the 46 recipient private schools were church-related, and 30% of all federal Chapter 2 funds went to the nonpublic schools. The Eastern District of Louisiana held in 1990 in *Helms v. Cody* (the original name of the suit) that the aid had the primary effect of advancing religion. Strangely enough, another judge two years later reversed this ruling in part, especially after some of its benefits had been terminated. But a third ruling, *Helms v. Picard* by the Fifth Circuit Court of Appeals, reinstated the ban.

The Supreme Court overruled these findings and reached back to render null and void some of the High Court's prior rulings on the subject. This relatively rare reversal by the nation's highest tribunal now makes substantial government aid to church schools a possible reality.

A Bad Week in June

The week of June 23 was not a good one for religious liberty and church-state separation at the Supreme Court. On Monday the Court reversed a perfectly sound 1985 precedent and weakened the wall of separation between church and state. On Wednesday it declined to review a bad 1990 precedent, which was based in part on a 1940 ruling the Court itself reversed three years later, and instead struck down an act of Congress intended to correct the 1990 ruling. On Thursday the Court reversed federal appellate rulings from New York and Washington State that had recognized a constitutional right to physician assisted suicide. In all three cases, ARL had filed *amicus* briefs on behalf of freedom of conscience. Let's look at the details.

Parochiaid

In 1985, in *Aguilar v. Felton* and *Grand Rapids v. Ball,* the Supreme Court, building on a long line of church-state precedents, ruled 5-4 that placing public school teachers in sectarian private schools violates the First Amendment's establishment clause. On June 23 the Court ruled 5-4 in *Agostini v. Felton* (O'Connor, Rehnquist, Scalia, Kennedy, Thomas on one side; Souter, Stevens, Breyer, Ginsburg dissenting) that several rulings since 1985 *(Witters* and *Zobrest)* had changed the Court's approach to the establishment clause, thereby setting the stage for a reexamination of *Aguilar,* The Court in *Agostini* also reached out and struck down part of *Grand Rapids v. Ball,* though that case was not before it, ruling that the "revised" establishment clause doctrine required the override.

The majority decision, written by Justice Sandra Day O'Connor, reasoned that *"Aguilar* cannot be squared with this Court's intervening Establishment Clause jurisprudence and is no longer good law." The majority concluded that there is no longer excessive entanglement between church and state in the administration of Title I programs and that the program in New York City "contained safeguards" against sectarian indoctrination. O'Connor asserted that "our understanding of the criteria used to assess whether aid to religion has an impermissible effect has changed significantly. . . . We have abandoned the presumption . . . that the placement of public employees on parochial school grounds inevitably results in the impermissible effect of state-sponsored indoctrination or constitutes a symbolic union between government and religion."

In another departure from long-established law, O'Connor asserted that "we have departed from the rule that all government aid that directly aids the educational function of religious schools in invalid."

In his carefully reasoned, eloquent dissent for himself and Justices Stevens, Breyer and Ginsburg, Justice David Souter explained how the majority had repudiated "the very reasonable line drawn in *Aguilar* and *Ball* and authorized "direct state aid to religious institutions on an unparalleled scale, in violation of the Establishment Clause's central prohibition against religious subsidies by the government." The dissenters also argued that the majority erred in accepting the appeal in *Agostini* by using a federal court procedure, Rule 60(b)(5), in an unprecedented and unwarranted way.

Souter's dissent invoked the lessons of history, referring to "the hard lesson over and over again in the American past and in the experiences of the countries from which we have come, that religions supported by governments are compromised just as surely as the religious freedom of dissenters is burdened when government supports religion." Souter further warned, "The human tendency, of course, is to forget the hard lessons, and to overlook the history of governmental partnership with religion when a cause is worthy, and bureaucrats have programs. That tendency to forget is the reason for having the Establishment Clause (along with the Constitution's other structural and libertarian guarantees), in the hope of stopping the corrosion before it starts."

Souter reminded the majority that they ignored two central facts: "A public educational agency distributes Title I aid in the form of programs and services directly to the religious schools" and "New York City's Title I program before *Aguilar* served about 22,000 private school students, all but 52 of whom attended religious schools."

Agostini involved federal Title I remedial education services, which the parochial schools insisted be provided in their buildings rather than in public schools. After the Court ruled in *Aguilar* in 1985 that the services could not be provided in sectarian school facilities, the nonpublic schools demanded that they be provided in mobile units parked near the parochial schools. This arrangement inflated the program's costs and segregated those students from the public school population.

Advocates of tax aid for sectarian private schools are claiming that *Agostini* is a green light for voucher programs. Defenders of church-state separation and public education are divided as to the ruling's possible consequences. Some believe that *Agostini* will allow a massive flow of tax aid to sectarian schools. Others believe the ruling stops short of a green light. Lisa Thurau, executive director of the National Committee for Public Education and Religious Liberty (PEARL), which defended *Aguilar* (and of which ARL is a member organization), takes the more pessimistic view. She said that "it is especially disconcerting . . . that the Court does not consider the government's provision of the core educational services of parochial schools as a subsidization of religion."

However *Agostini* is read, we are in for a major struggle to maintain church-state separation and protect religiously neutral public education. American voters have repeatedly shown that they strongly oppose tax aid to denominational schools and we have won an impressive string of court victories. Now we must redouble our efforts.

Rehnquist Court Lowers the Wall Still Further

The U.S. Supreme Court, by the narrowest of margins, held in June that a state-paid sign-language interpreter could be placed in parochial schools. The case, *Zobrest v. Catalina Foothills School District*, reached the High Court after a district court and the Ninth Circuit Appeals Court concluded that provision of these services to sectarian schools was unconstitutional because the interpreter would act as a conduit for a child's religious inculcation, thereby promoting religious development at government expense. The case was brought by parents of a deaf child who attends a Roman Catholic high school in Tucson, Arizona, after the local public school district refused to provide an interpreter.

The five to four majority ruling written by Chief Justice Rehnquist and joined by Justices Scalia, Kennedy, Thomas, and White (in his last church-state ruling before retirement), invoked the *Mueller* and *Witters* cases, which also represented a weakening of the wall of separation between church and state by granting aid to private and parochial schools under allegedly neutral laws which provide aid to a broad class of taxpayers.

In this case Rehnquist and Company held that government programs which neutrally provide aid to a broad class of citizens could not be tested for Establishment Clause violations when sectarian institutions receive benefits.

The majority seemed at pains to suggest that provision of a sign-language interpreter was aid only to the child, and at the request of a parent, thereby rendering aid to the school "incidental," even though Rehnquist noted that the parents in this case enrolled their son in Salpointe Catholic High School "for religious reasons."

The majority also sharply differentiated the sign-language interpreter's role from that of a teacher or guidance counsellor. "The sign-language interpreter . . . will neither add to nor subtract from the environment" of the sectarian school, they concluded. The interpreter, in Rehnquist's view, is only present to "accurately interpret whatever material is presented to the class as a whole." Rehnquist also cited two earlier parochiaid cases, *Wolman v. Walter*, in 1977, which held that provision of health services in public and nonpublic schools was allowable, and *Meek v. Pittenger*, in 1975, which made an exception for diagnostic speech and hearing services on sectarian school premises.

The dissent, written by Justice Harry Blackmun, joined by Justices Souter, Stevens and O'Connor, accused the majority of "disregarding longstanding principles of constitutional adjudication" by allowing the government to pay for an employee "whose duty consists of relaying religious messages in a parochial school classroom." Blackmun noted pointedly that regulations adopted under the Individuals with Disabilities Education Act (IDEA) forbid the use of federal funds to pay for "religious worship, instruction, or proselytization." Several previous court decisions by the Fourth and Sixth Circuit Courts and district courts in Ohio and the District of Columbia have strictly enforced that requirement. Blackmun further noted that the Arizona Constitution has been interpreted by the state's attorney general to prohibit the provision of sign-language interpreters to church-related schools.

In a direct rejoinder to his colleagues, Blackmun observed, "Until now, the Court never has authorized a public employee to participate directly in religious indoctrination. Yet that is the consequence of today's decision." Blackmun added, "It is beyond question that a state-employed sign-language interpreter would serve as the conduit for... religious education, thereby assisting Salpointe in its mission of religious indoctrination."

While acknowledging that some social-welfare services are acceptable in a nonpublic school environment, Blackmun stressed that the Court "has always proscribed the provision of benefits that afford even the opportunity for the transmission of sectarian views."

Blackmun cited the Faculty Empowerment Agreement at Salpointe Catholic High School, which emphasized that "religious programs are of primary importance" and "are not separate from the academic and extracurricular programs but are instead interwoven with them." The Faculty statement also requires teachers "to assist in the implementation of the philosophical policies of the school and to compel proper conduct..."

Blackmun held that provision of any state employee to a pervasively sectarian school violated the First Amendment's Establishment Clause. He wrote, "A state-employed sign-language interpreter would be required to communicate the material covered in religion class, the nominally secular subjects that are taught from a religious perspective, and the daily Masses at which Salpointe encourages attendance for Catholic students. In an environment so pervaded by discussions of the divine, the interpreter's every gesture would be infused with religious significance."

Finally, Blackmun and his three allies warn that state-provided personnel would likely be subjected to "religiously based rules of conduct" in church-run schools, which could lead to conflict. "To require public employees to obey such rules would impermissibly threaten individual liberty, but to fail to do so might endanger religious autonomy . . . The Establishment Clause was designed to avert exactly this sort of conflict."

The *Zobrest* ruling is likely to provoke considerable discussion, if not alarm among defenders of public education and religious liberty. Lee Boothby, general counsel for the Council on Religious Freedom, cautioned that the decision was decided by "the narrowest of margins" and "narrowly confined to the facts of me case." "The *Lemon* test is alive and well," he added.

Former Congressman Robert Drinan, now a professor of Georgetown Law School, warned in a recent *America* article, "The raw emotions that surround the issue of aid to church-related schools will surface again."

Supreme Court Upholds Bible Club Act

On June 4, the U.S. Supreme Court upheld Congress's 1984 Equal Access Law requiring public secondary schools that have noncurriculum-related clubs to also allow religious clubs to meet. We can now expect increased violations of family rights as school Bible clubs bring in adult missionaries—permitted under the law—to proselytize secondary school students as young as 11 or 12 without parental knowledge or consent. We can also expect increased divisiveness among students as many of them separate into sectarian clubs on school premises, as well as the disruption of schools by radical groups such as skinheads, the Klan, and anti-choice groups.

The Equal Access Law was originally passed as a sop to sectarian pressure groups after the defeat in the Senate of President Reagan's proposed amendment to authorize government-regimented prayer in public schools. As Congress is unlikely to repeal this misguided law, local school boards can defend students and families, as ARL's Edd Doerr pointed out in the *New*

York Times on July 6, by retailoring noncurricular programs to fit the Court's definition of "curriculum-related," thus keeping out religious and ideological clubs; by requiring written parental permission for students to attend all noncurriculum-related meetings on school premises; and by barring from clubs all outside adults who might try to proselytize students.

Writing for an eight-to-one majority in *Westside Community Board of Education v. Mergens,* Justice Sandra Day O'Connor held that the Equal Access Act did not violate the Establishment Clause because there was "a crucial difference between government speech endorsing religion, which the Establishment Clause forbids, and private speech endorsing religion, which the Free Exercise and Free Speech clauses protect."

O'Connor admitted that "the possibility of student peer pressure remains, but there is little if any risk of official state endorsement of coercion where no formal classroom activities are involved and no school officials actively participate."

The Act is activated if only one noncurriculum-related activity is offered. O'Connor broadened the concept somewhat by arguing that "a student group directly relates to a school's curriculum if the subject matter of the group is actually taught, or will soon be taught, in a regularly offered course." In a small glimmer of hope that opponents should remember, O'Connor wrote, "To the extent that a school chooses to structure its course offerings and existing student groups to avoid the Act's obligations, that result is not prohibited by the Act."

In a concurring opinion, the Court's two leading church-state separationists, William J. Brennan and Thurgood Marshall, concluded that while the Act was not patently unconstitutional it did "raise serious Establishment Clause concerns" if "the public schools are perceived as conferring the imprimatur of the State on religious doctrine or practice."

Brennan and Marshall wrote that the "schools bear the responsibility for taking whatever steps are necessary to make clear that their recognition of a religious club does not reflect their endorsement of the views of the club's participants." Furthermore, the school "must fully disassociate itself from the club's religious speech and avoid appearing to sponsor or endorse the club's goals."

The only dissent came from the Court's most consistent maverick, John Paul Stevens, who objected to the federal government's increasing intervention in local school activities. Stevens expressed concern that school authorities were losing their control over constitutional activities on campus. He complained of "a sweeping intrusion by the federal government into the operation of our public schools."

The first test of the *Mergens* decision came on June 22 when the U.S. Court of Appeals for the Third Circuit voted two-to-one to uphold a lower court ruling requiring the Centennial School District in Bucks County, PA, to permit the use of school facilities for religious organizations. The case *(Gregoire v. Centennial School District)* arose in 1987 when Student Venture, a branch of Campus Crusade for Christ, was denied use of a high school auditorium for a "Christian" magician's performance on Halloween. The group sued and won a temporary injunction permitting the performance, but the school district adopted a policy in 1988 barring religious groups from school facilities.

This case differs somewhat from other equal access rulings because the central issue involved off-campus groups that rented space on campuses. The Pennsylvania district in question had allowed more than 65 groups to use their facilities, creating what the appeals court called a "limited open forum" for advocacy. The court also observed, "granting a religious organization permission to use school facilities does not imply an endorsement of religious goals."

Americans for Religious Liberty had joined with other organizations in an *amicus curiae* brief to the Supreme Court opposing the Equal Access Act.

Religious Liberty Loses in Peyote Ruling

On April 17 the Supreme Court dealt a severe blow to religious liberty in its 6-3 ruling in *Employment Division of Oregon v. Smith*. The ruling, written by Justice Antonin Scalia, held that state law may override a "free exercise of religion" claim to protect sacramental use of the hallucinogenic drug peyote by Native Americans, even though 23 states and the federal government allow special exemptions from drug laws for such use.

Justice Scalia based his ruling in part on the Court's 1940 *Gobitis* ruling, which upheld a state law denying Jehovah's Witnesses children conscientious exemption from a compulsory flag salute law. Scalia ignored the fact that *Gobitis* was reversed by the Court in 1943 in *Barnette*. Scalia wrote that allowing conscientious objection in this limited case "would be courting anarchy ... in direct proportion to the society's diversity of religious beliefs," and that "we cannot afford the luxury of deeming presumptively invalid, as applied to the religious objector, every regulation of conduct that does not protect an interest of the highest order." He added that accommodation of religious minorities should be left to the political process.

Justice Sandra Day O'Connor concurred in the result but said that the Scalia majority (with Rehnquist, White, Kennedy, and Stevens) erred by overturning established precedents. She said that "the First Amendment was enacted precisely to protect the rights of those whose religious practices are not shared by the majority and may be viewed with hostility."

In his dissent, joined by Brennan and Marshall, Justice Blackmun wrote that the majority had overturned "a settled and inviolate principle of this Court's First Amendment jurisprudence," and showed little "judicial restraint" in "deciding the constitutionality of a criminal prohibition which the State [Oregon] has not sought to enforce."

A wide spectrum of constitutional scholars (such as Harvard's Laurence Tribe, Stanford's Gerald Gunther, NYU's Norman Redlich), religious organizations (such as the National Council of Churches and the American Jewish Congress), and the ACLJ have asked the Supreme Court to reconsider the *Smith* decision.

Commentators agree that the *Smith* ruling expands the power of the state while weakening individual liberty and promoting "moral majoritarianism."

'Creationism' Bites the Dust

The U.S. Supreme Court's June 19 ruling against Louisiana's law requiring that public schools give equal treatment to "creationism" whenever evolution is taught was a landmark victory for church-state separation, academic freedom, public education, and science. That the ruling in *Edwards v. Aguillard* was by a strong 7-2 margin means that little hope remains for the fundamentalist "creationist" movement to bring their essentially religious doctrine through the front door of the public school.

Americans for Religious Liberty joined the Anti-Defamation League of B'nai B'rith in filing an *amicus curiae* brief to the Supreme Court in the case. ARL executive Edd Doerr and ARL member Al Seckel originated the idea of having 72 American Nobel laureates in science file an *amicus* brief in the case.

In writing the majority opinion, Justice William J. Brennan held that the Louisiana law violated the constitutional test that legislation must have a secular purpose. Brennan noted that the state law clearly had as its main purpose "to restructure the science curriculum to conform with a particular religious viewpoint." The Brennan opinion upheld the lower federal court rulings against the state law.

The Court specifically held: "The Act does not further its stated secular purpose of 'protecting academic freedom.' It does not enhance the freedom of teachers to teach what they choose and fails to further the goal of 'teaching all of the evidence.' Forbidding the teaching of evolution when creation science is not also taught undermines the provision of a comprehensive scientific education. Moreover, requiring the teaching of creation science with evolution does not give school teachers a flexibility that they did not already possess to supplant the present curriculum with the presentation of theories, besides evolution, about the origin of life. Furthermore, the contention that the Act furthers a 'basic concept of fairness' by requiring the teaching of all the evidence on the subject is without merit. Indeed, the Act evinces a discriminatory preference for the teaching of creation science and against the teaching of evolution by requiring that curriculum guides be developed and research services supplied for teaching creationism but not for teaching evolution, by limiting membership of the research services panel to 'creation scientists,' and by forbidding school boards to discriminate against anyone who 'chooses to be a creation-scientist' or to teach creation science, while failing to protect those who choose to teach other theories or who refuse to teach creation science. A law intended to maximize the comprehensiveness and effectiveness of science instruction would encourage the teaching of all scientific theories about human origins. Instead, this Act has the distinctly different purpose of discrediting evolution by counterbalancing its teaching at every turn with the teaching of creation science.

"The Act impermissibly endorses religion by advancing the religious belief that a supernatural being created humankind. The legislative history demonstrates that the term 'creation science,' as contemplated by the state legislature, embraces this religious teaching. The Act's primary purpose was to change the public school science curriculum to provide persuasive advantage to a particular religious doctrine that rejects the factual basis of evolution in its entirety. Thus, the Act is designed either to promote the theory of creation science that embodies a particular religious tenet or to prohibit the teaching of a scientific theory disfavored by certain religious sects. In either case, the Act violates the First Amendment."

Chief Justice William Rehnquist joined Justice Antonin Scalia in a vitriolic 31-page dissenting opinion which made it clear that the two justices are determined to do anything they can to undermine the Supreme Court's long series of decisions upholding and applying the First Amendment separation principle.

Fundamentalist activists are unlikely to try to get "equal treatment" legislation passed again soon, but they will try to have individual teachers promote "creationism" in classes. Further, many fundamentalists are likely to try to keep their children out of biology classes or shift them to sectarian private schools, for which they will seek public funding.

Supreme Court Outlaws Parochiaid, School Prayer

After four years of seeming to drift toward Radical Right positions on church-state issues, the U.S. Supreme Court returned in June and July to its traditional fairly strong separationist stance.

On June 4 the Court ruled in *Wallace v. Jaffree* that an Alabama law prescribing periods of silence for "prayer or meditation" in public schools is unconstitutional. Two weeks later the Court struck down 8 to 1 a Connecticut law which gave employees an unqualified right not to have to work on their sabbath. On July 1, in *School District of Grand Rapids v. Ball* and *Aguilar v. Felton,* the Court ruled against state and federal programs of tax aid for sectarian private schools.

Americans for Religious Liberty entered the parochiaid and school prayer cases in coalition *amicus curiae* briefs. In addition, ARL board members Jay Wabeke and Florence Flast were key figures in developing the *Grand Rapids* and New York *Felton* cases. Attorney in the *Grand Rapids* case was Albert Dilley, a member of ARL, while the *Felton* case attorney was Stanley Geller.

The Alabama "silent prayer" ruling reaffirmed and fine-tuned the Court's earlier school prayer decisions. The Court did not forbid schools from setting aside moments of silence for meditation or reflection, and it has never forbade students to engage in totally voluntary personal prayer. The Court has simply held that lawmakers must keep their noses out of matters religious. Further, by singling out prayer as a prescribed activity for public school students, Alabama lawmakers had elevated that one religious activity over such others as good works, moral reasoning, or rationally thinking about religious subjects.

In the Connecticut Sabbatarian case, the Court held that state laws could require employers to make reasonable accommodations to workers' religious needs but may not elevate religious considerations absolutely above all others.

The parochiaid rulings are the most significant of the batch, if for no other reason than that tax aid for sectarian institutions involves hard cash and is the most geographically widespread and intensely pursued goal of the largest and most powerful sectarian special interests.

At issue were two programs in Grand Rapids, under which $3 million was spent annually to furnish publicly paid remedial and supplementary teachers to an assortment of Catholic, Lutheran, Calvinist, Adventist, and Baptist private schools, and New York's implementation of Title I of the 1965 Elementary and Secondary Education Act by placing public remedial teachers in parochial schools. (Incidentally, in the New York program, parochial schools were receiving *double* the amount of tax aid per student as public schools. In Grand Rapids, the various parochial school interests used the threat of not supporting tax levies for public schools to get public school officials to go along with their parochiaid schemes.)

The Supreme Court held that the Grand Rapids "shared time" plan not only had the primary effect of advancing religion but also entangled government in religious matters. The challenged programs impermissibly promoted religion by creating a "symbolic union of church and state" and by subsidizing "the religious function of the parochial schools by taking over a substantial portion of their responsibility for teaching secular subjects." The Court noted that the beneficiaries of the programs were "wholly designated on the basis of religion" and also "segregated by religion."

The New York City parochiaid program, and by implication all similar programs throughout the country (and costing taxpayers about $300 million per year), was held unconstitutional because attempting to operate it in a constitutional, religiously neutral manner would require an excessive degree of entanglement between religion and government.

Opponents of the Grand Rapids and New York rulings complained that poor children would be hurt by the withdrawal of tax-paid teachers from parochial schools and that the Court is hostile to religion. Supporters of the rulings point out that parochial students can receive the remedial instruction in local public schools, which was the intent of Congress when it enacted the program in 1965. Nor is the Court hostile to religion. It has repeatedly held that separation of church and state is the best policy for religion and religious liberty.

Why did the Court take so long to strike down federal aid for parochial schools? When the application of federal aid to sectarian schools was first challenged in 1966 (by ARL board member Florence Flast and ARL national adviser Leo Pfeffer), the lower courts held that federal taxpayers lacked "standing" to sue in federal courts. When the Supreme court upheld taxpayer standing in 1968, in *Flast v. Cohen,* it also approved a state law providing tax aid to parochial schools in the form of textbook loans and thereby threw a scare into those wishing to test federal parochiaid in court. So a cautious, incremental litigation strategy of challenging an assortment of state parochiaid plans first was followed. This wise strategy resulted in a series of Supreme Court rulings from 1971 to 1975 striking down teacher salary supplement, purchase of services, tuition tax credit, tuition grant, auxiliary services, and other forms of state parochiaid. The 1975 *Meek v. Pittenger* ruling against a Pennsylvania aid plan copied from the 1965 federal plan set the stage for a legal challenge to federal parochiaid, after federal education authorities declined to comply voluntarily with the *Meek* ruling. A New York suit was delayed at the district court level and was finally denied a hearing before the Supreme Court, leaving the *Felton* case to finally settle the matter. It took nineteen years to get this decision against federal parochiaid because challengers had to play by the rules of the game—something the parochiaiders don't like to do.

Reaction to the parochiaid and school prayer rulings was predictable. Supporters of religious liberty and the press generally hailed the rulings, but moral majoritarian and sectarian special interest groups attacked the Court viciously. Attorney General Edwin Meese, the nation's top law enforcement officer, speaking at the American Bar Association convention in July, denounced the Court for not acceding to the administration's anti-separationist views in the cases. Meese also attacked the Court for using the Fourteenth Amendment to apply the First Amendment to state and local government, a view shared only by Radical Right extremists. Actually, the Fourteenth Amendment, passed after the Civil War, was intended to apply the whole Bill of Rights to state and local government, but the Supreme Court refused to so apply it until after World War I.

Education Secretary William Bennett assailed the Court even more strongly in a speech to the Knights of Columbus. He said the Court was "misguided" in its efforts to keep government neutral toward religion, and added that "the Court had failed to reflect sufficiently on the relationship between our faith and our political order." Bennett said the Reagan administration would do all it could to nullify the church-state separation rulings.

Meanwhile, the administration is asking federal courts in New York, Missouri, and Kentucky to delay implementing the ruling against federally funded teachers working in parochial schools. It apparently hopes that Congress can be persuaded to provide tax aid to sectarian schools through a voucher plan or that the old plan can be continued by placing the tax paid teachers in mobile classrooms located adjacent to the private schools.

Chapter 5
Editorials

Voice of Reason, from its first issue, devoted significant space to the editorial function, explaining ARL's viewpoint on issues and events as they occur. Some editorials deal with broader issues, allowing the editors to explore the context and history of movements which may seem transitory. This editorial chapter also includes some commentary features, which present a more far-ranging exploration of some issues. Edd Doerr has long written most of *VOR*'s editorials, honing his skills as an expository writer, as well as a consummate writer of letters to the editor. A couple of guest editorialists, Joseph Chuman and Samuel Rabinove, also appear in this chapter.

Supreme Court: The Times They are A'Changin'

Every sentient being in the U.S. knows by now that President Bush named Judge John G. Roberts Jr., who has served for two years on the U.S. Court of Appeals for the District of Columbia Circuit, to replace Justice Sandra Day O'Connor. The long dreaded day when Bush could begin the process of extending the long arm of conservatism to encompass the third branch of government has now arrived.

First, we should remember some of the contributions of Justice O'Connor over the past quarter century. Ronald Reagan's first appointee, O'Connor proved to be a reliable conservative on some issues, particularly involving corporate interests and national security. But she began to carve out an independent posture on some issues, including those dealing with religious liberty and women's rights. Her argument for an "endorsement of religion" test proved to be compelling, and resulted in opposition to coercive types of school prayer and government efforts to promote symbolic veneers of religion. Her votes saved *Roe v. Wade* from being gutted, affirmative action from effective dismemberment, and prevented some, though not all, actions of government endorsement of religious symbols. She seemed increasingly sensitive to the plight of religious minorities in a public square dominated by religious majorities. But she was clearly wrong on the broad issue of government subsidies for faith-based private schools, arguing, erroneously in our view, that private choice of religious education by parents renders the Establishment ban irrelevant. Her demeanor and her unwillingness to engage in the kind of ideological rancor employed by Justices Scalia and Thomas, and her pragmatic, case-by-case approach to resolving cases may have been the glue that held a fractious and contentious Court together. She was the swing vote in many cases, and for good reason. Her surprise resignation pleased the Religious Right, one of whose spokesmen said, "Thank God Justice O'Connor has resigned." In a polarized nation, it is sometimes necessary to have a "moderate" on the High Court, and O'Connor proved to be the most moderate and least ideological of President Reagan's three appointees.

Judge Roberts appears to be a classic Establishment Republican, more attuned to the corporate world than to movement conservatism. His record on the D.C. Appeals Court and his few years as deputy solicitor general in the George H.W. Bush administration offer few clues to his performance. While working for Republican presidents, he wrote that *Roe v. Wade* was "wrongly decided." But in his confirmation hearings for the appeals court, he said the abortion decision was "settled law" and that his personal convictions, whatever they may be, would not clash with his duty to uphold precedent. In another case he defended, on behalf of the first Bush administration, the practice of prayers at high school football games in Texas, but whether that represents his settled opinion or merely the positions adopted by his superiors is unclear.

He should certainly explain his legal philosophy, and his view of the place of the Court in the American polity when his confirmation hearings begin in the Senate on September 6.

Roberts is certainly well qualified. A graduate of both Harvard College and Harvard Law School, he is often described as brilliant and as open to different points of view.

One fact in Roberts' resume has led to considerable discussion already: his Roman Catholic faith. He will be the tenth Catholic out of more than 100 justices if he is confirmed. This issue should not be a concern at all, given Article VI's ban on religious tests for public office. In an ideal world it would hardly matter. But it has already become a question of some concern. Some conservatives hope his religion will influence his decisions on issues that matter to them, such as abortion, gay rights, and religious participation in public funding. Some liberals worry that his personal views may color his thinking on the same issues. One scholar, David Yalof, a political scientist at the University of Connecticut and author of *Pursuit of Justices: Presidential Politics and the Selection of Supreme Court Nominees,* argues that religious affiliation is not a good predictor of judicial conduct. "We have a small sample of Catholic justices now, and there's no pattern on whether their Catholicism determined anything," Yalof told a *New York Times* interviewer. Justices Scalia and Kennedy bitterly disagree over capital punishment and school prayer, for example, and both are Catholic Republicans appointed by Ronald Reagan.

The battle lines have been drawn, and some elements in today's charged political environment are not above using religion as a wedge issue. Ironically, conservative Protestant Republicans are accusing liberal Catholic Democrats of bigotry because the Democrats plan to question Roberts at length about a host of issues. The Senate Judiciary Committee will be a target of the endeavors: Four of the eight Democrats are Catholics, as are two of the ten Republicans. The Religious Right is backing Roberts, hoping that his religion will prove helpful for their agenda. But *U.S. News & World Report* said that leading religious conservatives expressed "concerns" about Roberts' religious affiliation in private meetings the day after his nomination was announced. If Roberts is confirmed, the Supreme Court will have four Catholics, three Protestants and two Jews.

Many liberal and pro-choice groups have already announced their opposition to the Roberts appointment. A word of caution is in order, however. President Bush was reelected last November, and Republicans now hold 55 Senate seats. The voters knew - or should have known — that the makeup and character of the Court were major issues in the campaign. But 51% of the electorate chose Mr. Bush, knowing that in his hands rested the future of the Judiciary. If Mr. Roberts is rejected, it is altogether likely that someone even worse will be nominated. Bush's track record of in-your-face appointments to the Cabinet and to the federal courts is well established. It may be that Roberts is the least unacceptable under the circumstances. This is the hard reality of American politics in the year 2005. Those who believe in the broadest protection of religious and civil liberties may well be disappointed in this nomination. But the time to have prevented that was last November.

— Al Menendez

Conservatives are Guilty of Rewriting U.S. History

The surest way to control the future is to control the past.

This slogan could serve as the rallying cry of the Christian right in its interpretation of the religious views of America's Founding Fathers.

To promote their attack on the separation of church and state, secular government, and liberal values, the religious right vigorously espouses the idea that Benjamin Franklin, George Washington, John Adams, James Madison, and even Thomas Jefferson were evangelical Christians much like themselves.

The religious right also contends that the United States is founded on biblical values. This strategy bolsters the promotion of school vouchers, the teaching of scientific creationism alongside of evolution, and charitable choice, which places government funds directly into church coffers, by contending that such programs reflect the true intention of Americas founders. These claims are false. While the Founding Fathers believed in God and were in some sense Christian, the God they affirmed and the Christianity they professed bore no significant relationship to the beliefs of today's conservative crusaders. Theirs was a Christianity liberalized by the rationalism of the European Enlightenment and deeply skeptical of clerical authority.

Rather than worship the God of the Bible, many of the founders were attracted to deism. Deism, which flourished in America in the late 18th and early 19th centuries, is a religious view which holds that once God created the universe he let it unfold according to natural laws, without interference and uninterrupted by miracles.

Hence, Jefferson in the Declaration of Independence refers to "the Laws of Nature and Nature's God." Washington characteristically referred to God with impersonal designations such as "The Grand Architect of the Universe" and "Higher Cause." In his voluminous correspondence, there isn't a single reference to Jesus Christ, an odd omission if he had been an enthusiastic Christian.

Rather than basing the fledgling nation on biblical principles, the founders looked to near precursors such as John Locke and Isaac Newton, and ancient pagan philosophers such as Cicero and Seneca, with whom they were more familiar.

For our Founding Fathers, nature's laws, aided by reason, served as the source for individual rights and democratic government. Adams reinforced this basic fact when he wrote: "The United States of America is the first example of governments erected on the simple principles of nature."

The explicitly non-religious character of American government is dramatically illustrated by omission: The United States Constitution makes not a single reference to God, and its sole reference to religion, in Article 6, declares that no religious test shall ever be required as a qualification to hold public office.

"The no religious test" clause of Article 6 aroused a firestorm of protest at the time and was hotly debated, underscoring the deliberate intention of its framers. The Constitution is an exclusively secular document dedicated to protecting the rights of citizens, peacefully mediating disputes among them, and allowing for the pursuit of happiness.

The secular character of the Constitution reveals how the Founding Fathers understood the relationship of religion to the state. While they certainly believed that a democratic society could be sustained only by a moral citizenry, and many affirmed that religion was an important source of morality, they emphatically denied that it is government's function to either promote religion or ensure the moral character of the American public.

In their view, leaning on the thought of Locke, both religion and morals are exclusively private matters. It is not the role of government to be a moral teacher, a crucial fact deliberately forgotten by those conservatives who wish to enhance religion's power with government support in an effort to redress what they see as a deteriorating moral condition in American life.

If America is suffering a moral crisis (a point on which many would disagree), the founders would have expected religious leadership to look to itself, and not to government, for assistance.

The private character of religion impelled the founders to create the doctrine of the separation of church and state. They were close enough in time to the great European wars of religion to know that when the absolute truths of religion are merged with the political power of the state, the result, too often, has been a toxic and explosive brew. One needs only to look at the resurgent warfare and bloodletting carried along religious lines in places such as the Balkans, India, and the Middle East to reinforce a salutary lesson.

The creation of secular government and the separation of church and state is not an antireligious arrangement. It exists not only to protect government from the forces of religion, but also to leave religion uncorrupted by the petty and unholy preoccupations of the state.

Secular government is not an enemy of religion, but its most enduring and steadfast ally. In this regard, the founders realized what so many Americans seem to have forgotten: Religion that seeks and requires support by the state is, in a spiritual sense, deeply impoverished religion.

The founders' solution to the church-state problem was a true stroke of genius deeded to future generations of Americans. It has kept the United States relatively free of religious violence that tragically has consumed other societies around the globe, both historically and now. At the same time, it has ensured that religion flourishes, free of government entanglement, as it does nowhere else in the Western world.

It has taken centuries for us to put the tiger into the cage. We let it loose at our greatest peril.
— *Joseph Chuman*

Dr. Joseph Chuman is leader of the Ethical Culture Society of Bergen County in Teaneck, New Jersey. He teaches at Columbia University. This essay is reprinted by permission.

A Sad Day for Ohio

The Akron Beacon Journal recently informed its readers, "Literally in the dark of night, the Ohio legislature this month slipped language into a state budget bill to increase funding for Cleveland's private schools by more than 44% in the next two years.

"At the same time, public schools watched as lawmakers whittled their funding expectations by hundreds of millions of dollars.

"The $10.5 million in new state aid going to the Cleveland voucher program will cut operating losses at the Cleveland Diocese of the Roman Catholic Church. It also for the first time will give high school students an opportunity to receive taxpayer-funded vouchers to attend a private school."

Here is "parochiaid politics" at its worst. No debate. Dictation by church authorities to compliant public officials. The voucher aid has moved from $2,250 per child to $2,700 per child. The law also permits schools to collect the full difference between the voucher amount and tuition from parents whose income exceeds $36,800. Today one-third of voucher recipients come from those middle class families, though the voucher program was billed as a help for the disadvantaged.

There was no public debate on the issue. A legislative aide for the Republican chairman of the Ohio Senate Education Committee told *Education Week* that the provision raising the amount was "not controversial."

The Ohio mess points up the hard-nosed political facts of the voucher issue. Sectarian special interests will always up the ante, even at the expense of underfunded public schools. Legislators seem to accommodate their appeal with no fear of loss of public support. Long-range educational needs of the truly disadvantaged are ignored.

Ohio is a one-party state, with a Republican Governor, Bob Taft, who approved this raid on the public treasury, and a Republican legislature.

Where is the outrage? Where is the shame?

— Al Menendez

Are Religious Liberty Rankings Tainted?

For the second straight year the U.S. State Department has refused to designate U.S. Middle East ally Saudi Arabia as a "country of particular concern" for its treatment of religious minorities. An "Annual Report on International Religious Freedom" has been required by an official U.S. commission since the passage in 1998 by Congress of the International Religious Freedom Act. This annual report, based mostly on reports from U.S. embassy staffs, is submitted to the Committee on Foreign Relations (U.S. Senate) and the Committee on International Relations (U.S. House of Representatives). It is supposed to result in sanctions or pressures on countries which are harassing their citizens in religious matters.

This year's annual report lists the usual suspects: China, Iran, Iraq, Burma, North Korea and Sudan. These six nations have the worst records of discrimination against either religious minorities or against all religions. In some respects, the list is perplexing. While Iran is clearly a repressive "Islamic Republic," it does provide seats in its parliament for Christians and Zoroastrians.

Iraq has a vigorous and ancient Christian community, the Chaldean Catholic Church, whose liturgy is celebrated in Aramaic, the very language spoken by Jesus. Are these two countries really among the worst?

Then comes the real surprise. Saudi Arabia, which ruthlessly suppresses any religious expression other than Wahabbi Islam, has been left off the list for several years. It is arguably the worst nation on earth in regard to religious oppression. All non-Muslim worship is forbidden, even in private residences and even among the thousands of foreign workers who help the kingdom's economy. As recently as March 15, the country's defense minister, Prince Sultan, said in Riyadh, the capital, that no places of non-Muslim worship would ever be allowed in the nation which is home to the holiest shrines of Islam, Mecca and Medina. Prince Sultan said, "Those who want to establish churches are fanatics. There are no churches — not in the past, the present or future. Whoever said that [referring to complaints from abroad] must shut up and be ashamed."

A U.S. State Department spokesperson admitted that Saudi Arabia "came close" to being added to this year's list but said the Bush administration has decided to work with Saudi officials behind the scenes to improve the level of religious freedom. Critics say the decision is hypocritical and is related only to the nation's oil fields and to its decision to assist U.S. war efforts in the region.

The *Washington Post* commented acidly, "But leaving Saudi Arabia off the list is a particular affront to fact and logic. In the desert kingdom, as the human rights report details, no religion other than Islam may be practiced in public; churches and synagogues are illegal. Non-Muslim worshipers, in fact, can be lashed, and proselytizing for any non-Muslim faith is illegal. Muslims who convert to other religions can be executed. And even those who advance Muslim teachings not sanctioned by the government are imprisoned. Shiite Muslims are discriminated against, and their clerics have been detained for long periods; their testimony can be excluded in court. People are arrested, even put to death, for practicing 'magic.' What does it mean to have a list of egregious violators of religious liberty and not include Saudi Arabia?

"State Department spokesman Richard Boucher acknowledged that Saudi Arabia 'came very close to the threshold.' But he said the government's experts concluded unanimously that it was better to hold off and work with the monarchy to improve matters. One wonders whether Saudi Arabia and Uzbekistan would have been granted such a reprieve had they not been important American allies.

"To the extent the government contrives ways to keep American allies off its list, the designation process is a political joke. The law permits the president to waive the sanctions that being on the list normally triggers if America's national interests so require. But whether a country belongs on the list at all should be an empirical, not a political, question. The human rights report has become valuable over the years as it has become less political; it now describes honestly the human rights conditions in countries around the world — whatever their relations with the United States may be. The same honesty should determine designations of gross violators of religious liberty. It may be necessary to deal with evil governments. It is never necessary to pretend they are not evil."

Once again, the Bush administration shows that its concern for religion is tainted by politics.

A National Day of Prayer?

By every measure, Americans are among the most religious people on earth. About 90% say they pray daily, 95% believe in some kind of Supreme Being, almost two-thirds are members of a local religious congregation and about 40% say they attend services every week. More religious communities have found a place of welcome in the United States than in any other country in history.

Why then do we need the government to tell us to pray on the first Thursday in May, as required by an act passed by Congress and signed by President Truman in 1952? While participation is voluntary, such acts of government become institutionalized.

In this land of remarkable religious diversity and vitality such mandates by officialdom are unnecessary and, frankly, disturbing. It is sometimes perplexing how this could pass constitutional muster, when it clearly is "a law respecting an establishment of religion" prohibited by the First Amendment of the Bill of Rights.

Another reason why thoughtful Americans of every religious persuasion (including those who do not choose to participate in any organized religion) should be wary of this National Day of Prayer is that it has become politicized and has been captured by a vocal and powerful segment within America's faith communities. At the White House East Room ceremony on May 2, 2002, Shirley Dobson, "the chairwoman" of the National Day of Prayer Task Force, told the invited guests, "We are grateful to have a president who honors God and recognizes the need for prayer." As President Bush looked on, she added, "May the Lord put a shield of protection around you, your family, and the nation."

Adding his voice to the increasingly partisan ceremony, U.S. Senate chaplain Lloyd John Ogilvie said, "We pray for nothing less than a spiritual awakening in America and an unprecedented unity in Congress." While this was supposed to represent humor of a sort, and most of the 200 guests laughed, it may come across as decidedly unfunny to Americans who are not Republican conservatives or evangelical Protestants — the groups which formed the vast majority of the attendees at the 51ˢᵗ National Day of Prayer event at the White House.

Both the President and the First Lady added to the evangelical tone. Laura Bush praised her husband as a man "strong enough to bear the burdens and humble enough to ask God for help," while the President claimed that "a great people must spend time on bended knee in humility, reaching for wisdom in the presence of the Almighty."

This domination of a national event by the Religious Right is a clear violation of the spirit of tolerance and inclusion so often invoked by this President but so often ignored by him. It speaks volumes about exclusion and intolerance. And there is no reason to think that future events will be any less partisan and sectarian.

Congress should rethink whether such a requirement is in keeping with our highest principles and our constitutional framework. And religious people should consider: When prayer becomes political, is it really prayer?

Congress is not doing a very good job dealing with the things voters have asked it to do in taxation policy, Medicare and Social Security protection, balancing the budget, or questions relating to national security, international affairs, the global economy and the environment. Why, then, should it engage in religious activities, where it has no competence and no constitutional place? The same could be asked of the White House.

The American people are quite capable of deciding when and how to pray without government encouragement.

Roe v. Wade at 30

January 22 marked the thirtieth anniversary of *Roe* v. *Wade,* the Supreme Court's breakthrough 1973 ruling that acknowledged and recognized (not "created," as the Religious Right would have it) every woman's constitutional right to decide for herself whether or not to continue a problem pregnancy. *Roe* is comparable in importance to the Declaration of Independence, the Bill of Rights, and the Emancipation Proclamation.

While Americans hold an enormous variety of opinions on the morality or propriety of abortions for particular reasons, stages of pregnancy, or circumstances, a majority continues to agree that it is the individual woman and not government that should do the deciding.

The primary argument against the right to choose has it that "personhood" begins at "conception," that fertilized eggs, embryos, and fetuses are "persons" or "unborn persons." This is a view with very little historical precedent, essentially a Vatican invention in the latter part of the nineteenth century. It is a view that has little religious backing, as the Jewish and Christian scriptures do not condemn abortion and, indeed, the Hebrew word for person is "nefesh," which means one who breathes, i.e., is born.

Nor does the notion of early fetal personhood have scientific backing. In 1989 Americans for Religious Liberty arranged for an *amicus curiae* brief to be submitted to the Supreme Court in *Webster v. Reproductive Health Services* in which twelve Nobel laureates and over 150 other scientists pointed out that neuroscience shows that the brain functions associated with personhood are not possible until rather late in gestation, sometime after 28 weeks. (Over 90% of abortions are performed during the first trimester and over 99% by twenty weeks.) Interestingly, the great 13th century Christian theologian Thomas Aquinas did not subscribe to the Vatican's later "personhood at conception" view.

The real reason behind the anti-choice crusade is an interest in the maintenance of male dominance and the enhancement of religious hierarchical authority. It is no coincidence that the religious bodies that are the most anti-choice are those that refuse to ordain women and find various ways to keep women in subordinate positions.

Where do matters stand today, thirty years after *Roe* v. *Wade*? Thanks to conservative appointments, the Supreme Court has allowed choice to be eroded somewhat, while conservatives in Congress and many state legislatures have passed measures to increase reproductive health care costs and reduce access to services, particularly for poor and young women.

But the greatest threats to choice, to reproductive health care, and to freedom of conscience are the accession to power of George W. Bush and the extraordinarily strong influence of the Religious Right now over both houses of Congress.

On his first day in office in 2001 President Bush reinstated the Reagan/Bush I global gag rule on international family planning aid. In his first budget Bush removed contraceptive coverage for federal employees. He has fanatically promoted "abstinence only" education. (Frances Kissling of Catholics for a Free Choice makes the point that if abstinence only education does not work well in Catholic seminaries, why would it work anywhere else?)

Bush administration operatives have opposed condoms for HIV/ AIDS prevention and in 2002 Bush withheld $34 million in congressionally approved funds from the UN Population Fund even after his own mission to China had approved the funding.

In 2002 Bush withdrew U.S. support for the UN Convention on the Elimination of All Forms of Discrimination Against Woman and is pulling the U.S. back from support for the reproductive health care services pledged by the U.S. and 160 other countries at the 1994 UN Population Conference in Cairo. In October Bush removed medically accurate information from the HHS website. He froze $3 million in funding for the World Health Organization for reproductive health research and stopped $200 million in funding for programs to support women and deal with HIV/AIDS in Afghanistan.

In 2001 Bush appointed anti-choice zealot John Ashcroft to be Attorney General and an anti-choice governor Tommy Thompson to be HHS Secretary. He closed the White House Office for Women's Initiatives and Outreach. He has sought to appoint anti-choicers to federal appellate judgeships.

The Republican-controlled House of Representatives has passed bills to outlaw certain abortion procedures and to restrict stem cell research. In an effort to pave the way for eventual reversal of *Roe* v. *Wade*, the Bush administration is pushing for federal aid for fetal health rather than what is really needed, beefed-up programs for maternal health.

Meanwhile, on December 4, the U.S. Supreme Court heard arguments in *NOW v. Scheidler,* a suit originally filed in 1986 charging that the Pro-Life Action League, Operation Rescue, and other groups violated the 1970 Racketeer Influenced and Corruption Organization (RICO) law in their efforts to shut down clinics providing abortion services.

In short, what we have now, though far too many Americans seem neither to see nor care about it, is a national government increasingly under the influence and serving the ideological agenda of the zealous, well-organized Religious Right, which, clearly, represents only a minority of Christian and Jewish citizens.

Thoughtful Americans across the religious and political spectra will need to recognize the threat of the Talibanization of this country and take action to restore secular (i.e., religiously neutral) democracy.

— Edd Doerr

Scalia's Arrant Nonsense

Supreme Court Justice Antonin Scalia dragged himself out in frigid weather to deliver a mess of intellectual pottage to a tiny, freezing audience in Fredericksburg, Virginia, on January 12. The event was a commemoration of a 1777 meeting of Thomas Jefferson, George Mason, and other patriots in a tavern to draft what became the Virginia Statute for Religious Freedom. The Virginia document, passed in 1786, led to the First Amendment's guarantee of religious freedom. It is certainly an event worth celebrating, even though the Virginia remembrance was sponsored by the Knights of Columbus and the Knights Templar, two groups with nothing in common. What Scalia said on this occasion was disconcerting and oddly inappropriate. He claimed that "God had been excluded from the public forum and from political life." This is poor history. Both the Congress which drafted the First Amendment and the ratification debates surrounding the Constitution and the Bill of Rights rejected the multiple establishment argument advanced by Patrick Henry and others in favor of the clear separation doctrine advocated by Thomas Jefferson and James Madison. Scholars also agree that the adoption of Article Six and its ban on religious tests reflected a desire to separate religious and political institutions and to limit improper ecclesiastical influences on civil policy.

Numerous Supreme Court decisions have refuted the Scalia thesis. In *Abington* v. *Schempp* (1963) the Court held, "The state must be steadfastly neutral in all matters of faith, and neither favor nor inhibit religion." In *Wallace* v. *Jaffree* (1985), the Court ruled, "The government must pursue a course of complete neutrality toward religion."

And in *Lee* v. *Weisman* (1992) Justice David Souter wrote, in his concurring opinion, "The state may not favor or endorse either religion generally over non-religion or one religion over others. This principle against favoritism and endorsement has become the foundation of Establishment Clause jurisprudence ensuring that religious belief is irrelevant to every citizen's standing in the political community."

Justice Scalia, whose disastrous opinion in *Employment Division* v. *Smith* case in 1990 set back the cause of religious liberty, is hardly in a position to lament a weakening of religious free exercise. Scalia ridiculed in *Smith* religious liberty as a "luxury we may not be able to afford." Scalia's record on the Court indicates a repeated disinterest in and indifference to the claims of religious minorities, a preference for religious majorities, and a decided preference for the state against the individual in religious matters.

Jefferson's Wall of Separation at 200

On January 1, 1802, President Thomas Jefferson penned a letter destined to be ranked with the Declaration of Independence (which of course Jefferson also wrote), James Madison's 1785 Memorial and Remonstrance Against Religious Assessments, the Constitution, the Bill of Rights, and Washington's 1790 letter to the Touro Synagogue in Newport, Rhode Island. Addressed to the Danbury, Connecticut, Baptist Association, Jefferson's letter stated, in part:

> Believing with you that religion is a matter which lies solely between man and his God, that he owes account to none other for his faith or his worship, that the legislative powers of government reach actions only, and not opinions, I contemplate with sovereign reverence that act of the whole American people [referring to the First Amendment] which declared that their legislature should "make no law respecting an establishment of religion, or prohibiting the free exercise thereof," thus building a wall of separation between Church and State.

The importance of this letter can only be grasped in its historical context, in its influence on the US. Supreme Court's rulings from then until the bicentennial we celebrate now, and on what the present Supreme Court will make of it between now and Independence Day, 2002.

Jefferson's "wall of separation" metaphor was employed by the Supreme Court in its first religious liberty case, *Reynolds v. United States,* in 1879. Citing the quotation above, the Court held that, "coming as this does from an acknowledged leader of the advocates of the measure, it maybe accepted almost as an authoritative declaration of the scope and effect of the amendment thus secured."

The next time the Supreme Court utilized the "wall" metaphor was in the landmark 1947 case, *Everson v. Board of Education.* The Court stated, in Justice Hugo Black's ringing words, that,

> The "establishment of religion" clause of the First amendment means at least this: Neither a state nor the Federal Government can set up a church. Neither can pass laws which aid one religion, aid all religions, or prefer one religion over another. Neither can force nor influence a person to go to or remain away from church against his will or force him to profess a belief or disbelief in any religion. No person can be punished for entertaining or professing religious beliefs or disbeliefs, for church attendance or non-attendance. No tax in any amount, large or small, can be levied to support any religious activities or institutions, whatever they may be called, or whatever form they may adopt to teach or practice religion. Neither a state nor the Federal Government can, openly or secretly, participate in the affairs of any religious organizations or groups and vice versa. In the words of Jefferson, the clause against establishment of religion by law was intended to erect "a wall of separation between church and state" ... That wall must be kept high and impregnable.

Although the *Everson* passage, approved by every member of the 1947 Court, was cited favorably in three subsequent rulings and its spirit informed many more, the Supreme Court, thanks to several conservative appointments, has been drifting slowly away from the position of the *Everson* justices and such subsequent "separationists" as the late, highly regarded Justices William J. Brennan, Thurgood Marshall, and Harry Blackmun, toward the "accommodationist" stance of Justices William Rehnquist, Antonin Scalia, and Clarence Thomas, who have made it quite clear that they do not agree with Jefferson, the *Everson* court, and the court majorities until recently. Before the end of the Court's present term this coming July we will find out whether the serving justices will uphold Jefferson's wall or consign it to the rubbish heap. The crucial test will be the case involving a thus far successful challenge to the Ohio law that provides subsidies through vouchers to sectarian schools in Cleveland, a case scheduled for hearing within weeks.

It cannot be denied that if Jefferson's wall is allowed to crumble, religious freedom in America will be in serious trouble. The door will be open for government to compel taxpayers to support sectarian schools and other institutions that commonly practice forms of discrimination and indoctrination the vast majority of Americans would find intolerable, for sectarian religion to invade public education, and for women to be chained to medieval sectarian medical codes.

To understand our present predicament we must return to Jefferson's 1802 letter to the Danbury Baptists, which latter day "accommodationists," the heirs of the Virginia governor, Patrick Henry, defeated by Jefferson and Madison in 1785-86, will do anything to discredit. Typical of the accommodationist attacks is the one made twenty years ago at a Senate hearing on then President Reagan's school prayer amendment by televangelist Pat Robertson, the same Pat Robertson who joined with Jerry Falwell shortly after the terrorist attacks on September 11 in suggesting that God allowed the attacks to take place to punish Americans for their "liberal sins." Robertson misrepresented the Jefferson letter and said that the "wall" metaphor "only appeared in the constitution of the Communist Soviet Union." (Details maybe found in Robert S. Alley's 1996 book, *Public Education and the Public Good,* published by Americans for Religious Liberty.)

In reality Jefferson's letter was a response to a letter from the Danbury Baptists praising him and voicing a complaint against Connecticut's establishment of the Congregational Church, an arrangement finally ended in 1818. Jefferson received the letter on December 30 and replied two days later. Although Chief Justice Rehnquist brushed Jefferson's letter off in a 1985 ruling as merely "a short note of courtesy," our third President took it a great deal more seriously.

Jefferson sent the Baptists' letter along with a draft of his reply to Attorney General Levi Lincoln with this request:

> The Baptist address, now enclosed, admits of a condemnation of the alliance between Church and State, under the authority of the Constitution. It furnishes an occasion, too, which I have long wished to find, of saying why I do not proclaim fastings and thanksgivings, as my predecessor did. The address, to be sure, does not point at this, and its introduction is awkward. But I foresee no opportunity of doing it more pertinently. I know it will give great offense to the New England clergy, but the advocate of religious freedom is to expect neither peace nor forgiveness from them. Will you be so good as to examine the answer and suggest any alterations which might prevent an ill effect, or promote a good one, among the people?

At Lincoln's suggestion, Jefferson omitted his comments about proclamations so as not to "give uneasiness to some of our republican friends in the eastern states where the proclamation of thanksgivings etc. by their Executive is an antient (sic) habit and is respected." Another attack by accommodationists on Jefferson's "wall" is their insistence that the First Amendment's establishment clause was intended not to erect a wall but to permit nonpreferential aid to all religions. That, of course, was the Patrick Henry position which Madison and Jefferson defeated in the Virginia legislature the year before the Constitutional Convention was held in Philadelphia. The nonpreferentialist, accommodationist position was considered by the First Congress in 1789 and rejected in favor of the present language of the First Amendment.

Nor was the establishment clause drafted simply to block a single religious "establishment," as some accommodationists claim. By 1789 the colonial, European-style single establishments were virtually a dead letter, having given way to church-state separation, as in Virginia, or some sort of broad multiple establishment.

No establishment of religion means what Jefferson and Madison intended, what Washington lauded in his 1790 letter to the Touro Synagogue, what the Supreme Court held in 1947 and for decades afterward, and what far-sighted religious leaders, politicians, and ordinary people have always believed. Separation of church and state, the American experience has proven, is best for religion, best for democratic government, best for the liberties of the people.

The alternative is some greater or lesser form of Talibanization, the goofy agendas of Falwell and Robertson, or the dismal disastrous dystopia sought by the sectarian special interests seeking school vouchers, tax support for faith-based initiatives, organized school prayer, and the imposition on women of narrow theologies of embryonic personhood.

If history teaches anything, it is that separation of religion and government is essential to religious liberty, freedom of conscience, and democratic values.

—Edd Doerr

September 11, 2001

Images of devastation, death, and horror from the events of September 11 are burned into the psyches of people across the land and the world, joining the pictures of Pearl Harbor, the London blitz, Nazi death camps, Hiroshima, and the killing fields of Cambodia. We grieve with everyone else and support efforts by the United States and other governments to bring the remaining conspirators to justice, perhaps through tribunals similar to those at Nuremberg after World War II.

We support measures designed to reduce the risk of future terrorist attacks, but believe that such measures should not erode the liberties at the core of the American way of life.

We applaud President Bush's appearance at the Islamic Center in Washington and his condemnation of prejudicial actions aimed at Americans of Arab ancestry or Muslim faith. We agree that Arabs and Muslims in general must not be ill-treated or blamed for the actions of a few fanatics. We disagree, however, with Mr. Bush's use of the word "crusade" to refer to possible responses to the terrorist attacks. That term, best confined to the eleventh to fourteenth century military expeditions by European Christians to oust Muslims from control of Palestine, can only offend Muslims everywhere.

Speaking of religion, it should be noted, as commentators infrequently did, that the September terrorists all appear to have been fundamentalist fanatics. Why would reasonably bright men plan and train for a year or more for a suicide mission if they did not believe that their self-martyrdom would send them straight to paradise?

Which brings us to our domestic Taliban, televangelists Jerry Falwell and Pat Robertson. On the latter's "700 Club" gabfest on September 13 the Lynchburg loudmouth pontificated that the ACLU, People for the American Way, feminists, gays and lesbians, and supporters of abortion rights and church-state separation are partially responsible for the terror attacks on the World Trade Center and the Pentagon and the attack on the White House or Capitol foiled by the heroic passengers on the flight that crashed in Pennsylvania.

"I point the finger in their face and say, 'You helped this happen'," Falwell spewed. "God Almighty," Robertson chimed in, "is lifting his protection from us," echoing the former Moral Majority honcho's comment about God "lift[ing] the curtain and allow[ing] the enemies of America to give us probably what we deserve."

Falwell and Robertson have tried to back away from their extremist rhetoric, but they cannot erase their implication that God and the terrorists might be collaborating. They have been spouting nonsense for too many years for their apologies to be taken very seriously

Our nation needs to protect itself from both foreign terrorists and our would-be domestic Taliban.

What's Scientific About Creation Science?

Reading the Book of Genesis and interpreting it literally, one can hardly escape the conclusion that our earth is flat. Indeed, for many centuries, Jews and Christians believed just that.

But, as we knew, that is not all. Genesis teaches that the earth is the center of the universe, that the earth was created first (followed by the sun, moon and stars), all of which revolve around the earth.

There aren't many people today who believe that the earth is flat but, incredibly, there still are some who insist that the sun and stars revolve around the earth because the Bible says so, and the Bible is the inspired word of God, scientifically and historically true in every detail. This is a triumph of faith over fact, which leads directly to so-called creation science.

Creation science is an attempt to cloak fundamentalist religion in the language of science. It matches the biblical account of creation, as set forth in Genesis. Public school systems have been pressured to revise biology curricula to enable the teaching of this account as an explanation for the origin of life. To advance this objective, bills have been introduced in recent years in at least 15 states to require public schools to teach this story of creation.

In 1925, John T. Scopes was tried for teaching Darwin's theory of evolution to high school students, in violation of Tennessee law. He was convicted. Evolution, which was regarded as heresy by fundamentalist Jews and Christians, was virtually absent from American public schools for many years. In contrast to fundamentalists, most mainstream churches and synagogues interpret at least some of the Bible as allegory, and hence are open to evolution as an explanation for the origin of the species.

Only in the past 50 years has evolution been expounded in biology textbooks. In 1968, in the case of *Epperson v. Arkansas,* the US. Supreme Court ruled unanimously that a statute that, for religious reasons, made it unlawful to teach evolution in public schools violated the First Amendment.

The two pivotal points of conflict between creationists and evolutionists concern the beginning of mankind and the age of the earth.

To the creationists, any theory that man evolved from lower forms of life is anathema because of the biblical account of God's special creation of Adam and Eve. They believe that all basic types of plants and animals were made by direct acts of God during the week of creation, and revealed in Genesis. And while evolutionists cite overwhelming scientific evidence that the earth is several billion years old, creationists place the earth's age at about 10,000 years.

In 1980, Arkansas passed another law, this time requiring equal time for creation science in public school science classes whenever evolution is taught. This law was challenged in the case of *McLean v. Arkansas.* It was overturned as unconstitutional in federal district court as an attempt to teach religion in public school.

At one point during the trial, Judge William Overton, a Methodist, asked, "What kind of scientific theory is this that is not subject to revision — ever?" His decision against the law was never appealed. But in 1987 *Edwards v. Aguillard,* a challenge to a similar Louisiana law reached the Supreme Court. The court ruled that laws requiring equal teaching of creation science, when evolution is taught in public school science classes, are unconstitutional since creation science is a religious belief and not a scientific theory (Imagine a state law requiring equal treatment of astrology whenever astronomy is taught.)

Like any scientific theory of course, evolution can and should be subjected to critical scrutiny. Evidence either for or against it can be adduced, examined and either accepted or rejected. Creation science, on the other hand, is not really a theory at all. Rather, it is an article of faith.

While those who now accept evolution are free to change their minds if new evidence is found, the creationists enjoy no such freedom. For them to change their minds would be to reject the word of God, which is unthinkable.

Creation science is a throwback to the Dark Ages, when religious zealots hounded men of science, like Copernicus and Galileo, when the scientists' observations failed to conform to the dogma of that time. It does not belong in public school science classes.

— *Samuel Rabinove*

Rabinove is the former legal director of the American Jewish Committee. This article originally appeared in the White Plains Reporter Dispatch.

Humanae Vitae at 30

Thirty years have passed since Pope Paul VI, ignoring the recommendations of his own advisory commission, issued his notorious encyclical *Humanae Vitae* condemning contraception and abortion. What has happened between 1968 and 1998?

Contraception is readily available in developed countries and is gradually becoming more available in the developing world. Abortion is now legal and generally available in most First

World countries, generally illegal and risky in much of the rest of the world.

World population has grown by more than 50% since *Humanae Vitae* and since the mysterious suppression of the National Security Study Memorandum 200 report ordered by President Nixon and approved by President Ford. Birth rates have shrunk to near replacement levels in the First World but have only slowed somewhat in the Third World, where illegal, unsafe abortions are common, large numbers of children die each year from malnutrition and disease, and women's lives are seriously endangered by lack of reproductive health technology. Meanwhile, the lives and health of hundreds of millions are threatened by resource depletion and environmental degradation.

While most Catholics in the U.S. and elsewhere disagree with the Vatican ban on contraception and abortion, that church's hierarchy somehow retains the political clout to block or retard progress in making reproductive health care and information universally available. Abortion is still illegal in Brazil, the world's largest Catholic country, which has an abortion rate double that of the U.S. While Mexico, beset by poverty and corruption, has begun debating its law against abortion, the Catholic bishops have gone all out to oppose any liberalization of the law, even though an estimated 1,500 women there die each year from unsafe, illegal abortions; the Vatican's envoy to Mexico has threatened excommunication for anyone obtaining or helping in an abortion.

Catholic bishops in the U.S. have continued to exert pressure wherever possible to impede access to reproductive health services, aided and abetted by misogynist fundamentalist militants.

Humanae Vitae greatly accelerated the secularization of ordinary Catholics in the U.S. and elsewhere, as measured by the sharp decline over the past 30 years of church attendance, donations, church school enrollment, religious vocations, support for clerical celibacy and the all-male priesthood, and other indices of traditional orthodoxy. While the U.S. bishops are often progressive on economic issues, their campaigns against reproductive rights and for tax support for nonpublic schools are regressive and contrary to the public interest. In contrast, many Catholic lawmakers in Washington and state capitals are strong supporters of women's rights, public education, and church-state separation.

There was a time when society appeared to be divided by vertical denominational lines. Now, however, the divisions are more generally horizontal, with moderates and progressives of all faiths ranked against those immersed in various militant fundamentalisms.

Justice William J. Brennan, Jr.

On July 24 death claimed the most distinguished defender of civil liberties and religious freedom ever to serve on the U.S. Supreme Court, Associate Justice William J. Brennan, Jr. For 34 years, in 1,360 opinions over his name, Brennan contributed more than any other justice to the defense of individual liberty and the Madisonian-Jeffersonian wall of separation between church and state.

Among his significant rulings was *Aguilar v. Felton* in 1985, which was overturned in June of 1997 in *Agostini* (see separate report in this issue).

Ever the firm defender of church-state separation, Brennan wrote majority, concurring, or dissenting opinions in cases involving government aid to church schools and colleges, church taxation, religious devotions in public schools, rights of Sabbatarians, clergy in political office, religion in the military, state regulation of church soliciting, Sunday closing laws, and legislative chaplains.

In 1987 Brennan wrote the majority opinion in *Edwards v. Aguillard,* which struck down a Louisiana law aimed at giving "creation science" equal time in public school science classes.

Brennan strongly supported equal rights for women and reproductive freedom. His 1972 opinion in *Eisenstadt v. Baird* paved the way for the 1973 ruling in *Roe v. Wade,* which recognized a woman's fundamental right to choose whether or not to continue a problem pregnancy. In *Eisenstadt* he wrote: "If this right to privacy means anything, it is the right of the individual, married or single, to be free from unwanted governmental intrusions into matters so fundamentally affecting a person as whether to bear or beget a child." Although Justice Harry Blackmun authored the majority opinion in *Roe v. Wade,* Brennan did more than anyone else to shape it.

Not only was Brennan a driving intellectual force on the Court, he also had the ability to bring his colleagues to consensus.

In the pantheon of American freedom and democracy, we honor the 18th century's James Madison as the chief architect of the Bill of Rights. In the 19th century we had Lincoln's revitalization of the ideas of the Declaration of Independence in his Gettysburg Address and in the creation of the Fourteenth Amendment by two forgotten members of Congress, Bingham of Ohio and Howard of Michigan. In the 20th century we have had William Brennan, whose remarkable third of a century on the Supreme Court strengthened the Bill of Rights, expanded its coverage and protections, and taught us how the judiciary should function.

And, just as Martin Luther King, Jr., taught that the content of one's character is more important than the color of one's skin, so William J. Brennan, Jr., a devout Catholic, reminded us that one's actions and values are more important than one's formal religious affiliation.

The U.S. Census and Religion

The Heritage Foundation's recommendations that Congress "mandate a census question on religious practice" and that the President "direct the Bureau of the Census to record levels of religious practice in the census for the year 2000" are not only absurd, but indicate a substantial misunderstanding of the constitutionally limited role of government in the religious life of the people of this nation.

One of the primary purposes of the First Amendment was to limit governmental involvement in religious activity, something that the founding fathers found abhorrent. Why should Congress "know the level and intensity of religious practice in America?" as *The Heritage Report* urged. Congress is not permitted to discriminate for or against individuals on the basis of their religious convictions or practices, let alone the degree to which individuals may chose to practice their religions. The recommendations raise serious constitutional problems. Warning signals should immediately be activated when proposals like these are advocated. What will Congress do with this kind of information? Will the taxes of religiously observant people be lowered, to reward them for their fealty? Will sanctions be placed on the nonreligious or the mildly religious? Will contributions to religious charities be treated differently in the tax code from other kinds of charities? One can only ponder the mischievous ways in which such information could be misused.

And what happens if individuals refuse to answer census questions about religion? Will they be fined or imprisoned? Will the data thus attained be skewed by nonparticipation and noncompliance?

This proposal is an insidious one. It may please religious sociologists and demographers who might have easier access to a mass of new religious data, but it will not please those who place constitutional principles at the forefront of American life.

Furthermore, there are already a host of social science and public opinion organizations which routinely gather data on the religious beliefs and practices of the American people *without government involvement or encouragement.* There is the Princeton Religion Research Center (PRRC), a branch of the Gallup Organization, in Princeton, New Jersey, which exists for the sole purpose of gathering, analyzing and disseminating data on U.S. religious practice. The National Opinion Research Center (NORC) at the University of Chicago has been gathering religious data as part of the General Social Surveys for two decades. The Barna Research Group in California annually surveys religious opinion, belief, activity and practice. So do numerous other university research centers. The National Survey of Religious Identification (NSRI) conducted in 1990 by the Graduate School of the City University of New York, produced a wealth of data on American religion. A replication is planned for the year 2000. The Glenmary Research Center in Atlanta, in conjunction with the National Council of Churches, has published comprehensive and detailed volumes on American religious group membership since 1971. Do we really need any more? Americans may rightly claim to be over polled and over researched. But these nongovernmental agencies rely on voluntary participation. An official U.S. Census question, or questions, about religion would presumably be compulsory in nature.

Previous government censuses of religion (1890,1906,1916, 1926, and 1936) provided some useful information, but social scientists have long been divided as to their overall merit and value. Even they were based solely on data provided by the religious groups themselves, not by individual citizens.

In a nation that is arguably more sensitive to religious liberty and church-state separation today than six or seven decades ago, a religious census question would undoubtedly provoke strong opposition and massive resistance. This is not an idea whose time has come; it is an idea whose time has long passed.

To Die in Pensacola

The killings of Dr. John Britton and James Barrett, and the wounding of June Barrett, in Pensacola, Florida, on July 29 were not mere murders. They were political assassinations, impersonal assassinations committed by a militant extremist fanatic.

Not only were the killings horrible crimes against two innocent victims, they were also attacks aimed at intimidating the millions of women who are led by their consciences and circumstances to exercise their fundamental right to choose to terminate problem pregnancies, and at intimidating the health professionals who must regularly brave threats from extremists to serve the medical and counseling needs of these women.

Of course the Pensacola killings, and the firebombing of a Virginia clinic only hours later, are but part of a vast wave of violence and intimidation aimed at shrinking the sphere of the rights of conscience and at imposing a narrow sectarian moral code on all women. In the last year and a half another physician was assassinated in Pensacola and still another was shot in both arms in Kansas. Since 1982 there have been 146 incidents or attempts at bombing or arson against clinics in 31 states. From 1977 to the present, according to National Abortion Federation records, there have been 178 death threats, 347 cases of unlawful entry, 568 acts of vandalism, and 35 incidents of burglary. Tens of thousands of zealots have been arrested for attempts to blockade or interfere with clinics.

Because local law enforcement has not always been effective in dealing with attacks on clinics and their personnel, Congress finally passed and President Clinton signed in May the Freedom of Access to Clinic Entrances Act (FACE), designed not to limit legitimate freedom of expression by anti-choice protesters but to guarantee freedom for women to act on their right to choose if and when to become mothers.

We join with most Americans in urging strict enforcement of the FACE law and vigorous prosecution of those who resort to violence, terror, and intimidation to weaken constitutional freedoms.

Finally, while some large anti-choice groups disavow any connection with extremist violence, it should be obvious that years-long campaigns of propaganda and rhetoric about "murdering babies" and "American holocausts" contribute to an atmosphere conducive to acts of violence. If the vast and powerful "pro-life" movement is serious about its professional goal, it would put its enormous resources into helping save the lives of hundreds of millions of children and adults in the third world who are threatened by readily preventable or curable diseases, starvation, economic dislocation, war, and environmental degradation. That is a cause we can all support.

The Bill of Rights: 200 Years and Still Counting

Bells should have been ringing all over this country on December 15, the 200th anniversary of the ratification of the Bill of Rights. For slowly but surely the United States has moved in the direction of the great vision of the nation's Founders, a society where individual freedoms are not only celebrated but are protected, guaranteed and enforced by all levels of government.

The existence of an enumerated Bill of Rights means that no government at any level can deny or substantially limit freedom of religion, speech, assembly, the press, privacy or a host of other liberties. It means that majorities, however large, can not trample on the rights of minorities. Certain basic, inherent, inalienable rights endure in the human spirit and are not subject to the whims of the electorate.

First and foremost, the Bill of Rights amendments to the Constitution protect the people from arbitrary actions of government. In an age when virtually all governments were capricious and arbitrary, this limitation represented a major leap forward in human history.

The Bill of Rights is also a profoundly moral document. Roger Rosenblatt, writing in *Life* magazine recently, observed "That jerry-built, troublesome afterthought to the Constitution did not merely guarantee a range of personal freedoms; it said in effect that Americans are free to discover their moral selves—to say and write whatever we wish, within reason, and thus to realize by the exercise of that freedom who we are and might become."

The touchstone of the Bill of Rights is the First Amendment, which limits government actions relating to religion, press, thought and assembly. Roger Rosenblatt again: "The First Amendment has always been dearest to our hearts because it allows us to see where our hearts are located. Hope is what the First Amendment is based on, the hope that citizens, left to their own rafts and rivers, will behave well toward one another. The belief in potential human virtue underlies the whole idea of the Bill of Rights."

This is why the Bill of Rights has a peculiar freshness, an urgency that belies its 18th century origins and language. It is relevant today. Indeed it remains a beacon of hope to the oppressed of all nations. All of us today must pledge our efforts to preserve and extend its protections to all Americans today and in the future.

What Religious Freedom Means

In August 1790 President George Washington wrote to the congregation of the Touro Synagogue in Newport, RI, the oldest in North America, that, "It is now no more that toleration is spoken of as if it was by the indulgence of one class of people that another enjoyed the exercise of their inherent natural rights. For happily the Government of the United States, which gives to bigotry no sanction, to persecution no assistance requires only that they who live under its protection should demean themselves as good citizens, in giving it on all occasions their effectual support."

To mark the bicentennial of the Washington letter and subsequent visit to Newport, the Touro Synagogue held a three-day celebration the weekend of August 17-19, 1990. The program included a panel discussion of current religious liberty problems, featuring actor Ed Asner, writer Robert Alley, American Jewish Committee attorney Samuel Rabinove, and ARL executive director Edd Doerr. The final ceremony at the Touro Synagogue included a reading of Washington's letter by Ed Asner and the following short address by ARL's Doerr.

Religious freedom, to many Fourth of July orators, is simply a matter of one's being free to believe as one pleases and to attend the church or synagogue of one's choice. This definition *will not do,* neither here and now, nor in any place at any time.

Religious freedom—as that concept has been forged into shape over the centuries on the anvil of practical experience by Madisons and Jeffersons, by farsighted judges and lawmakers and religious leaders, by writers and ordinary people—means at least this:

Religious freedom means the right of every individual to believe or not believe, to profess or not profess, any religious proposition or creed on the basis of his or her own experience, education, study, or reasoning, and the concomitant right to change one's beliefs.

It means the right to worship or not to worship, to be or not be a member of a religious group, to change or discontinue a religious affiliation. It means the right to express one's religious views and to attempt to persuade others of their correctness, the right to travel for religious purposes, the right to use one's home and property for religious purposes.

Religious freedom means the right to live one's life according to one's own beliefs, up to the point, of course, at which that free exercise of religion begins to interfere with the equal rights of another person. It means the right to make and follow one's own moral judgments and decisions of conscience on such matters as marriage and reproduction. It means the right to provide religious and moral instruction to one's children. It includes the right to access to information and opinion.

Religious freedom means the right to determine whether and to what extent one will contribute to the support of any or all religious institutions or programs. It means no taxation whatsoever for any religious institutions or programs, as Madison made clear 205 years ago in his Memorial and Remonstrance Against Religious Assessments, in which he declared that such "establishments of religion" inevitably produce "bigotry and persecution."

As religious freedom includes the right of persons to form or belong to religious or lifestance organizations, these associations must enjoy the freedom to order their own worship, educational, charitable, and other activities; to formulate and change their teachings and doctrines; to determine their own forms of organization and governance; to set their own standards for membership and positions of authority; to operate programs of missionary outreach; to interpret to the public their views and principles.

Religious liberty means that government may not discriminate against or in favor of any person because of his or her religious beliefs or disbeliefs, for religious association membership or nonmembership. It means that government may not impose religious tests for public office or enact policies based on principles that depend for their validity on the doctrines or ethos of particular religious bodies.

The edifice of religious freedom, though still not completed, is one of the grandest and most magnificent ever erected by humankind. Yet it rests on the not always steady shoulders of all of us, of We the People. We must never allow it to wobble, to crack, to erode, or to be destroyed. We must resolve that that shall not happen.

Bork Nomination Threatens Basic Liberties

President Reagan's nomination of Robert Bork to replace retiring Justice Lewis Powell on the U.S. Supreme Court, if confirmed by the U.S. Senate, would seriously endanger the liberties of Americans until well into the next century.

Reagan's appointment of Antonin Scalia and Sandra Day O'Connor to the Court to join Chief Justice William Rehnquist and Justice Byron White narrowed the Court's pro-civil liberties, pro-church-state separation, and pro-women's rights majority to a shaky five to four. Replacing Powell with Bork would place in jeopardy most of the Court's forty years of rulings favorable to civil liberties and personal freedom.

Bork is an admirer of Chief Justice Rehnquist, who pontificated in a 1985 school prayer dissent that, "the 'wall of separation between church and state' is a metaphor based on bad history, a metaphor which has proved useless as a guide to judging. It should be frankly and explicitly abandoned." This shows, of course, how out of touch both Bork and Rehnquist are with history and with the reasoning of the country's founders, particularly the two most important, Thomas Jefferson, author of the Declaration of Independence and the Virginia Statute for Religious Freedom, and James Madison, chief architect of the Constitution and Bill of Rights.

Bork has made it clear that he disagrees with *Roe v. Wade,* the 1973 Supreme Court decision which recognized that the Constitutional right to privacy covers a woman's right to freedom of conscience on abortion. Bork claims that there is no right to privacy in the Constitution, although the Supreme Court explained that right in 1965 in *Griswold v. Connecticut* with regard to the privacy right to practice birth control.

Bork has indicated that First Amendment freedom of expression applies only to political expression and not to other forms of speech and press, an eccentric view that is almost unique to him.

Perhaps the most telling insights into Bork's thinking are found in a speech, "Tradition and Morality in Constitutional Law," which he delivered at an American Enterprise Institute conference in 1984 in Washington. Your editor was present at the speech and remembers thinking at the conclusion of the address, "Bork is just a Jerry Falwell in striped pants."

In his AEI speech, Bork placed the power of government and the power of majorities, whether permanent or transitory, over individual liberties. Bork said, "One of the freedoms, the major freedom, of our kind of society is the freedom to choose to have a public morality. As Chesterton put it, 'What is the good of telling a community that it has every liberty except the liberty to make laws'?"

Bork does not seem to grasp that the American democracy posited in the Declaration of Independence and institutionalized by the Constitution, Bill of Rights, and Fourteenth Amendment requires that majority rule, in carefully limited spheres, must be balanced by the widest possible latitude for individual freedom. Bork could weaken individual liberties in the interest of enhancing the power of big government and big religion over individual liberties. He would erect a "moral majoritarian" prison of conformity over the ashes of the Bill of Rights.

But Bork's appointment to the Supreme Court has not yet been confirmed by the Senate, which has the power to reject the nomination or to delay confirmation until President Reagan leaves office or replaces Bork with a more moderate nominee. Until then, the Supreme Court can function quite adequately with eight justices.

All Americans who appreciate the importance of our Constitution and Bill of Rights, and who value individual liberty, freedom of conscience, and our constitutional principle of separation of church and state must join in the effort to get the Senate to reject the Bork nomination.

Sectarian Intrusion

The most overlooked church-state problem in America, and surely one of the most serious, is the intrusion of sectarian missionaries into the public schools. What is especially astonishing is the sheer magnitude of the problem coupled with the fact that it has not been challenged in the courts.

In our Fall 1983 issue we reported that an *Education Week* study had found that about 4,500 adult professional missionaries were then operating in public schools. Young Life had over 400 paid missionaries; Campus Life, the high school program of Youth for Christ, 800 missionaries; Bill Bright's Campus Crusade, 120 missionaries; Fellowship of Christian Athletes, 168 paid missionaries and 3,200 volunteer leaders and coaches, etc.

The problem worsened in 1984 when Congress passed so-called "Equal Access" legislation requiring secondary schools (seventh grade and up in most states) to allow student-originated groups to meet in public schools and permitting adult missionaries to be brought into the meetings. Moral Majority leader Jerry Falwell told the *Philadelphia Inquirer* during the congressional debate that, "We knew we couldn't win on school prayer [President Reagan's proposed school prayer constitutional amendment was defeated in the Senate in March 1984], but equal access gets us what we wanted all along." What Falwell wanted was made clear in his *Fundamentalist Journal* in September 1984 in an article describing the public schools as "a larger mission field than many countries."

The most successful single public school evangelist is probably Jerry Johnston, a 26-year-old preacher headquartered in Shawnee Mission, Kansas. Johnston claims to have spoken to two million students in about two thousand public schools in 25 states. In a promo piece for his "Life Public School Assembly" program he states: "In the public junior and senior high school age bracket there are approximately 40 million teenagers in the United States. This large group of young people represents one of the greatest virgin mission fields existent today and yet by and large, they are unreached by the Christian community" (sic!). Johnston reiterated his "virgin mission field" spiel in a long broadcast interview in October with Dallas radio evangelist Marlin Maddoux.

In the same promotion piece Johnston declares, "It is imperative that the youth minister learn the protocol of how to approach the public school administration and develop the open door policy of continued contact with secular youth at the local public junior and senior high school campus." Johnston urges "youth pastors" to use the "Equal Access" legislation to gain entry to "Christian clubs" begun, at least ostensibly, by students in public schools.

"I realized several years ago," Johnston continues, "that I could literally go into a public high school and speak to the entire student body on a neutral, secular theme that was relevant and valid, develop rapport to [sic!] the students by my presentation and later invite them to a gospel service. This is what I call pre-evangelism. We develop rapport to later present the claims of Jesus Christ. As a ministry we are now offering a highly successful, valuable tool for the youth minister that will allow him to get into the public school in health class, a social concerns class or a high school convocation, present a program, develop an identity with the students and establish himself as a counselor with regard to these social problems which establishes a bonified [sic!] relationship for future and further activity."

Johnston provided a good example of his modus operandi in Pinellas County (Tampa Bay area), Florida, in November. In apparent collaboration with Trinity Baptist Church in Clearwater, Johnston conned county school officials into allowing him to conduct half-hour assembly programs in eleven public middle and high schools. The assembly programs—for which Johnston was paid $250 each, though it is not certain whether the fees came from school or private funds—dealt with drug and alcohol abuse and teen suicide as a buildup to a persuasive invitation to an "all you can eat" free "pizza blast," to be held on Thursday, November 14, in Clearwater's Jack Russell Stadium.

About 4,000 students showed up at the stadium, largely unaware that they were going to be treated to a religious revival service for two hours before they got their free pizza on the way out. The kids were asked to fill out cards with their name, address, age, grade, school, and church affiliation. Buckets were passed for donations. The stadium rally also marked the end of a five-day revival Johnston was conducting at Trinity Baptist Church.

The St. Petersburg Times editorially blasted the whole affair. "Administrators who should have known better, and who were forewarned, allowed an evangelist to use the Pinellas County public schools this week to recruit students for a mass religious rally. It defies belief that such a thing could happen so many years after the U.S. Supreme Court explained why it should not... Some 30 years after the Supreme Court began to draw the line on religion in the public schools, its decisions are still sadly misunderstood by too many people. They are among the wisest decisions the Court ever handed down because they recognize that freedom of religion means nothing if the power of government—in this case, the public schools—can be used for the purpose of religious indoctrination."

(After hearing Johnston speak at a school assembly in his Wooster, Ohio, public school last April, 12-year-old Dana Golub went home and hanged himself. According to *Education Week*, there were reported to have been marked increases in suicide threats and attempts in both the Wooster and Akron areas after students heard Johnston speak.)

No one knows how successful Johnston and other fundamentalist proselytizers are in what are supposed to be religiously neutral public schools. But such activity clearly violates the First Amendment, offends many if not most state constitutions, destroys the neutrality which our pluralism requires of our schools, and undermines the religious integrity of countless families. What parent wants Johnny or Janie to come home from school converted to another religion as a result of activities sponsored, approved, or allowed by school authorities?

And matters are not helped when the U.S. Secretary of Education, William Bennett, publicly expresses approval of teachers and school officials attempting to influence students' religious views.

The intrusion of sectarian proselytizers into our public schools, which we called "the Invasion of the Soul Snatchers" in our Fall 1983 report, is an epidemic which must be brought under control. And it can be brought under control, if citizens will get off their apathy.

Concerned citizens can check with their local school districts to find out what policy is regarding "equal access" groups or outside evangelists or "youth ministers" operating in the schools. Policies to keep the schools properly neutral should be urged on local school boards. Intrusions into the schools by Jerry Johnston or missionaries from Young Life, Campus Crusade, or any other group should be protested (a quiet approach is best, as it helps shield school officials from pressure from fundamentalist interests). When school officials refuse to keep the schools in their charge neutral, legal action should be considered, though this is a serious step which requires national coordination.

ARL members encountering local sectarian intrusions into public schools should send us all the information possible on the situation. Local violations of church-state separation are also excellent opportunities for organizing ARL chapters or bringing ARL speakers before local audiences.

Let us resolve that during 1986 we will make some progress toward getting the missionaries out of our public schools.

"Secular Humanism"

It is bad enough that Radical Right propagandists, such as Tim La Haye and Jerry Falwell, have worked hard to generate prejudice against Americans of the Humanist persuasion and to peddle the "big lie" that American public schools teach the "religion of secuar humanism." Now both Congress and the Reagan Department of Education have made matters even worse.

Last summer Congress included a prohibition on using funds under the Education for Economic Security Act for "courses of instruction the substance of which is secular humanism." According to Sen. Daniel P. Moynihan, the prohibition was inserted by Sen. Orrin Hatch as the price for his support for the act's "Magnet Schools" section, which many senators considered necessary to help school districts undergoing desegregation efforts.

Now the Education Department has proposed rules for implementing the act which do not define "secular humanism" and which leave defining it to individual school districts.

Unless these rules are changed, many schools will face witch hunts led by Radical Right groups to find and root out "secular humanism." People for the American Way has provided examples of what can and will happen.

In Arizona, showing of an Eagle Forum (Phyllis Schlafly's group) film on "secular humanism" led a school board to eliminate Homer, Hawthorne, and Hemingway from required reading lists, and cost a teacher his job.

In two districts in Oregon, attacks on "secular humanism" were used to undermine school guidance and counseling programs.

In Texas, Mel and Norma Gabler used the "secular humanism" charge for years to censor school textbooks.

In Buffalo, NY, a child-abuse prevention and sex education program is under attack for promoting "secular humanism."

In Tennessee, a Radical Right group sued to eliminate textbooks which promote "secular humanism" by "talking about evolution, death and dying, and the struggle for equality."

Our public schools are required by the Constitution and the pluralistic nature of our society to be religiously neutral. They may not teach or promote "secular humanism" any more than Catholicism, Methodism, Judaism or Hinduism. No credible evidence has ever been produced in court that "secular humanism" is taught or promoted in any public school. Several years ago the federal courts found that Transcendental Meditation was being promoted in five New Jersey public schools, held TM to contain substantial religious elements, and ordered TM out of the schools. The court should do the same if "secular humanism" or any other religion is proven to be taught or promoted by public schools.

But no legislation is needed to prohibit the teaching of "secular humanism." Indeed, the law passed by Congress last summer singles out Americans of the Humanist persuasion and makes them the targets of suspicion and prejudice. The "secular humanism" section of the 1984 law bears an unmistakable resemblance to Nazi laws against Jews and our old colonial laws against Quakers, Baptists, Catholics, and non-trinitarians.

In practice, moral McCarthyites will put anything in the schools they dislike under the "secular humanist" label and use the law and Education Department rules to try to get rid of it. This has the potential for causing turmoil in every state.

Congress should repeal the "secular humanism" section or the courts should strike it down. Meanwhile, the Education Department should issue rules to prevent local witch hunts, rules to help school districts understand that "secular humanism" is not simply a net into which everything disliked by Jerry Falwell, Tim La Haye, and Phyllis Schlafly can be dumped.

Humanists believe in democracy, peace, evolution, situation ethics (which is not, "if it feels good, do it"), freedom of religion, church-state separation, civil liberties, science, pluralism, the right to birth control and divorce, etc. But so too do most Catholic, Protestant, Jewish, and other Americans.

If the Education Department does not issue rules to prevent Radical Right witch hunts, public education, educators, and Americans of all faiths will be the losers.

Legislating Morality

The controversy over abortion rights often gets down to the question of whether morality should or should not be the subject of legislation. Pro-choice people sometimes say that morality should not be legislated, while anti-choice people tend to say yes, it should, and go on to cite laws against murder, robbery, rape, etc., and insist that civil law is derived from the Ten Commandments (which, in any event, do not mention abortion).

Generally speaking, the purpose of law in a society whose government is based on the social compact idea, as ours is—the Declaration of Independence states that government must represent the people and exists to protect the equal rights of the people, while the Constitution stipulates that We the People establish a government to carry out specific secular tasks—is to protect mutually agreed upon rights, maintain order, defend against external enemies, and promote the general welfare. Morality is an individual and cultural matter of enormous importance but one is separate from but often linked with government in very complex ways.

But down to brass tacks. Government does not prosecute murderers and rapists because they are immoral but because they have violated the law and someone's rights.

Opponents of free choice on abortion argue that if government cannot legislate against abortion, then it cannot legislate against murder, rape, arson, or robbery because that would be legislating morality. It's not that simple. We have laws against murder, rape, arson, and robbery primarily because we have a secular consensus that these activities violate the rights of people. There is also, as it happens, a consensus on the immorality of these acts so broad that it encompasses the whole religious spectrum. (Torching abortion clinics or school buses is illegal but is deemed "moral" by some of a moral majoritarian bent.) And surely these acts were regarded as wrong before Moses came down from Mount Sinai (or to whatever we owe the Ten Commandments) and in societies where the Judeo-Christian tradition was or is unknown. Morality, from whatever source derived, is clearly as important as civil law.

The trouble with the abortion question is that there has never been any consensus in our civilization over the notion of fetal personhood, on which the anti-abortion position rests today. Jewish tradition treated personhood as beginning at birth. The Christian Church during most of its history frowned on abortion not because of a fetal personhood theology, which it usually did not have, but because it regarded abortion, contraception, and sterilization as a frustration of the procreative purpose of sex. (The Vatican has a hard time explaining how it tolerated the practice of castrating boys to keep their soprano voices for its choir.) In any event, abortion was generally practiced in all western countries right up to the present. Since men wrote history, and childbirth and abortion were considered only the concern of women, not much was written on this subject until quite recently. Indeed, abortion was legal and practiced in the United States during the lifetimes of the constitutional framers, becoming generally illegal under state laws late in the nineteenth century for reasons having to do mainly with the consolidation of the medical profession and for health reasons which made sense then.

In 1973 the Supreme Court simply recognized that the constitutional term "person" had never applied to fetuses, that there is no consensus as to when a fetus becomes a person, and that the constitutional right to privacy protects a woman's right to personal moral choice about continuing or discontinuing a problem pregnancy. The law simply reverted to what it was during the early generations of our republic.

We appreciate the sincerity of those generally rather conservative Catholics and Protestants who believe that fetuses are persons and that abortion is therefore wrong. We support their right to follow their beliefs and to try to persuade others to do so. But we must draw the line at attempts to enact a theology of fetal personhood into law. (We won't expand on the view of many pro-choice people that the personhood near conception theory is reductionist and materialistic, that personhood, our humanity, is acquired from our families and the wider social environment after we are born.) President Reagan and his moral majoritarian backers clearly want to legislate their particular nonconsensus, rather sectarian morality.

The words of theologian John C. Bennett in his *Christians and the State* are right on target. "No church, no matter how powerful, should bring pressure on the state to enact laws which are based upon principles that depend for their validity on its own doctrine or ethos."

There is a broad, probably universal, secular and religious consensus behind laws against murder, rape, robbery, assault, segregation, arson, and other invasions of individual rights. Most Americans support choice on abortion and a large number of religious bodies—such as the thirty Protestant, Catholic, Jewish, and other bodies in the Religious Coalition for Abortion Rights—support the right to individual moral choice in this intensely personal area. President Reagan, Jerry Falwell, and certain Catholic bishops are wrong when they seek to impose their essentially sectarian morality into law.

Invasion of the Soul Snatchers

American public schools are required to be religiously neutral both by the Constitution (the First Amendment) and by the pluralistic nature of our society. Indeed, our country's religious pluralism may accurately be said to have been both cause and effect of our adoption of the principle of separation of church and state in the First Amendment and state constitutions. No country enjoys our level of religious liberty or has anything like the degree of pluralism found here.

While implementation of the principle of religious neutrality in public education has gone on and would go on without help from the courts, Supreme Court and lower court rulings have accelerated the process and have provided useful, fairly firm guidelines for state governments and local school districts.

In 1948 the Supreme Court ruled that religious instruction classes could not be conducted in public schools. In 1962 and 1963 the Court outlawed government sponsored or mandated group prayer and devotional Bible readings in the schools, while leaving intact the right of individual students to voluntarily engage in personal prayer and while encouraging schools to teach objectively and neutrally *about* religion. In 1968 the Court struck down a religiously motivated state law banning the teaching of evolution. In 1980 the Court overturned a state law requiring the posting of the Ten Commandments.

Lower courts have barred the distribution of religious literature in schools, the teaching of Transcendental Meditation (a religious movement which tries to disguise itself as secular), the requirement that equal time be given in science classes for the teaching of "scientific creationism," the use of schools during the school day for student religious group meetings, and state-mandated periods of silence "for prayer or meditation."

Sticky problems remain in many school districts regarding religious holiday observances (Is Halloween a pagan religious festival? Are Christmas hymns other than sung prayers?), while an unknown number of schools have yet to comply with the Supreme Court's prayer rulings.

Congress adjourned before Thanksgiving without passing President Reagan's proposed constitutional amendment to authorize government sponsored group prayer or bills to require schools to allow student religious group meetings, but the struggle over these measures will resume in early 1984.

Our main concern in this editorial, however, is with the growing sectarian intrusions into public schools, a veritable "invasion of the soul snatchers," to borrow from a popular movie title.

Some fundamentalist creationist groups are encouraging individual teachers, whose own scientific and professional training seem to be inadequate, to bootleg "creationism" into science classes, a practice that violates the First Amendment as much as the Arkansas law requiring the teaching of "creationism." Other groups are encouraging fundamentalist teachers to promote their religious views in the classroom. If a school may not constitutionally promote a religion, then an individual teacher, a public functionary, may not do so either.

A more serious and growing problem is that of professional adult missionaries operating in public schools. According to a recent report in *Education Week,* about 4,500 such missionaries operate in and around public schools, reaching an estimated 10% of the nation's high school students.

Their usual modus operandi is to hang around school athletic and other events and circulate in school cafeterias and corridors, *with the permission of the school administration,* to make friends with students. Later many of the missionaries try to get onto school staffs as volunteer assistant coaches or tutors.

While the missionaries seem to reserve overt, hard-sell proselytizing for meetings held off-campus, they use the schools to make contacts, to post notices of their meetings (they have been known to use school public address systems), and to persuade kids to attend off-campus religious meetings.

The purpose of this activity is clear: "to build relationships with kids in order to expose them to the Gospel," as one Young Life missionary put it; "to introduce adolescents to Jesus Christ and His relevance to life today," according to another.

The proselytizing groups are not those often referred to pejoratively as "cults" but, rather, fundamentalist or conservative evangelical groups drawing members and support from people of a number of conservative Protestant denominations and, occasionally, conservative Catholics.

The main groups are: "Young Life, with over 400 paid missionaries and a $15 million annual budget; Campus Life, the high school program of Youth for Christ, with 800 paid missionaries; Student Venture (formerly Student Life), an operation of Bill ("I Found It") Bright's Campus Crusade for Christ International, with 120 paid missionaries; High School Huddle and Junior High Huddle, programs of The Fellowship of Christian Athletes, with 168 paid missionaries and 3,200 volunteer leaders and coaches.

We do not question the religious beliefs of the missionaries operating in the schools, or their right to proselytize. What is objectionable and unconstitutional is the use of public schools for proselytizing. While schools may admit outside adults as resource persons in classrooms or as volunteers, these must be utilized solely for legitimate academic purposes.

No missionaries of any kind should be allowed to operate in the schools. And the responsibility of keeping such activity out falls to school principals, superintendents, and boards. Schools and school districts should adopt and enforce policies against even indirect proselytizing in the schools.

Concerned citizens and groups should be prepared to litigate in cases where school districts refuse to halt proselytizing. In that connection, ARL members and chapters would do well to check the policies of their local school boards. ARL's national office will assist local members and chapters in dealing with these problems.

Now is the time for us to finish the job of bringing all our public schools into compliance with the religious neutrality required by the Constitution and needed to preserve the religious liberty of all our students.

Chapter 6
Book Reviews

We are particularly proud of our book coverage. At a time when more book titles are being issued in the U.S. than ever before, fewer book reviews are appearing. Books with church-state implications are appearing with increasing frequency, but are often ignored by the major media sources. VOR's editors are committed to locating and reviewing the most important books in our field, including those from less well known publishers. We owe it to our readers and to the authors, who, often unsung and unappreciated, make contributions to our understanding of vital issues.

VOR reviewed 618 books in its first 106 issues. The all-time record is 22 reviews in Issue 105, followed by 21 reviews in Issue 103, 20 reviews in Issue 84, and 19 reviews in Issue 102.

We try to cover the whole gamut of books related to religion and politics. On occasion we will group titles by subject. In Issue 36, for example, we reviewed four books on "Religion, Russia and the Future," i.e., the return of Russian Orthodoxy to political influence and power in the former bastion of communism. Issue 84 was devoted primarily to books about the Catholic Church and its challenges today.

In this chapter we have selected 20 of our book reviews, mainly of books that received considerable national attention.

The Republican War on Science, by Chris Mooney, Basic Books, 342 pp., $24.95.

This exhaustive and comprehensive overview of a little-discussed topic is an eye-opener. Based on hundreds of interviews, thorough research and buttressed with over 60 pages of end notes, this study demonstrates "how cultural conservatives have disregarded, distorted, and abused science on the issues of evolution, embryonic stem cell research, the relation of abortion to health risks for women, and sex education."

That's not all. "Today's pseudo-conservatives have captured at least a major portion, if not the central mechanism, of the Republican Party and largely control the Bush Administration." The result has been detrimental to the importance of sound scientific thinking in the formulation of public policy. Science has become "politicized" by these forces, says the author, a journalist who specializes in the often troubled relation between science and politics. No wonder that 48 Nobel laureates in the sciences endorsed the Kerry-Edwards ticket last November. While the entire Republican Party is not guilty of all of the excesses, it is noteworthy that Richard Nixon fired his scientific advisers and that the Reagan and both Bush Administrations have ignored the consensus opinion of the scientific community on a host of vital issues.

It is not only religious conservatism that comes into play, says Mooney. "The Right has a strong track record of deliberately attempting to undermine scientific work that might threaten the economic interests of private industry."

Mooney praises the Union of Concerned Scientists and the National Center for Science Education. He also calls for the restoration of the Congressional Office of Technology Assessment and "safeguarding scientific advisory committees" as ways to counter the anti-science trends in U.S. public life. His conclusions should be heeded:

"The advent of the modern conservative movement, its takeover of the Republican Party, and its ultimate triumph under the administration of George W. Bush have brought us to a point where a true divorce between democratic government and technocratic expertise seems conceivable. In this context and considering its track record, we have no choice but to politically oppose the anti-science right wing of the Republican Party. This does not necessarily entail an outright partisan agenda. Encouraging the electoral success of Republican moderates with good credentials in science could potentially have just as constructive an effect as backing Democrats. But if we care about science and believe that it should play a crucial role in decisions about our future, we must steadfastly oppose further political gains by the modern Right. This political movement has patently demonstrated that it will not defend the integrity of science in any case in which science runs afoul of its core political constituencies. In so doing, it has ceded any right to govern a technologically advanced and sophisticated nation."

This is a provocative, indeed excellent, book.

— Al Menendez

Divided by God: America's Church-State Problem and What We Should Do About It, by Noah Feldman, Farrar, Straus and Giroux, 306 pp., $25.00.

Noah Feldman, a professor at New York University Law School, proposes to end America's church-state crisis with a simple formula: No coercion and no money. What is this crisis? "Religious division threatens the unity of the American nation more clearly than at any time in a century," he writes. To defuse the crisis, he endorses "greater latitude for public religious discourse and religious symbolism, and at the same time insistence on a stricter ban on state funding of religious institutions and activities." In other words, "The State may neither coerce anyone in matters of religion nor expend its resources so as to support religious institutions and practices." He adds, "We should permit and tolerate symbolic invocation of religious values and inclusive displays of religion while rigorously protecting the financial and organizational separation of religious institutions from institutions of government."

There are problems with this proposal. Symbolism and government endorsement of religious values are replete with contradictions. Whose religious values deserve governmental approbation? Will minority religions be protected? Will individuals not wanting to identify with any religion be marginalized? Feldman seems naive and not well informed when he argues that "public manifestations of religion — at least at the national level — are becoming increasingly pluralistic. . . . In some instances pluralistic public religion even holds out the possibility of enabling new religious minorities to participate fully in the American public sphere." If anything, the increasing power of the Religious Right makes it likely that evangelical Protestantism will continue to dominate the U.S. public square, whether at presidential inaugurals, National Days of Prayer, or at the U.S. military academies.

Feldman insists on dividing the American people into two broad categories, which he labels "values evangelicals" and "legal secularists," though the totality of the U.S. seems much broader and more diverse than this. He claims that values evangelicals can include Catholics, Jews and Muslims, or anyone who holds ethical values. Legal secularists are those who believe religion should be a private concern that has little or no impact on public policy. Most Americans would probably feel uncomfortable being categorized in this fashion. Values evangelicals include all who "care primarily about identifying traditional moral values that can in theory be shared by everyone." But he never identifies what these values are or how they shape the public discourse.

He is certainly correct in this assessment: "The deep divide in American life is not primarily over religious belief or affiliation; it is over the role that belief should play in the business of politics and government."

Commendably, he condemns the view that opposition to state aid for faith-based schools rests solely on a tradition of 19th century anti-Catholicism. "The framers who prohibited establishment at the federal level, and the Constitution drafters who did likewise in the states both before and after the framing, were not yet in the grips of bigoted anti-Catholic politics." But he says the opponents of aid to Catholic schools should have "accommodated Catholic public school children either by exempting them from practices they saw as Protestant, or by taking those rituals out of the schools altogether."

Church-state separationists will endorse some of Feldman's thesis, particularly when he writes, "The tradition of institutional separation that must be reasserted goes beyond funding for religious schools. All attempts to use government resources to institutionalize religious practices countermand the American tradition of nonestablishment, grounded historically in the belief that government has no authority over religious matters."

Feldman aims for even-handedness. "Secularists must accept the fact that religious values form an important source of political beliefs and identities for the majority of Americans, while evangelicals need to acknowledge that separating the institutions of government from those of religion is essential for avoiding outright political-religious conflict."

But Feldman should have acknowledged that religious neutrality on the part of government, in both the symbolic and financial realms, is much more likely to guarantee religious liberty and to preserve and advance freedom of conscience than any form of politically-motivated accommodationism. Religious freedom is safe and secure when a secular government neither advances nor inhibits religion — anybody's religion.

— Al Menendez

Evolution vs. Creationism: An Introduction, by Eugenie Scott, introduction by Niles Eldredge, Greenwood Press, 296 pp; Hardback $49.95, Paperback: University of California Press, $19.95.

Eugenie Scott's book is a fascinating hybrid: analyses of the C-E debate, critique of creationist claims from the viewpoints of scientists, teachers, theologians and the law, and a critical edited compilation of major creationist documents and arguments. The result is a one-stop resource for the newcomer and veteran alike. Anthropologist Scott, an ARL National Adviser, draws on her experience of 20 years or more as executive director of the National Center for Science Education to provide a sweeping overview of the multiple forms of antievolutionism. NCSE is the principal organization devoted to evolution education and critiquing creationist claims [Disclosure note: I am an NCSE Board Member].

Major sections of the book are "Science, Evolution, Religion, and Creationism," "A History of the Creation-Evolution Controversy," and "Selections from the Literature." Unfortunately, the "Intelligent Design" writers were not forthcoming with permission to reprint their own arguments, very unlike the case in normal academic discourse (and unlike the more traditional creationists, as well). This Part Three may otherwise be the most valuable aspect of the book, with exerpts on cosmology, astronomy, geology, patterns and processes of biological evolution, legal issues, educational issues, religious issues, and "the nature of science." Earlier, Chapter Six on Neocreationism is especially important, addressing the current state of affairs—especially the "Intelligent Design Movement" with deep roots in conservative Christianity but professing to be secular (unless one scratches the surface ever-so-gently to find admissions by its leading lights that they are using I.D. as a "wedge tactic" to get religion taught in the science classroom). The August 2005 comments by President George Bush advocating I.D. teaching demonstrate the political reach of this movement.

Creationism is a handmaiden to a mixture of resurgent anti-intellectualism, anti-elitism, and an array of conservative cultural values. There are many divisions in the "fellowship" of creationist leaders, but a general reaction against evolution education sews together this sometimes divergent group into a potent political force often willing to overlook otherwise large theological, political and cultural differences. Scott shows how science and religion are different and argues that they are not necessarily in conflict.

As an introduction to a huge problem facing science and religion, this book is very valuable and should be on the shelf of teachers, clergy, students – and politicians. Extensive bibliographies and suggested readings give good leads to each topic in vastly greater detail than a survey volume can include.

— John Cole

John Cole holds a Ph.D. in anthropology from Columbia University and is a member of the board of the National Center for Science Education.

What's the Matter with Kansas? How Conservatives Won the Heart of America, by Thomas Frank, Metropolitan Books, 306 pp., $24.00.

Frank's central argument is both impeccable and empirically verifiable. A large segment of working class Americans now routinely vote against their best economic interests and widen the gap between rich and poor because they have been convinced by religious conservatives that personal "morality" issues are the only important ones. He uses his home state of Kansas as an example. Rural Kansas, especially, is a burned-over district of poverty, out-migration and economic deprivation, and voters there routinely elect right-wing Republican advocates of "limited government," economic non-regulation, taxation inequality, and religious indoctrination of a conservative Protestant variety. All the while, the privileged upper classes in the Kansas City suburbs, who shun and disdain this kind of religion, reap the economic benefits of this stupidity.

"My home state of Kansas, a reliable hotbed of leftist reform movements a hundred years ago, today ranks among the nations most eager audiences for bearers of backlash buncombe." The Democratic Party has been reduced to almost third-party status, except for the governorship, while Republicans dominate everything else and have even increased their share of total registered voters. (Colorado is the only other non-Southern state with a growing Republican majority.)

Frank argues, "Over the last three decades, conservatives have smashed the welfare state, reduced the tax burdens on corporations and the wealthy, and generally facilitated the country's return to a nineteenth-century pattern of wealth distribution. The leaders of the backlash may talk Christ but they walk corporate. Values may matter most to voters but they always take a backseat to money once the elections are won." Fundamentalist Protestant religion has corrupted and debased political life. "Kansas has trawled its churches for the most aggressively pious individuals it could find and has proceeded to elevate them to the most prominent positions of public responsibility available, whence these saintly emissaries are then expected to bark and howl and rebuke the world for its sins. What makes the Kansas way so remarkable and so dysfunctional is that in each case the state's lawmakers combine this flamboyant public piety with a political agenda that only makes the state's material problems worse."

Kansas Republicans are now anti-abortion, anti-evolution and anti-public education and these "bitter" views have "poisoned political activity right down to the roots of the grass."

The politico-religious disease affecting Kansas may not be a regional aberration. "Things that began in Kansas — the Civil War, Prohibition, Populism — have a historical tendency to go national. Maybe Kansas, instead of being a laughing stock, is actually in the vanguard."

— *Al Menendez*

Constantine's Sword: The Church and the Jews, by James Carroll, Houghton Mifflin Co., 756 pp., $16.00.

Hitler's extermination of six million Jews did not happen in a vacuum. The Shoah, or Holocaust, could occur only because the way had been prepared by many centuries of Christian anti-Semitism. In this extraordinarily detailed, comprehensive, nuanced, gripping book, Catholic author James Carroll, a former priest now married and with two children, traces the development of anti-Semitism from its origins nearly two millennia ago, through Christian theological developments that contributed to and shaped anti-Jewish sentiment, the Crusades (whose first victims were not Muslims but Jews), the Inquisition, and trends since the Reformation leading eventually to the Nazi death camps. Like Catholic authors Garry Wills and John Cornwell, whose books we also reviewed recently, Carroll criticizes Pope Pius XII and the Vatican for their failure to adequately respond to Hitler's murderous designs. One sentence near the end of the book pretty well summarizes his findings. Carroll writes (p. 603) that "Catholic history, while not causing the Shoah, was a necessary, unbroken thread in the rise of genocidal antisemitism as well as the source of the Church's failure to openly oppose it." *Constantine's Sword* is so richly detailed, documented, and readable that no short review could do it justice.

— *Edd Doerr*

Papal Sin: Structures of Deceit, by Garry Wills, Doubleday, 326 pp., $25.00.

In 2000, the U.S. House of Representatives passed a resolution (H. Con. Res. 253) by 416 to one (Rep. Pete Stark, D-CA) "strongly objecting to any effort to expel the Holy See" from the UN General Assembly as a "permanent observer." The resolution, sponsored by Rep. Chris Smith (R-NJ), was aimed at countering the See Change campaign, initiated by Catholics for a Free Choice and supported by more than 500 organizations in the U.S. and abroad (including Americans for Religious Liberty) which seeks to terminate the arrangement whereby the Catholic Church (the Holy See) enjoys a preferred status at the UN denied to all other religious groups. The church has used that privileged status to thwart efforts to have the UN deal more adequately with population and women's rights issues.

Smith's resolution garnered near-unanimous support because a great many members of Congress mistakenly fear offending Catholics, a fear based on the erroneous notion that the pope and bishops speak for and represent a majority of Catholics. As I have pointed out often, the Vatican's authoritarian leadership is out of sync with most Catholics on such key issues as contraception, abortion, divorce, clerical celibacy, ordaining women, and education.

The Smith resolution highlights the importance of this useful book by eminent historian and devout Catholic Garry Wills. Wills makes it abundantly clear that the papacy has long engaged in an Orwellian "selective manipulation of history" in the interest of advancing papal power at the expense of truth and such basic human values as freedom of conscience. He zeros in on the Vatican's misrepresentations regarding the Holocaust and anti-Semitism a topic explored by John Cornwell in *Hitler's Pope)* and on its "dishonesties" in dealing with contraception, clerical celibacy, ordination of women and cover-ups of clerical child abuse.

Wills wants a reformed and democratized Catholicism, and repeatedly decries the "structures of deceit" which have for so long been such a notable feature of papal power politics and centralized authoritarianism. Politicians and Americans generally of all persuasions need to recognize that there are in reality two Catholic churches, one a power-hungry oligarchy and the other the vast majority of quite ordinary people who, we might note, put Bill Clinton in the White House twice.

— Edd Doerr

The Next Christendom: The Coming of Global Christianity, by Philip Jenkins, Oxford University Press, 20 pp., $28.00.

Historian Philip Jenkins argues forcefully and with a commanding sense of history and demography that Christianity will soon be a Southern Hemisphere, largely Third World phenomenon. This demographic shift, now underway and accelerating, will have a major impact on world politics and on the internal dynamics of all Christian churches.

Even now, about 65% of the world's Roman Catholics live in Latin America, Africa and Asia, and over 40% of the cardinals who will choose the next pope reside in the Third World. By 2020, over 72% of Catholics will be Third World residents. While this change could lead to more political emphasis on social justice issues, it might lead to wholly unexpected developments. Jenkins says, "Traditional mappings of left and right are ill fitted to comprehend present and future religious changes."

Jenkins warns Western and U.S. liberals that the future may well not be to their liking. "The liberal issues dear to American or West European Catholics are irrelevant or worse to the socially traditional societies of the south. While the ordination of women may seem an essential point of justice to Westerners, it is anathema for much of the emerging world." Jenkins adds, "For the foreseeable future, the characteristic religious forms of Southern Christianity, enthusiastic and spontaneous, fundamentalist and supernatural-oriented, look massively different from those of the older centers of Christianity in Europe and North America. This difference becomes critically important in light of current demographic trends. In the coming decades, the religious life characteristic of the regions may well become the Christian norm."

Other data, cited by Jenkins, support these interpretations. At present, in the Anglican Communion, conservative African and Asian bishops outnumber those from Europe and the United States. In a quarter century, the differences will be even greater.

Among American Roman Catholics, "One sixth of the priests currently serving American parishes have been imported from other countries," and "of the seminarians about to be ordained in the United States, 28% have been born outside the country." The ancient Christian nation of Great Britain "today plays host to some 1,500 missionaries from fifty nations" bent on reconverting England.

These trends affect Protestantism as well, and conservative immigrants from Latin America and Korea will strengthen the evangelical wings of American Protestant Christianity. Eastern Orthodoxy will decline, because it is almost entirely a European-based faith.

Muslims will continue to expand, and clashes between Christians and Muslims may intensify. Jenkins writes, "At the turn of the third millennium, religious loyalties are at the root of many of the world's ongoing civil wars and political violence, and in most cases, the critical division is the age-old battle between Christianity and Islam."

This is a sobering assessment of religion's future impact.

— Al Menendez

Hitler's Pope: The Secret History of Pius XII, John Cornwell, Viking Press, 430 pp., $29.95.

This scathing indictment of the papacy of Pius XII (Eugenio Pacelli) is receiving justifiable national and international attention. While little of its material is wholly new, it has organized and summarized a critical view of Pacelli's policies toward Nazi Germany and in particular its attempt to wipe out world Jewry.

Cornwell, an English journalist and author a decade ago of a book debunking rumors that Pope John Paul I had been murdered in 1978, had access to much unpublished documentation in numerous archives. While he does not solve the perplexing case of why Pius XII did little to mitigate the suffering of Europe's Jews — or even of his fellow Catholics in Poland and elsewhere who opposed Hitler — he does offer a number of reasonable suppositions.

Cornwell's research is particularly strong in dealing with Pacelli's early career as a canon lawyer and a Vatican diplomat in Weimar Germany. Pacelli worked ceaselessly to craft a concordat with Germany that would guarantee the rights of the church hierarchy over its members, particularly in matters of education and family life. Cornwell argues that both Hitler, Germany's führer when the concordat was finalized, and the Vatican got most of what they wanted. The Vatican strengthened its control over the German Catholic bishops and people while Hitler received respectability and was assured of the loyalty of Catholics to his regime, even though most Catholics had voted against him in the 1932 elections.

Cornwell writes that the Vatican favored centralization over conciliarity in its relationship to local hierarchies. Church officials preferred to deal with high state officials to achieve their objectives. The Vatican also showed little or no interest in the religions freedom of Protestants, Anglicans, Jews or Orthodox Christians.

According to Cornwell, the concordat with Germany gave the Vatican unprecedented control over German Catholic life. It also led to the enfeeblement of Catholic political life and limited the possibilities of Catholic dissent toward Hitler's policies, even though courageous individual Catholic laity and clergy continued to oppose Hitler. But he says that a "Vatican policy of compliance" virtually ignored Hitler's crackdown on Catholic schools and institutions.

Cornwell charges that the Vatican ignored the centrist and moderately progressive Catholic political parties in Italy (the Popular Party) and Germany (the Center Party), preferring right-wing Catholic parties in Austria, Spain, Portugal and elsewhere.

From the outset of his reign, Pacelli tried flattery and appeasement of Hitler, according to Cornwell. He refused to publish a denunciatory encyclical prepared by his predecessor, Pius XI, and did not recall the papal nuncio from Berlin.

Why now? Why has Cornwell waded into a controversy that had already been addressed for three decades by respected scholars, including Guenther Lewy, Saul Friedlander, and Carlo Falcone? Cornwell clearly has an agenda of his own. He has produced a literary version of "the devil's advocate," a one-time Vatican official whose role, until abolished in 1983, was to argue against canonization of individuals being considered for sainthood.

For thirty-five years, Vatican officials charged with implementing the complex, arcane procedures surrounding canonization have been moving Pius XII's case forward. The first step, beatification, is said to be near. Cornwell, a former Catholic seminarian, is clearly trying to undercut the effort, feeling that elevating Pius XII to sainthood would be a disastrous setback to Catholic progressives and to the ecumenical movement.

One question could be asked: Do non-Catholics care which individuals are elevated to sainthood? The answer is a surprising yes. Canonization clearly has political, economic, geographical and theological implications. It represents a seal of approval, of sorts, over certain lifestyles, values and principles. Individuals who are canonized are said to be exemplars to believers. Cornwell writes, "The beatification process for Pacelli is fraught with political significance, both within and outside the Church. If it succeeds, Pacelli's policies will be dramatically confirmed - endorsing the modern ideology of papal power and justifying Pacelli's wartime record."

Cornwell argues that canonizing Pacelli will send the wrong message to world Catholicism because "Papal autocracy, carried to the extreme, can only demoralize and weaken Christian communities." He adds, "In many parts of the world, the Catholic Church enjoys the benefits of a pluralism widely undervalued by its traditionalists. In an era largely hospitable to religious freedom it is difficult to assess the full extent of the moral and social enfeeblement of the local churches. It has been the urgent thesis of this book that when the papacy waxes strong at the expense of the people of God, the Catholic Church declines in moral and spiritual influence to the detriment of us all."

Cornwell's eloquent and provocative study ends on this note, "I am convinced that the cumulative verdict of history shows him to be not a saintly exemplar for future generations, but a deeply flawed human being from whom Catholics, and our relations with other religions, can best profit by expressing our sincere regret."

Cornwell makes his case effectively, but there remain areas of interpretation that many scholars of this period will challenge. It is perhaps a bit naive to affirm, for example, that "Had Catholics protested, specifically, Kristallnacht and the rise of anti-Semitism, the fate of the Jews in Nazi Germany and indeed throughout Europe might have been different." The monstrous policies of Hitler and his allies, coupled with his growing military might, required comparable challenges from other nations. Dictators rarely listen to the pleadings of individual citizens, or ecclesiastical entities. (Cornwell cites the somewhat effective Catholic opposition to German euthanasia of the mentally and physically infirm and the removal of crucifixes from classrooms in 1941.)

Cornwell also argues that Pius XII had a grand design for Catholic evangelization in Eastern Europe, to bring about eventual reunion between Eastern Orthodoxy and Rome. Thus, he refused to protest the atrocities committed by a fanatically Catholic government in Croatia — which Cornwell says the Vatican knew about relatively early. Without additional historical evidence to substantiate this charge, it must remain in the realm of speculation.

—*Al Menendez*

God and the Gun: The Church and Irish Terrorism, Martin Dillon, Routledge, 244 pp., $27.50.

To what extent is religion an integral part of the seemingly unending conflict in Northern Ireland? For thirty years that question has been considered, and often carelessly dismissed, by observers, participants, and others. Martin Dillon, a longtime BBC correspondent in Northern Ireland, is an ideal person to tackle this knotty problem. His insights and experience lend credibility to this analysis. And an earlier book, *The Shankill Butchers,* showed the religious motivations for a series of sectarian murders in the 1970s.

Basically, Dillon concludes that religious conditioning has led inexorably to violence. Ireland, especially in the North, has long been a society where religious convictions and identities have led to separation of the different communities, even in education, residential location and, often, career choices.

While this is changing, especially among the educated middle classes and in the Republic, there remains a tenacious religious intensity among the North's fundamentalist Protestants, whose entire worldview is shaped by religious fears and preconceptions.

Dillon found the clergy, both the higher echelons and parish ministers, reluctant to discuss the role of religion in the conflict, saying, "It was easier to get terrorists to talk than priests and ministers."

While clergy claim they oppose violence, there is considerable ambivalence in their message. He writes, "For the Protestant community, the slogan 'For God and Ulster' carries the imprimatur of religious conviction and defense of faith." "Catholicism, nationalism and republicanism are interconnected," he adds. So, too, he notes, "The folk tradition of the gun in both communities, carries with it a moral crusade in defense of the respective traditions."

Dillon argues convincingly that "the British army and military intelligence identified the Catholic Church as an integral part of the conflict and therefore of the enemy." Dillon reveals that British military intelligence services even bugged confessionals in the 1970s, which could have led to international condemnation had it been known. His extensive interviews reveal how "paramilitaries have reconciled killing with their religious convictions."

Dillon became more disillusioned with the lack of integrity on the part of the clergy of both traditions, admitting that he was "frightened, saddened and shocked" by much of what he learned. He concludes, "In an unholy war, the caricatures of religion starkly reflect the obscene justification of violence. Layers of consciousness have produced a divided society of two tribes with their respective and blunted perceptions of righteousness. In Northern Ireland, history and religion are more important than in any modern European country. Faith and Fatherland are indivisible ingredients of the conflict and have produced the barbarity associated with an unholy war."

— *Al Menendez*

American Evangelicals and the U.S. Military, 1942-1993, by Anne C. Loveland, Louisiana State University Press, 356 pp., $55.00.

Loveland, a professor of American History at LSU, has produced a one-of-a-kind study, history at its most engaging and exhilarating. Her painstaking research traces the role of evangelical Protestants in the U.S. military, from initial hostility to immense power in shaping policy and determining the overall religious orientation of the armed forces.

She writes that today the U.S. has "a military community largely populated by born-again Christians, in which conservative Protestantism set the standard of theological and ethical values. The dominant religious conservatism allowed aggressive, intolerant behavior on the part of its adherents but frowned on overt expressions of religious liberalism." Some of this is due to a simple fact: "The increasing number of high-ranking officers, both active-duty and retired, who assumed leadership positions in various parachurch groups involved with the armed forces also testifies to the growing approbation evangelical religion enjoyed among upper-echelon military men."

Evangelicals initially disliked the military command, because its leadership belonged largely to the mainline churches, especially the Episcopal Church, to which 40% of the military leadership adhered. But since evangelicals now control the military, they have forged a close identification with military policies, especially during the Reagan administration.

The coziness began under Eisenhower and intensified for several reasons, according to Loveland. "Another factor that contributed to a more harmonious relationship between evangelicals and the military leadership was that although some leaders continued to regard evangelical religion as theologically alien, they recognized that ideologically it was sympathetic to and supportive of the military."

This commonality of interest came to full bloom in Vietnam. "The Vietnam War proved to be a watershed event in the history of evangelicals in the United States. Evangelicals' support for the war policies of the Johnson and Nixon administrations strengthened their influence in the federal government.... . The Vietnam War facilitated a dramatic change in evangelicals' image and status within the military."

Loveland argues that evangelicals supported the Reagan military buildup, the Star Wars initiative and opposed the nuclear freeze for both political and religious reasons. Evangelical influence in the military led to some clashes with what she calls "the plural ideal, the wide-ranging religious pluralism among military personnel and in the chaplaincy." Evangelicals adhered to a "sectarian ideal" which, Loveland asserts, reveals "the uncompromising sectarianism so characteristic of evangelicals, the notion that their faith constituted 'true Christianity' while others represented 'half truth' or 'sub-Christian' views or even total falsehood." She adds, "Besides sectarianism, the sectarian ideal military evangelicals followed in the 1970s and 1980s embraced moral absolutism." Finally, evangelicals adhered to the "custodial notion that the dissemination of religious 'half truth' and moral relativism must be stopped or at least challenged because it subverted the faith of others and put them in danger of damnation."

As a consequence, many military evangelicals bitterly opposed the inclusion of Buddhist and Mormon chaplains in the armed services, though their efforts were unsuccessful. They were successful, however in promoting the philosophy of James Dobson inside the military.

Loveland notes that a devout fellow evangelical, Army Chief of Staff General John A. Wickham, Jr., "engaged a prominent evangelical, James C. Dobson, to help implement the development of a comprehensive army family policy." She adds, "That it was enunciated during General Wickham's tenure as chief of staff ensured that it carried the stamp of his professional, personal, and religious convictions." Loveland also notes that "the two men quickly developed a close relationship based on shared religious convictions and mutual respect." In addition, she says, "No one did more than Dobson to advertise Wickham's evangelical credentials. . . . Dobson also paraded the chief of staff before the Focus on the Family organization team."

During the first Clinton administration, evangelicals fought tooth and nail against the president's proposal to ban discrimination against gay and lesbian members of the armed forces. About the evangelical military lobby Loveland writes, "Though still a minority, they were insiders who wielded influence disproportionate to their numbers." Their attitudes toward those of other religious positions and/or lifestyles remained unfavorable. "By the 1990s many evangelicals still had difficulty fully accepting religious pluralism within the armed forces." Their campaign against the Clinton proposal was fierce, according to Loveland. "Military evangelicals fought an impassioned campaign against the lifting of the ban. The arguments they presented during the campaign made two basic points: That the issue was preeminently a moral one which ought to be decided on biblical grounds and that lifting the ban would be deleterious to the religious and moral welfare of the armed forces."

Military evangelicals worked closely with Religious Right allies and with Senators Dan Coats and Strom Thurmond of the Senate Armed Services Committee, both fellow evangelicals. Their campaign did not go unnoticed by the military command, says Loveland. "All of the religious activity in the Pentagon and the Washington, D.C. area focusing on the homosexual issue surely made an impression on the military leadership."

Loveland's conclusion to her seminal historical examination should, if anything, settle the argument that evangelical Christians are an oppressed, persecuted minority in the United States. "Military evangelicals' response to the issue of homosexuals in the military showed the influence they were capable of exerting by the 1990s. Fifty years after the beginning of the evangelical mission to the military, conservative Christians remain a minority in the armed forces, but they made up for their lack of numbers by their zeal and cohesiveness. The growth of evangelical religion in the civilian sector over the fifty-year period also contributed to their strength. Evangelicals' mission to the military and their campaign to influence national policy generally developed along parallel lines.... If anything, the controversy over homosexuality in the military suggested that military evangelicals, separately or allied with fellow believers in the civilian sector, constituted a force to be reckoned with in the future."

The words "definitive" and "seminal" are used carelessly in book reviewing circles. But in the case of this excellent study, both are appropriate.

— *Al Menendez*

Active Faith: How Christians Are Changing The Soul Of American Politics, by Ralph Reed, The Free Press, 311 pages, $25.00.

Ralph Reed, the Christian Coalition's youthful executive director, is at it again, trying to "prove" how reasonable his (actually, televangelist Pat Robertson's; Reed is just the hired CEO) movement is and how it is merely carrying on the grand old tradition of progressive Christian activism. He claims, for example, that "religious people are not motivated by partisan ideology but rather by a transcendent ethic of moral concerns that are grounded in faith." Well, so are "non-religious" people. And many so-called religious activists are, and have always been, mean-spirited partisans who lack respect for those of other viewpoints.

Reed shows himself to be a highly partisan Republican who claims that "the majority of the House Republican freshmen are committed evangelicals or devout Roman Catholics" and that the GOP "stands on the brink of long term majority status" because of evangelical support at the polls.

His heroes remain "professing Christians" like Governors David Beasley of South Carolina and Kirk Fordice of Mississippi. He writes that anti-choice, pro-voucher Representative Henry Hyde (R-IL) is "a man so sweet, so gentle, and so genuine in his faith that I have sometimes wondered if he was not an angel in a blue suit roaming the halls of Congress."

He expresses admiration for Pat Buchanan. "For us, Buchanan's candidacy represented an altogether fortuitous opportunity for religious conservatives by virtually ensuring that the ultimate presidential nominee would keep the pro-life plank in the party platform."

To his credit, Reed denounces coercive school prayer and Reconstructionist theology as "religious tyranny" and threatening to civil liberties. He claims that his movement is slowly evolving from "lily white" to "multiracial." But much of this may be strategic rather than fundamental, an attempt to soften Religious Right ideology to make it more compatible to moderate voters. He says there has been in his movement "a shift from a clergy-based leadership class to lay men and women, which has tended to shift the rhetoric of both leaders and their supporters from the evangelical idiom to the less apocalyptic vernacular of the legislative arena."

Reed admits that "politics is not the sole or even the primary answer to our nation's moral decay" and claims, without any proof, that "involvement in politics has corrupted the religious faith of liberals." Is there any reason to think that this, if it is true, would not happen to religious conservatives also?

Behind what Reed intends to be a facade of benign reasonableness lurk agendas, neither spelled out nor justified in the book, that would seriously undermine religious liberty, weaken or wreck public education, reduce women to the status of second class citizens or worse, fragment our society along religious and other lines, and stir up ancient antagonisms.

Finally, Reed's writing exhibits a colossal, unwarranted egotism rather inappropriate in one of such tender years.

— *Al Menendez and Edd Doerr*

A Justice for All, by Kim Isaac Eisler, Simon and Schuster, 303 pp., $22.00.

Legal correspondent Kim Eisler has produced a first-rate biography and legal study of Justice William Brennan, whose 34 years on the Supreme Court represented a high point for church-state separation and civil liberties.

Ironically, Brennan was selected because Cardinal Francis Spellman lobbied President

Eisenhower to have a Catholic on the Court. There had been none on the Court for a number of years until the vacancy in 1956. Eisenhower, playing politics just before the 1956 election, agreed that his next appointment should be a Catholic and preferably a Democrat. Ike, totally uninterested in the judicial philosophy of his Court nominees, selected Brennan. Spellman was furious. He had good reason, as Brennan became a leader for women's rights, reproductive choice, and church-state separation.

Brennan was a major player in the school prayer decisions. "His *Schempp* opinion was a tour de force," says Eisler. Brennan helped shape the Court's opinion that government sponsored school prayer was unconstitutional, an opinion written by Justice Tom Clark. Eisler says that *Schempp* was "the most wrenching personal decision of his career." Brennan had, after all, gone to parochial schools, attended Mass every week, and was a very firm Catholic. "He was a religious man, but on the Court, the Constitution was the Bible," writes Eisler. Brennan, in fact, frequently made clear that he was sworn to uphold the Constitution and would not allow his personal religious opinions to have any sway over his rulings.

Brennan was a major player in *Griswold v. Connecticut,* which guaranteed the right to birth control. He lobbied exhaustively to concentrate on the Ninth Amendment and the right to privacy, while other justices, like Douglas, wanted to promote the freedom of association argument. Brennan wrote that the rights actually listed in the Constitution were "just examples which do not preclude applications or extensions of those rights to situations unanticipated by the Framers." He thus laid the groundwork in *Griswold* for *Roe v. Wade.*

Brennan played a major role in the great abortion rights decision, though he did not write the majority opinion. He lobbied strongly for defense of a woman's right, while other justices, particularly Blackmun, were mainly concerned with the right of doctors to practice their profession. Blackmun and others were interested in a narrow definition but Brennan was "outspoken in his belief that the anti-abortion laws of the states (Georgia and Texas) were definitely unconstitutional." Brennan's concern "from the outset was for the pregnant woman," and said that abortion "should be held to involve a basic constitutional right." He also fought hard in the *Eisenstadt v. Baird* case from Massachusetts concerning the distribution of contraceptives to unmarried women. Brennan wrote, "if the right to privacy means anything, it is the right of the individual, married or single, to be free from unwarranted governmental intrusion in matters so fundamentally affecting a person as the decision whether or not to bear a child." Thus, "It was William Joseph Brennan, not Blackmun, the opinion's author, who laid the framework for the most controversial decision in Supreme Court history." Eisler adds that, "If Blackmun's original draft had come down as an opinion of the Court, it would have meant that states did not have the power to restrict abortions, they just had to be clear and reasonable about it." Brennan insisted on a very strong defense of freedom of conscience in this area.

Eisler regards Brennan as one of the brightest stars in our judicial firmament. It will be a long time before we see his like again.

—Al Menendez

The Culture of Disbelief: How American Law and Politics Trivialize Religious Devotion, by Stephen L Carter, Basic Books, 328 pp., $25.00.

This Yale law professor's provocative book is important mainly because it has been touted by Yale Law alumnus Bill Clinton.

Carter is concerned that "our political and legal cultures treat religious beliefs as arbitrary and unimportant" He writes, "There may have been times in our history when we as a nation have tilted too far in one direction, allowing too much religious sway over politics. But in late-twentieth-century America, despite some loud fears about the influence of the weak and divided Christian right, we are upsetting the balance afresh by tilting too far in the other direction—and the courts are assisting in the effort."

He stresses this point. "Our secular politics is unlikely to become the servant of any single religious tradition; the nation has become too secure in its diversity to allow that travesty to occur. But it is quite possible for religion to become the servant of secular politics." Clearly he underestimates the power of religious militancy and extremism and the impact that religiously intolerant and authoritarian groups are having on the political, educational, and legal frameworks of our society.

Carter is right on some issues but abysmally wrong on others. On the good side he refers to church-state separation as "the durable and vital doctrine that shields our public institutions from religious domination and our religious institutions from government domination." He also affirms that "religions that most need protection seem to receive it least," referring to free exercise claims of minority religious groups under the Rehnquist Supreme Court. He says that "religious pluralism and equality—*never* mere 'toleration'—should be essential parts of what makes American democracy special."

On government-sponsored creches and religious symbols on public property he says, "In a world of religious equality this plain religious preference by the government is insupportable." He worries that "the political process will protect only the mainstream religions, not the many smaller groups that exist at the margins." There is ample evidence to support that view.

Carter criticizes government-sponsored school prayer. "By choosing among possible prayers, and then forcing its choice on impressionable children who look to their schools for guidance, the state in effect coerces religious adherence. . . . The powers of the state should not be used to coerce religious belief, and it is impossible to design a noncoercive approach to school prayer."

Unfortunately, Carter is wrong on many other subjects. A conservative Episcopalian, who sends his children to private religious schools where their religion can be "celebrated and not demeaned," he thinks it unfair for parents not to be able to receive tax support for their children to attend private and church run schools. He buys the argument that there is strong public support for "voucher programs and other tax support for private schools, including religious schools," ignoring the referenda in almost twenty states over the last quarter century that indicate the opposite. Instead, he accepts highly questionable polling data. He also says that private and parochial schools are more integrated than public schools. This statistical sleight of hand is simply not mathematically or rationally correct In one section it compares apples with oranges. He says that the percentage of black children in Catholic schools in Washington, D.C., is about the same or slightly lower than that for the city as a whole. He should not compare the Catholic school population to the whole population in Washington, but to its public school population, and he will find that about 64% of Catholic school students are black, compared to 95% in public schools. He also says parents who seek religious education for their children are more concerned with reinforcement of family values than they are in specific religious aspects. Even if that were true, it does not make tax aid to those schools any more constitutionally permissible.

He is also wrong when he says, "our history suggests that the Founders intended to allow states to establish religions, and, certainly did not intend to proscribe state support for religion." Many constitutional scholars have shown this interpretation to be faulty.

In some areas Carter overstates his case. He says, "The potential transformation of the Establishment Clause from guardian of religious liberty into a guarantor of public secularism raises prospects at once dismal and dreadful." There are very few separationists and/or religious or political liberals who would use the Establishment Clause to obliterate religion in America or persecute religious people. Carter claims, "When citizens do act in their public selves as though their faith matters, they risk not only ridicule, but actual punishment." If this were true, why is it that virtually every member of Congress and every state legislature claims a religious affiliation?

Carter wants to preserve church-state separation without "trivializing" faith, but such trivializing is not a constitutional issue. He argues, "Our culture has come to belittle religious devotion, to humiliate believers, and, even if indirectly, to discourage religion as a serious activity," adding that "democracy is best served when the religions are able to act as independent moral voices interposed between the citizen and the state." Carter's fears are exaggerated. After all, in the U.S. more people attend church and are more involved in religious activity than in any other major nation in the world.

Carter is concerned about how religion is taught in public school, as are many thoughtful Americans. He believes that religion deserves a more vital role in the curriculum, and is aware that teaching about it objectively is difficult. But again he overstates his case when he writes, "One problem with the public school curriculum is that the concern to avoid even a hint of forbidden endorsement of religion has led to a climate in which teachers are loath to mention religion." The real situation is much more complicated.

He argues that religion is unfairly excluded from political life but shows no concern that religious based political parties or movements are inherently dangerous to democracy. Carter shows little sensitivity to the dangers of religious oppression in America, evidence of which is found abundantly both in our history and in the history of other nations. He ignores Chief Justice Warren Burger's warning that "political division along religious lines" was one of the principal evils that the First Amendment was designed to prevent.

There are many errors in the book. The *Lee v. Weisman* graduation prayer case came from Rhode Island, not Long Island. The author or his editor apparently does not know the difference between a jeremiad and a jihad. Kansas is no longer a "dry" state, having abolished statewide prohibition in 1958. The Catholic theologian is Richard *McBrien,* not *O'Brien.* The Supreme Court has not upheld tuition reimbursement tax credits, but only limited tax deductions. John Dewey was not anti-religious.

Finally, though Carter's book is stimulating and thoughtful, it is riddled with confused interpretations of fact and history, lapses of logic, and fuzzy thinking. And from the book's extensive notes it is clear that the author relied too heavily on conservative sources.

—*Al Menendez and Edd Doerr*

The American Hour, by Os Guinness, Free Press, 458 pp., $24.95.

Os Guinness, an English expatriate living in the U.S. since 1984, is the main architect of the so-called "Williamsburg Charter" in 1988 and the "living With Our Deepest Differences" curriculum on religious liberty for public school use published in 1990, both of which this newsletter has analyzed and criticized as seriously flawed and deficient (Copies of our critiques are available for $1.00 from ARL, P.O. Box 6656, Silver Spring, MD 20916.)

In *The American Hour* Guinness wrings his hands about an alleged "current crisis of cultural authority" in the U.S. and discusses the role of religion in American culture. He writes glowingly about the importance of religious liberty but then spends a great many pages attacking implementation of the church-state separation principle. Through most of the book the author remains floating in the stratosphere of high level abstractions, borne aloft on a seemingly inexhaustible stream of hot air. On the rare occasions when he descends to somewhere near the real world he carefully avoids discussing any of the real church-state conflicts which the country has faced and makes it clear, to those readers who have the stamina to wade through this opus, that he really does not like church-state separation or its defenders (as this reviewer learned in five years of interactions with the author), thinks ill of religiously neutral American public schools, and disapproves of the right of women to freedom of conscience on abortion.

Among the book's many absurdities: repeated assertions about the "decline of the Christian Right" (the author must have slept through 1992); criticism of Jewish "overreactions" to proselytism "especially when the Jewish community enjoys so much growth through mixed marriage" (which actually results in a net membership loss to the Jewish community); an absurd attack on humanism for lacking "supernaturalism"; a claim that Mormons are not Christian; confusion of "libertarianism" with "civil liberties."

The book should be mentioned in the Guinness Book of Records (published, I believe, by some of the author's relatives) for having the highest content of cliches and non-sequiturs per page. Its pompous pretensions toward profundity take shallowness to record depths.

The author winds up offering "faith" as the solution to the "crisis of cultural authority" without specifying or describing what faith he has in mind. When he writes (p. 299) that "Power is only for those who can exercise it effectively and well" and scorns leaders who resort to "constant consultation with the governed, we might be able to detect more than a faint odor of some sort of tory authoritarianism.

— *Edd Doerr*

Lead Us Not Into Temptation, by Jason Berry, Doubleday, 407 pp., $22.50.

New Orleans journalist Jason Berry, an articulate Catholic liberal, surveys the tragic nationwide epidemic of child abuse by Roman Catholic clergy. The greater tragedy, he finds, is the coverup by high church officials, who transferred errant clergy from parish to parish and tried to silence dissent within and without the church. However, "The cover-up shattered against two pillars of democracy: the court system and a free press," writes Berry.

The resulting scandals and trials have cost the church and its insurers $400 million, a figure which may grow to $1 billion. Some observers believe that church leaders will redouble their efforts to win public funds for parochial schools and other church-run institutions to make up for the drain.

Berry warns that "the corruption of ecclesiastical culture is part of a psychological and sexual crisis that has been building for years," but fears that "Vatican clericalism refuses to acknowledge that the problems need a remedy." He writes, "Rome's response toward the clergy sexual crisis shows how far ecclesiastical leaders have drifted from ideals they espouse ... Denying the existence of this decay is one symptom of a spiritual cancer. Arresting the illness requires a structural change in the ecclesiastical concept of the Church, and history suggests the Vatican will resist that to the bitter end."

Berry mentions two church-state aspects of the scandal. One is the failure of some civil officials, such as New Orleans District Attorney Harry Connick, to prosecute priests because it might embarrass the church of which they are members. Also, some bishops have suggested that church officials remove damaging material from their files and send them to the Vatican's embassy in Washington, D.C., which has international immunity and cannot be subpoenaed by U.S. courts. Berry comments acidly, "Hiding things was one strategem in a psychology of power rooted in fear." Berry also cites Alfred P. Rubin, a law professor at Tufts University, who warns that such actions would lead to a break in diplomatic relations between the U.S. and the Vatican.

Priest-sociologist Andrew M. Greeley's powerful foreword calls Berry's story "the greatest scandal in the history of religion in America and perhaps the most serious crisis Catholicism has felt since the Reformation." Greeley adds a personal note: "It is my strong impression that the situation is actually much worse than it appears in this book . . . Bishops have with what seems like programmed consistency tried to hide, cover up, bribe, stonewall."

— Al Menendez

Earth in the Balance: Ecology and the Human Spirit, by Senator Al Gore, Houghton Mifflin, 407 pp., $22.95.

Senator Gore's analysis of our planet's ecology/population crisis is right on target in this brilliant, readable, sophisticated book. He shows very clearly that the only result of increasing environmental degradation and resource depletion, coupled with rapid population growth, can be a global disaster. His prescriptions for remedies are those of a politician/statesman, in the best sense of that term, realistic and achievable, and aimed at pulling together the widest possible spectrum of people. With remarkable deftness he attacks environmental shortsightedness while appealing for cooperation to both the self-interest and values of groups heretofore indifferent to the ecology/population crisis or unfriendly to serious efforts to slow or halt population growth. Gore's book ought to be read by everyone.

— Edd Doerr

The Population Explosion, by Paul R. Ehrlich and Anne H. Ehrlich, Simon and Schuster, 320 pp., $18.95.

Our planet's steadily growing human population, now at 5.3 billion, has become too large for nature to sustain at decent living standard levels for all. Increasing consumption of nonrenewable resources, coupled with overuse, misuse, and waste of nonrenewable resources, clearly threatens the future of civilization. The Ehrlichs, eminent scientists both, spell out the details of this overarching problem in this very readable and convincing book. They show that halting population growth and bringing world consumption into line with the carrying capacity of our world environment is imperative, that time is running out much more rapidly than most people think, and that we must either control our numbers and our resource consumption rationally, humanely, and fairly or nature will do it for us brutally and nastily.

The authors score the Vatican's position on birth control and challenge the do-nothing population-environment policies of the Reagan and Bush administrations.

Harvard biologist, and ARL advisor, E.O. Wilson calls this book "a primer of the global environmental crisis (and what to do about it!) that I can recommend to all."

— Edd Doerr

Abortion and Divorce in Western Law: American Failures, *European Challenges,* by Mary Ann Glendon, Harvard University Press, $10.95, 197 pp.

Harvard law professor Glendon's book is a strange mix of good and bad. Her factual data on U.S. and Western European abortion and divorce law are most useful, as is her discussion of the failure of U.S. family law to provide as adequately for children and the poor as Western European laws. Where she is wildly wrongheaded is in her prescription for American abortion law, aired not only in this book but also on Bill Moyers' TV show and in *The New Republic.* Glendon blasts the U.S. Supreme Court for recognizing a constitutional right to freedom of conscience on abortion, preferring instead the European way of regarding abortion as a matter for legislative compromise and of legislatively-conferred privilege, which can be taken away or modified. Glendon suffers from a severe case of legal tunnel vision. She shows no understanding of American poll findings, neglects to mention the significance of Italy's abortion referendum, overlooks what science and history have to say about the controversy, totally ignores the church-state and religious liberty angles, cites European compromise legislation without describing how or why the compromises were arrived at, confuses morality with legality, and betrays no hint that she knows anything about the women's rights movement. Though her book was published before the Supreme Court's 1989 *Webster* ruling, Glendon clearly prefers the Borkian, moral majoritarian "solution" of allowing each state to inhibit the fundamental right to reproductive choice as its male-dominated legislature sees fit, even though this would mean that a woman's rights could change radically each time she crosses a state line.

With "friends" like Glendon, women need no enemies.

— Edd Doerr

Civil Religion and the Presidency, by Richard V. Pierard and Robert D. Linder, Zondervan Publishing House, 359 pp., $10.95.

Two of America's leading scholars of civil religion have performed a valuable service for informed Americans by describing how the civil religion of the American experience both reinforces and conflicts with the personal religions held by many of our citizens. The authors begin by building their definition of civil religion as a kind of transcendent public or civic religion rooted in Christianity but distinct from it. They say, "Historically speaking the Presidency has been intimately linked with civil religion, and this has bonded the Presidency to religious Americans. The very uniqueness of the American political arrangement demands this. The First Amendment to the Constitution guarantees religious freedom and forbids the establishment of any church or religion in the United States. The result is a strict separation of the institutions of church and state but not of religion and politics as such. Americans have always been a fundamentally religious people and this extends to every level of life including politics."

Pierard and Linder also note that the Presidency occupies a special place in American life that has almost a high priestly role and consequently the religious views of presidential candidates have always intrigued a percentage of American voters and have been considered important political issues. The authors also maintain that "the connection between religion and the Presidency has intensified in recent times, beginning with the Eisenhower administration."

Most of the book concentrates on detailed and very impressive study of the religious views of Washington, Lincoln, McKinley, Wilson, Franklin Roosevelt, Eisenhower, Nixon, Carter, and Reagan. Each president approached religion in a unique way and helped to add his own perspective to civil religion. The authors also suggest that the phenomenon will undoubtedly continue into the future. They say that there are certain inherent tensions in American society between civil faith and particular religious expressions and they criticize in many respects the concept of the president as high priest, while recognizing that it is likely to continue. They warn about the dangers of civil religion in a passage that is worth heeding, "The civil religion reading of American history with its emphasis on 'special providence' and the 'chosen nation' have done untold mischief, as it served first to justify the destruction of the indigenous Indian culture and then foreign intervention, war, and the imposition of American values, institutions, and commercial enterprises on other peoples. . . . Moreover, Christians must recognize that the beliefs of American civil religion are not those of Christianity but of another faith. In fact, civil religion comes dangerously close to blasphemy when it identifies God with the national destiny and in essence reduces the universal God of the Bible to the tribal God of America."

—Al Menendez

The Naked Public Square: Religion and Democracy in America, by Richard John Neuhaus, William B. Eerdmans Publishing Company, 280 pp., $16.95.

There isn't much to rely on in this ponderous work by an eminent Lutheran cleric.

The title, with its inept but spicy metaphor, is a come-on, as the author virtually admits. That public square isn't naked—it is a cluttered, teeming, bumper-stickered place ("Jesus Saves," for example, vying with "The Moral Majority is Neither"). Close by are chaplains, politicians and judges invoking the deity and uttering semi-official pieties.

What is Neuhaus's beef? It is that the pieties aren't fully official. He wants legal recognition, sanction, and support of Christian public morality, and embraces Jerry Falwell as prophet, though from time to time he complains of Falwell's "vulgarities," excesses, and steamroller tactics.

Neuhaus gives mere lip service to democratic principle. He insists on majority rule precisely in the area where it should not apply—over the individual's mind, conscientious beliefs, and personal way of life. With the crudest demagogues, he prates that freedom "of" does not mean freedom "from" religion—clearly implying that unbelievers cannot escape the pressure of their neighbors, backed by the state. Yet, ironically, Neuhaus occasionally expresses impatience with the tyranny of polls and the "trendy," orally bankrupt policies they encourage.

Rote recitation forms of obeisance are cited as democratic models. Neuhaus says the Ten Commandments are an "obvious example" of public morality which it would be unthinkable to do without. Well, if we look deeply into American thought and practice—which Neuhaus professes to do—we will find a pioneer religious liberty champion, Roger Williams, expelled from Massachusetts in 1635 for "dangerous opinions" bearing on this very point. Williams had been preaching, among other things, that the Commandments (particularly, the first four) should not be regarded as part of the Bay colony's criminal code because one's duty to God was not enforceable by civil power. In exile, Williams founded Rhode Island and aimed it in the direction of separation of church and state. Today we may hear Williams turning over in his grave at news of the Supreme Court's 1984 ruling (5 to 4) in the Pawtucket crèche case, in which the Court managed to completely ignore the views of Rhode Island's founder. Neuhaus does mention Williams, as well as Paine, Jefferson and Madison, but always obliquely and condescendingly.

Theory aside, Neuhaus is way off-base in pretending that Christian public morality is a proven, practical bulwark against totalitarianism. He cites fascism, Nazism and communism but fails to acknowledge that Mussolini, Hitler, and Lenin took power in countries long accustomed to state piety and Christian public morality – countries, in fact, where such practices as prayer and religious indoctrination in the schools were commonplace.

So selective is Neuhaus in handling the historical record that he describes Father Charles Coughlin as a pioneering electronic preacher who in the 1930s "had for a time considerable clout . . . until he broke with Roosevelt and tried to lead his radio millions into electoral politics under his own banner." No mention of Coughlin's fascistic doctrines or the riotous, Jew-baiting street corner meetings his Christian Front followers staged in large cities. Nor does Neuhaus mention Protestant counterparts of Coughlin such as the Revs. Gerald L.K. Smith and Gerold Winrod — or the cross-burning symbolism of the Ku Klux Klan.

Neuhaus is similarly cavalier in his treatment of the few court rulings he cares to discuss. A "we are a Christian people" observation in a 1931 ruling in a Supreme Court conscientious objector case *(U.S. v. Macintosh)* is dredged up without regard to the 1946 ruling *(Girouard v. U.S.)* which overturned it. Understandably, Neuhaus does not deal at all with the embarrassing experience of Justice David J. Brewer, who in an 1893 *(Holy Trinity v. U.S.) obiter dictum* took the theocratic line only to find himself later obliged to publish a book *(The United States A Christian Nation)* explaining away the misconceptions to which his ill-considered observations had given rise.

Political cartoonists have lately enjoyed drawing the Supreme Court and Court buildings with crosses affixed to their tops. Don't laugh — any day, now, we may see construction crews pulling up to make this alteration, and it is hard to imagine Neuhaus objecting.

— Stan Lichtenstein

Chapter 7
ARL: Founders and History

ARL's founders, Edward L. Ericson and Sherwin T. Wine, contributed their reflections and observations about the organization and its history on three occasions in *VOR*.

ARL at 25

ARL's co-founders Edward L. Ericson and Rabbi Sherwin T. Wine reflect on our March 1982 founding and offer their insights on the role we continue to play in the world of 2007 and beyond.

ARL – A Job That's Just Begun

Twenty-five years after the organization of ARL, the situation is stark: The enemies of freedom of belief are steadily gaining ground. In the guise of promoting freedom of religious expression, respect for diversity of belief is disparaged or ignored.

A wearisome drumbeat of misinformation intones the claim that "freedom of religion does not mean freedom from religion." The corollary of that astonishing presumption is the pretension that what I propose to promote as religion is constitutionally privileged, while your differing opinion has no constitutional standing.

A variation of this claim asserts that the First Amendment was intended to protect religion from the state, but was never meant to insulate the state from religion. The two-pronged provision of the Amendment refutes that claim: "Congress shall make no law respecting an establishment of religion, or prohibiting the free exercise thereof." To be consistent with that doctrine, both requirements must be met. Neither promotion nor prohibition can be countenanced. (Justice Hugo Black liked to remind the Court that "no law means no law!")

Under cover of such specious arguments as the religious zealots make, the separation of church and state – so explicitly defined in the language of the Amendment quoted above – is so poorly grasped (often deliberately, one must conclude) that even the late Chief Justice Rehnquist purported to believe that the constitutional principle of church-state separation was a "myth."

As a result of a decades-long endeavor of obfuscation and deceit, millions of our fellow citizens have come to disbelieve that the Constitution means what it says. They suppose that we have gone "too far" in excluding "religion" from the courthouse and other public institutions, including public education. Both Federal and state constitutional prohibitions against using public revenues to advance religious indoctrination are waved aside as politicians cater to powerful sectarian lobbies. (For example, in my native state of Florida, our recent governor, Jeb

Bush, with the concurrence of a like-minded legislature, simply ignored Florida's Constitution, which forbids the use of state revenues to promote "directly or indirectly" sectarian enterprises. The result: Expenditure of state funds for church-basement "schools" where a fundamentalist reading of biblical texts supercedes science and history.)

For the past twenty-five years, *Voice of Reason* has documented hundreds of instances of gross denial of a liberty that every American has a constitutional right to enjoy. We—and millions of others—have stood up in defense of our freedom.

For those of us who founded Americans for Religious Liberty a quarter-century ago, the grim flow of events holds one stunningly bright recompense. We know now that our mission was not only worthwhile; it was—and is—absolutely essential, if future generations are to enjoy liberty of conscience, an atmosphere where science is unshackled, the mind is free and reason prevails. The would-be theocrats continue to gain ground, but we must counter their thrusts inch by inch. As their claims become more extravagant and unjust, and their hubris expands, they will surely overreach, and fall. Vigilant people, we among them, can help make that happen.

—*Edward L. Ericson*

Voice of Reason

Twenty-five years ago Americans for Religious Liberty was established to oppose the political agenda of the Religious Right. Jerry Falwell had created the Moral Majority. The Republican Party had embraced Jerry Falwell. A powerful new political "army" had emerged to bend the government of the United States to its will. The separation of religion and government was in grave danger.

Over the last twenty-five years the marriage between the Religious Right and the Republicans has grown more intense. During the past six years, with the active support of the Bush administration, the political agenda of the Christian fundamentalists has been aggressively promoted. Partisans of the Religious Right have been appointed to important government jobs. Defenders of the religious presence in government now fill the judiciary. Federal money has been given to religious organizations for religious programs. Military institutions are promoting Christian fundamentalism.

The Religious Right is no longer new. But political success has emboldened it. The presidential election of 2004 revealed that "values" is a primary issue in the minds of millions of voters. It was the issue that gave victory to President Bush despite the disaster in Iraq. Millions of poor people voted Republican because they were appalled by the prospect of gay marriage. The "culture war" is an ongoing battle promoted by the leaders of conservative religion.

The election of 2006 was a "blow" to the Religious Right. The Republican loss of the House and the Senate was traumatic. The Republican Party is on the defensive. Many of its former supporters, angry about the management of the war in Iraq, turned against the President and the Party. While many Republicans have soured on the alliance with the Religious Right, others see the fundamentalists as the one remaining force that can rescue them from defeat in 2008. "Values" would again be revived as a central issue.

The Democratic victory in November has given us hope. The stem cell controversy is also another source of hope. The fundamentalist assault on science has backfired. Questioning or denying evolution is not an important issue for most Americans. But undermining the possibility of medicine to restore health and to promote human survival *is* an important issue. Vetoing embryonic stem cell research is not supported by a majority of American people. The fundamentalists may have pushed the wrong button. Denying science the freedom to do its healing work is only attractive to a fanatic minority.

The work of Americans for Religious Liberty and its courageous leader Edd Doerr has never been more necessary. The threat of the Religious Right is still ominous. The defense of the secular state is one of the foundations of a society of freedom and dignity. And I remain proud of my connection to the history of ARL.

— Sherwin T. Wine

ARL's First Twenty-Five Years: Some Highlights

1982

Americans for Religious Liberty was founded in the spring of 1982 when the leaders of its two predecessor organizations, the Voice of Reason and the Center for Moral Democracy, agreed to a merger. The Voice of Reason had been founded in 1981 in Michigan by Rabbi Sherwin T. Wine, Lynne Silverberg-Master, and others in response to the upsurge of political fundamentalism championed by televangelist Jerry Falwell and others. The Center for Moral Democracy was started around the same time in New York by Edward L. Ericson, leader of the New York Society for Ethical Culture, the Rev. Bruce Southworth, minister of Community Church (Unitarian Universalist) in New York, and others. Because of their similarity, the two groups were enthusiastic about combining.

The birth of ARL was marked by a National Summit Conference on Religious Freedom and the Secular State in New York in March. Featured speakers included Sherwin Wine, Edward Ericson, writer Isaac Asimov, Biblical archaeology professor Gerald Larue, ACLU attorney Arthur Eisenberg, American Ethical Union director Jean Kotkin, Unitarian Universalist Association board member Donald Field, biologist Ernst Mayr, and former *Church & State* magazine editor Edd Doerr, who was named executive director of the new organization. Lynne Silverberg-Master became president.

• ARL executive director Edd Doerr (and Catholics for a Free Choice executive director Frances Kissling) testified at the Senate Judiciary Committee hearings in opposition to the nomination of Robert Destro to the U.S. Commission on Civil Rights.

1983

• ARL's board voted to change the organization's name from the original Voice of Reason to Americans for Religious Liberty.

• Cleveland attorney and church-state activist Anne Lindsay was elected president, succeeding Lynne Silverberg-Master.

• ARL was a co-sponsor of the ACLU's 1983 Bill of Rights Lobby Conference and *Free Inquiry* magazine's James Madison conference.

1984

• ARL joined amicus curiae briefs to the Supreme Court in two important church-state cases, *Grand Rapids v. Ball* (tax aid to church schools) and *Wallace v. Jaffree* (school prayer).

• Maury Abraham joined the ARL staff. He was the main organizer of a March 5 rally at the U.S. Capitol opposing President Reagan's proposed school prayer amendment.

1985

• Ethicist, author, civil libertarian, and peace activist John M. Swomley was elected president of ARL.

• *ARL* joined other organizations in *amicus curiae* briefs to the Supreme Court in abortion rights, "equal access," and tax aid to religious colleges cases.

1986

• ARL and the Anti-Defamation League filed an *amicus* brief to the Supreme Court in the Louisiana creationism case. ARL's Doerr originated the strategy of having Nobel science laureates sign an *amicus* brief in the creationism case.

1987

• ARL and 33 other religious and civil liberties groups filed suit in federal court in New York challenging federal and state aid to sectarian private education. The suit, *PEARL v. Secretary of Education,* challenged remedial services and related programs under Chapter 1 of the 1965 Elementary and Secondary Education Act. It also targeted the constitutionality of a New York statute providing publicly-funded vans and neutral-site leasing, as well as Chapter 2 funds for computer software, audiovisual equipment, library materials and supplies for use on the premises of religious schools.

• ARL opposed the nomination of Judge Robert Bork to the U.S. Supreme Court on the grounds that his confirmation "would seriously endanger the liberties of Americans well into the next century." Doerr made 30 appearances on radio, television, and before audiences speaking on the Bork nomination.

• ARL sponsored the first interdisciplinary conference on the scientific, ethical and legal aspects of fetal personhood and the abortion rights issue. The conference attracted nationally distinguished scientists, ethicists, and theologians.

1988

• ARL and national ACLU filed suit on February 1 challenging the constitutionality of a congressional appropriation of funds for religious schools in France, Egypt, Indonesia, Israel and the Philippines. The suit, *Lamont v. Shultz*, was filed in federal district court in New York.

1989

• ARL filed an *amicus* brief in the U.S. Supreme Court in *Webster v. Reproductive Health Services,* a case challenging a Missouri law which barred all public funding of abortions, banned privately paid abortions in public hospitals, prohibited publicly paid health care professionals and counselors from providing information to clients, and defined human life as beginning at conception. The ARL brief, signed by 167 distinguished scientists, including 12 Nobel laureates, was praised by NOW as the strongest brief filed in the case.

• ARL co-sponsored the April 9 "March for Women's Lives" on the Mall in Washington, DC.

1990

• ARL joined with more than 50 medical, women's, religious and other groups in an *amicus* brief to the U.S. Supreme Court in *Rust v. Sullivan*, which involved the Reagan administration's 1988 cutoff of federal aid to family planning and reproductive health services.

• ARL joined with the National Coalition for Public Education and Religious Liberty in *Pulido v. Cavasos*, a Missouri case on appeal to a federal court. The case involved the distribution of federal remedial services to faith-based schools. ARL also joined in a National PEARL *amicus* brief in the *Helms v. Cody* case in Louisiana. The case involved federal and state aid to faith-based schools.

• ARL joined the state coalition opposing a tuition tax credit scheme to aid private and parochial schools in Oregon. ARL also joined pro-choice groups in referendum elections involving freedom of choice in Nevada and Oregon. All three referenda were on the ballot in November 1990.

• ARL supported a federal court challenge to the Boy Scouts of America, involving charges of religious discrimination against nontheists, in *Welsh v. BSA*.

1991

• ARL and five Nashville taxpayers challenged the constitutionality of $15 million in tax exempt bonds for construction at a pervasively sectarian college. The suit, *Steele v. Industrial Development Board*, was filed in federal district court in Nashville. The college involved was David Lipscomb University, affiliated with the fundamentalist Churches of Christ.

• ARL participated in the coalition in Washington State to guarantee freedom of conscience in the abortion rights controversy.

• ARL filed an *amicus* brief with the U.S. Supreme Court in *Lee v. Weisman*, a public school graduation prayer case from Rhode Island. The ARL brief, prepared by General Counsel Ronald A. Lindsay, argued that government sponsorship of invocations tends to degrade religion and violates the Establishment Clause of the First Amendment.

• ARL worked closely with the anti-voucher coalition in Pennsylvania, where the State House of Representatives rejected a $300 million voucher plan for private and parochial schools.

• The U.S. Second Circuit Court of Appeals ruled in favor of the ARL/ACLU challenge to distribution of U.S. Agency for International Development funds for sectarian schools overseas. The case, renamed *Lamont v. Woods*, held that the $14 million grants to Jewish and Catholic schools in Egypt, Israel, Jamaica, the Philippines, Micronesia and South Korea were unconstitutional.

1992

• ARL joined a broad coalition of mainstream groups, the Coalition for the Free Exercise of Religion, in supporting the Religious Freedom Restoration Act (RFRA). RFRA's main purpose was to redress the balance against free exercise of religious belief and practice which an increasingly conservative Supreme Court enunciated in the 1990 *Employment Division v. Smith* case.

1993

• ARL and several teachers' groups helped to block a proposed voucher pilot program in Maryland. Executive director Doerr testified against the measure at both House and Senate hearings in Annapolis.

• ARL joined the California coalition to oppose vouchers in a November 1993 referendum election.

• ARL and Minnesota ACLU filed suit to stop a shared time program aiding parochial schools in St. Paul. The state court suit was *Stark et al. v. St. Paul Public Schools.*

• ARL opposed the naming of Raymond Flynn as U.S. ambassador to the Vatican (Holy See), though the U.S. Senate declined to allow testimony from groups opposed to the diplomatic connection inaugurated by President Reagan in 1984 as a violation of the Constitution.

• ARL joined in an *amicus* brief to a California appellate court, challenging a 1987 state law which removed abortion and pregnancy-related care from the category of "necessary medical care" for minors. The case, *American Academy of Pediatrics v. Lundgren*, was supported by many religious, feminist, and civil libertarian groups.

1994

• ARL joined with People For the American Way, RCAR, the Anti-Defamation League, and the American Jewish Congress in an *amicus* brief to the U.S. Supreme Court in *Madsen v. Women's Health Center,* a case involving access to family planning clinics.

• ARL filed a brief with the U.S. Supreme Court in *Board of Education of Kiryas Joel v. Grumet*, a challenge to a New York State law creating a school district for the exclusive use and under the control of one religious group.

• ARL signed a national statement, "A Shared Vision: Religious Liberty in the 21st Century," issued by more than 80 individuals and organizations. It affirms the importance of individual freedom of conscience, affirms the constitutional principle of church-state separation, and stresses the importance of religious neutrality in public education.

• ARL joined with National PEARL, a coalition of educational and civil liberties groups, in an amicus brief to the Fifth U.S. Circuit Court of Appeals in a school prayer case from Mississippi, *Ingebretsen v. Jackson Public School District.*

1995

• ARL and 35 other national organizations issued a comprehensive statement, "Religion in the Public Schools: A Joint Statement of Current Law," to advise public school districts of the legal standards surrounding the issue. The statement warned politicians and policymakers that "tampering with our basic religious liberty safeguards is a dangerous and divisive cause of action."

• ARL joined with Zero Population Growth and other organizations in supporting the programs endorsed by the U.N. Conference on Population and Development, held in Cairo.

• Research director Albert Menendez was named associate director of ARL at the April board meeting.

1996

• ARL participated in a Washington State coalition against a voucher referendum. The voters rejected vouchers.

1997

• ARL filed an *amicus* brief with the U.S. Supreme Court in the rehearing of *Aguilar v. Felton*, a 1985 case ruling that sending tax paid teachers into sectarian private schools was unconstitutional. ARL joined the Council on Religious Freedom's brief.

• ARL reprinted Indiana State University historian Richard V. Pierard's article, "Vouchers: The Wrong Medicine for the Ills of Public Education," and distributed them to every member of Congress.

1998

• Doerr presented a statement to the U.S. Commission on Civil Rights in connection with a hearing on religion and public education. He warned against proselytizing in public schools and about the difficulties of teaching adequately and fairly about religion in religiously pluralistic schools.

• ARL joined coalitions to defeat a tuition tax credit scheme for the support of nonpublic schools in Colorado and in opposition to a ban on late-term abortions in Washington State.

1999

• ARL joined the Minnesota Civil Liberties Union and other groups in an *amicus* brief to the Eighth Circuit Court of Appeals in a challenge to Medicare/Medicaid funding of "religious non-medical health care institutions." The suit sought to halt $50 million in federal tax support for Christian Science facilities. ARL also filed an *amicus* brief in conjunction with other organizations in *CHILD v. Vladeck*, a case challenging 1997 federal regulations creating and defining "religious nonmedical health care institutions." The brief was filed in the Eighth Circuit Court of Appeals.

• ARL joined Catholics for a Free Choice and 67 other organizations from around the world in a petition to the U.N. requesting a review of the Holy See's Non-Member Permanent Observer stratus. The campaign asserts that the U.N. special status gives preferential treatment to one religion and interferes with progress on women's rights and health.

• ARL joined the PEARL *amicus* brief in the *Mitchell v. Helms* case, involving aid to faith-based schools, before the U.S. Supreme Court.

2000

• ARL asked the U.S. House of Representatives to reject the nomination of the Rev. James Wright to be the House Chaplain. In a letter to every House member, ARL President John Swomley said the selection process was "deeply flawed and ...violated Article VI of the U.S. Constitution, which bans religious tests for public office."

• ARL worked with coalitions in California and Michigan to defeat school voucher ballot initiatives.

2001

• In a letter to President George W. Bush, ARL asked his "assurance that you will not tolerate religious discrimination in any programs funded with taxpayer dollars." ARL opposed the administration's "Community Solutions Act," the so-called faith-based initiative, as potentially unconstitutional. ARL joined with religious and civil liberties groups in opposing HR 7, the administration's "Community Solutions Act," which included substantial public money for church-related organizations.

• ARL joined more than 150 civic, labor, civil liberties, religious and other groups on September 20 in a declaration, "In Defense of Freedom," urging the U.S. government to preserve civil liberties and constitutional rights in its response to the terrorist attacks on our country.

• ARL joined an *amicus* brief filed by the National Committee for Public Education and Religious Liberty (PEARL) with the U.S. Supreme Court, supporting the Sixth Circuit Court ruling against the Ohio school voucher scheme.

• ARL filed a brief before the U.S. Court of Appeals for the Sixth Circuit in a case, *Steele v. Industrial Development Board,* that involved public aid to a "pervasively sectarian" college in Tennessee. The Court ruled two-to-one against the church-state separation position, and the case was appealed to the U.S. Supreme Court.

• ARL and other organizations in PEARL (the National Committee for Public Education and Religious Liberty) filed an amicus brief with the U.S. Supreme Court in the Cleveland voucher case (*Simmons-Harris v. Zelman*).

2002

• A New ARL board of directors was elected in February, with constitutional law Professor Burton Caine as chair. Doerr's title was changed from executive director to president.

• ARL filed an *amicus curiae* brief in the Third Circuit U.S. Court of Appeals in a case challenging the constitutionality of a Ten Commandments plaque at the Chester County, Pennsylvania, courthouse.

• ARL joined two dozen other religious and civil liberties groups that urged the state of Nevada to adopt a Religious Freedom Act which strengthens and ensures that the state constitution's free exercise clause is protected.

2003

• Edd Doerr was the featured speaker at a meeting of the Woman's National Democratic Club in December.

• ARL filed an *amicus curiae* brief with the U.S. Third Circuit Court of Appeals, urging affirmation of the district court ruling in *Freethought Society v. Chester County.* That ruling enjoined the removal of the Ten Commandments plaque from the Chester County Courthouse. The ARL brief was written by professor Burton Caine of Temple University School of Law and chair of the ARL Board of Directors.

• Veteran White House journalist Helen Thomas was the recipient of the 2003 Religious Liberty Award presented by ARL. She was cited for "her distinguished career in journalism and her devotion to religious freedom and church-state separation."

• ARL joined 40 other civil liberties, religious and educational groups in urging Congress to reject a $10 million voucher appropriation for the District of Columbia.

2004

• ACLU president Nadine Strossen was the recipient of the 2004 ARL Religious Liberty Award. She was cited for her many contributions as a "champion of civil liberties and religious freedom," for her work on behalf of "the struggle for human dignity" and in recognition of her and the ACLU's "decades of work and leadership in defense of civil liberties, religious freedom, and church-state separation."

2005

• ARL expands and improves its web site, www.arlinc.org, to include a wide range of information and analysis.

• *Voice of Reason,* ARL's quarterly newsletter, becomes a journal and expands its size and coverage.

• ARL joins several Jewish groups in an *amicus curiae* brief to the U.S. Supreme Court in *Van Orden v. Perry,* a Ten Commandments case from Texas.

• ARL joins a Baptist Joint Committee *amicus* brief to the Florida Supreme Court urging it to uphold a lower court ban on the state's voucher program.

• In other *amicus* briefs, ARL supported Oregon's physician-assisted suicide law. (*Gonzales v. Oregon*), free exercise of religion for prisoners (*Cutter v. Wilkinson*) and religious free exercise (*Gonzales v. O Centro Espirito*).

• Edd Doerr addressed the New York Society for Ethical Culture in May and Al Menendez spoke to the National Education Association's annual conference in Los Angeles in June. The texts of both speeches are available on ARL's website.

2006

• *Voice of Reason* is redesigned to include more news and analysis.

• ARL signs on to an *amicus* brief in a Missouri Supreme Court case, *Planned Parenthood v. Nixon*, involving reproductive rights and freedom of speech.

• ARL joins with 50 other groups in releasing a public statement, "The Truth About Vouchers," summarizing flaws in the voucher movement and its threat to public education.

• ARL signed an *amicus* brief in *Gonzales v. Carhart* and *Gonzales v. Planned Parenthood*, urging the Supreme Court to uphold freedom of conscience in reproductive health matters.

The ARL Bookshelf

During the past quarter century, ARL has produced more than two dozen books and monographs on vital church-state issues. Here they are, in chronological order:

1988

• Edd Doerr's *Religious Liberty in Crisis,* an introduction to the major church-state issues of the day, was ARL's first book.

1989

• *Abortion Rights and Fetal Personhood*, edited by Edd Doerr and James Prescott, included a collection of addresses from the ARL conference on abortion rights that refuted the unscientific claims propounded by some anti-choice activists.

1991

• *The Great Quotations on Religious Freedom,* edited by Edd Doerr and Albert J. Menendez, included 561 quotations that covered the full range of history and U.S. Supreme Court decisions.

• *Church Schools and Public Money: The Politics of Parochiaid*, by Edd Doerr and Albert J. Menendez, thoroughly examined the campaign to get taxpayers to support nonpublic schools.

• *Religion and Public Education,* by Menendez and Doerr, focused on the problems involving religion in public schools. The comprehensive guide covered religious observances, course offerings in the curriculum, and included relevant court rulings on all aspects of the controversy.

1992

• Doerr and Menendez contributed a chapter on referendum elections and parochial school aid in *Why We Still Need Public Schools: Church-State Relations* and *Visions of Democracy,* published by Prometheus Books and edited by Art Must.

• *Visions of Reality: What Fundamentalist Schools Teach,* by Albert J. Menendez, examined religious, racial, cultural and political bias in many fundamentalist private schools that would be eligible for voucher aid under national Republican proposals.

1993

• *The December Wars: Religious Symbols and Ceremonies in the Public Square,* by Albert J. Menendez, issued by Prometheus Books, surveyed the history of Christmas and Hanukkah controversies throughout history and showed how the conflicts fit in the larger context of church-state relations.

• *Catholic Schools: The Facts,* by Edd Doerr, was a realistic, contemporary portrait of the nation's largest private school system based on official church data.

• *Abortion Rights at the Polls,* by Albert J. Menendez, reviewed the 1992 abortion rights referendum in Maryland, showing how political, economic, educational and religious influences intersect on the abortion issue.

• *Religious Liberty and State Constitutions,* compiled all state constitutional provisions dealing with religion, and was edited by Doerr and Menendez.

1994

• *Abortion and Public Policy*, by John Swomley, defended of freedom of conscience in the sensitive area of medicine, ethics and religion. *Religious Political Parties*, also by Swomley, warned against the dangers of religion-based political movements. An appendix to the book by research director Menendez surveyed religious political parties from Afghanistan to Venezuela.

1995

• *The Case Against School Vouchers* (Prometheus Books) was a comprehensive hard-hitting analysis of voucher plans, written by Doerr, Menendez and Swomley.

1996

• *Myths About Public School Prayer,* by John Swomley, explored and examined the misinformation purveyed by prayer amendment backers.

• Associate director Menendez published two books on national politics, both of which explored religious influences on recent elections. Published by Prometheus Books were *Evangelicals at the Ballot Box* and *The Perot Voters and the Future of American Politics.*

• *Public Education and the Public Good,* by Robert S. Alley, defended a free, democratically-controlled system of public schools, while *The Religious Right in Michigan Politics,* by Russ Bellant, documented the increasing domination of Michigan's politics, especially its Republican Party, by extreme right-wing fundamentalists. ARL published both.

• *Church and State in Canada,* by Albert J. Menendez, was published by Prometheus Books, which also issued a trade edition of *The Case Against School Vouchers.*

• *Home Schooling: The Facts*, by Albert J. Menendez, critically examined the growing phenomenon.

1997

• *Confronting Church and State: Memoirs of an Activist,* by John Swomley, recounted the ARL president's more than fifty year career crusading for world peace, civil liberties and religious freedom.

• *Three Voices of Extremism,* by Albert J. Menendez, exposed three prominent exponents of the Religious Right, Charles Colson, James Dobson and D. James Kennedy.

• A monograph, *The Red Mass: A Fusion of Religion and Politics?,* by Menendez, considered the ongoing Roman Catholic Church practice of seeking to influence judicial and legislative leaders by invoking natural law arguments.

1998

• *Who Goes to Nonpublic Schools: A Study of U.S. Census Data,* by Albert J. Menendez, revealed that four factors (religious affiliation, high income, ethnic ancestry, and the racial profile of local public schools) were significantly correlated with high private school enrollment throughout the United States.

1999

• *Colorado 1998: Another Voter Defeat for School Vouchers,* by Albert J. Menendez, analyzed the 1998 tuition tax credit/voucher referendum.

• Edd Doerr's *Vox Populi: Letters to the Editor,* was a collection of recently published letters on church-state issues.

• *Compulsory Pregnancy: The War Against American Women,* by John Swomley, was an anthology of articles on abortion rights and reproductive freedom.

2000

• ARL published an updated version of Doerr's *Catholic Schools: The Facts.*

2001

• *The Case Against Charitable Choice: Why President Bush's Faith-Based Initiative is Bad Public Policy,* by Menendez and Doerr, pointed out the flaws in the Bush policy.

2002

• A revised, updated and greatly enlarged edition of *Great Quotations on Religious Freedom* by Menendez and Doerr was published by Prometheus Books. More than 700 quotations on various aspects of religious liberty and separation of church and state are included.

2006

• *Here I Stand,* by Edd Doerr, ARL's most recent book, is a collection of essays, speeches, magazine articles, letters to the editor and book reviews celebrating freedom of conscience and the principle of church-state separation.

ARL staffers have also published numerous articles in magazines and newspapers, and have contributed chapters to several book-length anthologies.

Special Feature

As ARL passed its first twenty years, we solicited these reflections from our two founders.

Sherwin T. Wine

Americans for Religious Liberty came into existence 24 years ago in response to the emerging danger of the Religious Right. Jerry Falwell was trumpeting his hatred of "Secular Humanists." The prophets of the Moral Majority were mobilizing the social conservatives. The Republican Party, under Ronald Reagan, was embracing the Christian fundamentalists. A new political force had arisen in America to threaten our freedom and to subvert the separation of religion from government.

The social conservatives had been around for a long time. They had their strongest bases in the white Protestant south and in the wing of the Roman Catholic Church that rejected Vatican Council II. Most of its advocates had been veteran voters for the Democratic Party, either because they were white southerners or because they were part of the Catholic working class. But Communism and the Black Liberation Movement had turned them from an amorphous mass into a self-aware constituency. The life style revolutions of the sixties—feminist and sexual —had only reinforced their anxieties. They were ready for "war" with the enemy.

The Religious Right had been transformed by an ambitious leadership. Church services were turned into political rallies. Radio stations were purchased and converted into propaganda machines for the fundamentalist message. School boards were infiltrated and changed into agents for the conservative religious agenda. Republican candidates for public office were inundated with promises of support. The American political arena was radically altered.

Both The Voice of Reason in Michigan and The Center for Moral Democracy in New York arose to confront this formidable threat to a free society. Creationists, anti-abortionists and censorship advocates suddenly appeared as armies of protestors. "Secular Humanist" and "Liberal" became pejorative terms in their mouths. A sense of aggressive triumphalism filled them with energy. The merger of the Michigan and New York resistance into Americans for Religious Liberty was inevitable in the face of this remarkable foe.

The discipline and ambition of the Religious Right has been unyielding since that time. The Republican Party is now under the control of the social conservatives and their southern white leadership. Missionaries of Christian fundamentalism have taken over the allegiance of millions of poor patriotic people form the heartland of America and have infiltrated the ranks of poor non-whites, especially Hispanics, to create an odd alliance of the rich and the poor. The befuddled Democrats have difficulty understanding that economics may not be the primary issue for most Americans. Values and culture are.

The re-election of George W. Bush reawakened all the fears that motivated our activism in 1980. A fundamentalist president with a fundamentalist constituency has been reconfirmed in power. The guarantors of freedom, from the Congress to the Supreme Court, are now being prepared for a major transformation. The foundations of the secular state are now being readied for assault. Victory has given the Bush devotees a new lease on determination and optimism.

As in 1980 — but, even more so — the organized resistance to the Religious Right and its Republican prophets is urgent. Americans for Religious Liberty, like all the other resisters to fundamentalist tyranny, is a moral necessity. The enemy is strong and dangerous — but not invincible.

Edward L. Ericson

Today an administration sits in Washington that is determined to rip apart the social fabric of American democracy. The reigning power-holders hate dissent and have made a science of manipulating public opinion. They demonize the secular state that alone makes religious equality and free expression possible.

Without the inclusion of a deeply imbedded bloc of crusading religious zealots, Mr. Bush's regime would not be in power—and they know it. To keep their partisans in line, the administration—by presidential fiat—diverts billions of dollars of public funds into the coffers of so-called "faith-based" programs.

Cynical politicians of the Right care little about religion, but much about the exploitation of "faith." As an astute observer has remarked, Mr. Bush has never served any interest other than that of his privileged class. If "patriotism" hypes fervor for an extremist agenda, he will invoke it. If piety stifles debate, he will support it.

To get people to act against their interest requires guile and indirection. Thus, tax supported "faith-based" giveaways.

Many well-meaning citizens see no harm in an innocuous public graduation prayer, or—to slide further down the slippery slope—to drop a few million into the pocket of your friendly neighborhood con-man (for charity's sake, of course)! The result is a perfect formula for long-term one-party rule, the time-honored fusion of Cross and Crown.

When more than 20 years ago, Rabbi Sherwin Wine and I sat down to consider the organizational merger that created Americans for Religious Liberty, we knew that the country was headed in the wrong direction. We knew also that the fight would be long and desperate.

In the 1980 election the Radical Religious Right had demonstrated its ruthlessness and effectiveness. By using sophisticated voter profiles and extensive direct mailing lists, aided by thousands of foot soldiers in fundamentalist churches, the Rightists came in "under the radar" and purged candidates from the presidency and Congress to local school boards.

But even in the aftermath of 1980, few foresaw how seriously this juggernaut would maim the political process and install the permanent reaction that now looms before us.

ARL's mission remains the same: To uphold the secular basis of democratic government, to defend religious and philosophical freedom, and to safeguard the future of church-state separation that makes such freedom possible. Liberty-loving citizens must take a page from our opponents' manual: Organize! Organize! Organize!

We must reach every ear that can hear, open every eye that can see, and awaken every mind that can think.

ARL needs to be there—with you!

ARL at Fifteen

Founded in the spring of 1982, Americans for Religious Liberty is completing its fifteenth year of work on behalf of religious freedom, church-state separation, and the constitutional ideal of secular democracy. ARL was formed by the merger of two organizations begun the previous year in response to the rise of Religious Right political groups. The predecessor organizations were the Center for Moral Democracy, founded by Ethical Society leader Edward L. Ericson, Unitarian Universalist minister Bruce Southworth, and others, and Voice of Reason, founded by Rabbi Sherwin T. Wine and others.

From the beginning ARL's goals included defending the religious neutrality of public education, strengthening church-state separation, heading off efforts to divert public funds to sectarian private schools, and defending reproductive rights.

ARL's first president was Michigan educator Lynne Silverberg-Master, followed by Ohio attorney Anne Lindsay, and current president John M. Swomley, a noted civil liberties activist and professor emeritus of ethics at the St. Paul School of Theology in Kansas City. Edd Doerr, a former teacher with years of experience in the church-state field, was named executive director in 1982. ARL's staff has remained small. Maury Abraham, now an attorney, served on the staff for several years and is now a board member. Writer-researcher Albert J. Menendez joined the staff in 1990.

U.S. Senator Frank Church was among ARL's founders. At an early 1982 meeting of the organization in New York he warned against "any group which presents its program for political action wrapped in the pages of the Bible and the folds of the flag." Early on ARL attracted such supporters as science writer Isaac Asimov, evolutionary biologist Ernst Mayr, American Baptist minister Carl Flemister, women's rights advocate Harriet Pilpel, public education activist Florence Flast, and church-state expert Leo Pfeffer.

ARL has members in all 50 states and several Canadian provinces.

Even a brief account of ARL's activities over the past 15 years would require a great many pages, so we will try to merely summarize the high points.

ARL's work has encompassed research, publishing, education, media appearances and debates in all sorts of forums, litigation, coalition building, and providing information and assistance to attorneys, students, journalists, scholars and other organizations.

Following publication of Ed Ericson's 1982 book, *American Freedom and the Radical Right,* ARL has produced 23 additional books and studies, more than have been published by any similar organization. (See our book ad in this issue.) Eight titles have been published by Prometheus Books, a major east coast publisher, and three by Centerline Press in California. ARL's book *The Case Against School Vouchers,* by Doerr, Menendez, and Swomley, went through three printings by ARL before being issued in trade paperback by Prometheus. Articles by Swomley, Doerr, and Menendez have appeared in numerous periodicals.

ARL Board members, National Advisory Board members (living and deceased), and staff have published an aggregate of over 750 books.

ARL's president and staff have been guests on radio and TV talk and panel shows, and have spoken at meetings, conferences, universities, seminaries, churches, and synagogues throughout the U.S. and elsewhere.

In 1987 ARL sponsored the first interdisciplinary conference on fetal "personhood," brain development, and abortion rights, the papers for which were published in the book *Abortion Rights and Fetal "Personhood"* The conference and book, in turn, contributed to an important *amicus curiae* brief to the Supreme Court in 1989, signed by 12 Nobel laureates and 155 other scientists and physicians, in the *Webster v. Reproductive Health Services* case.

Earlier, ARL originated the idea of having Nobel laureates in science sign an *amicus* brief in *Edwards v. Aguillard,* the case that resulted in the 1987 Supreme Court ruling against teaching "creationism" in public school science classes.

ARL has been active in the courts, often in coalition lawsuits and *amicus curiae* briefs. ARL joined with the ACLU in a successful challenge, in *Lamont v. Baker,* to use of federal funds for support of sectarian schools in other countries. ARL is currently supporting a court challenge to an attempt to get government development bond assistance for a sectarian college in Tennessee, and has been involved with the National Committee for Public Education and Religious Liberty (PEARL) in a number of cases. ARL was involved in all three of the Supreme Court's major church-state cases in June of 1997.

In 1987 ARL opposed Robert Bork's nomination to the Supreme Court because of the nominee's unfriendliness toward church-state separation.

Over the years ARL has been involved in coalitions dealing with state referenda on parochial school aid and abortion rights in Massachusetts, Maryland, Michigan, Arkansas, Colorado, California, Oregon, and Washington State. Since the early 1990s ARL has been part of the broad coalition supporting the Religious Freedom Restoration Act, recently struck down by the Supreme Court. In 1995 ARL joined 35 religious and civil liberties organizations issuing the statement on "Religion in the Public Schools," which was the basis for President Clinton's speech on the subject in July of that year.

Throughout its fifteen years ARL has been in the forefront of the struggle to defend the Jeffersonian-Madisonian principle of separation of church and state.

ARL's First Ten Years

Americans for Religious Liberty completed its first ten years in March 1992. From its modest beginnings, it has grown to a membership of over 8,000 and has made an impact on the national scene well out of proportion to its small size. It has submitted important amicus curiae *briefs to the Supreme Court and is supporting federal court litigation challenging religious liberty and church-state separation violations. Its president and executive director have addressed audiences from coast to coast. In the last three years ARL has published four significant books covering the major current religious liberty problem areas. (An interesting bit of trivia—ARL's staff, board, and advisory board members have published an aggregate total of nearly 1,000 books and uncounted thousands of articles.)*

To mark ARL's tenth anniversary, its principal founders, Edward L. Ericson and Sherwin T. Wine, contributed the following articles.

Edward L. Ericson

The events that led to the birth of ARL read like a fictional adventure in serendipity. (Readers will recall that the word was coined by Walpole from a tale in which a series of remarkable chance encounters produces astonishing results.)

Two separate beginnings—in Michigan and New York—each unknown and unrelated to the other—led to the ultimate formation of ARL as it exists today. I took the initiative in New York City and Rabbi Sherwin Wine did similarly in Michigan Each of us contemplated a nationwide effort to defend secular democracy and the separation of church and state.

During the presidential campaign of 1980, I became increasingly concerned by the strident attacks of the Radical Right on religious diversity and the principles of secular public education. When that September, following summer recess, I opened the new season of the New York Society for Ethical Culture, where I served as Senior Leader, I announced my determination to organize a broadly-based grassroots movement to counter the New Right's political juggernaut.

At a Sunday meeting devoted to this challenge, a well-known Unitarian layman, Donald Field, chanced to be present and offered to help organize our fledgling effort, especially to involve Unitarian Universalists. The Rev. Carl Flemister, Executive Minister of the American Baptist Churches of Metropolitan New York—a respected black leader of an integrated denomination—also joined in. My friends Isaac Asimov and his wife Dr. Janet Jeppson were early and generous supporters.

Through his Unitarian Universalist connections, Don Field recruited Sen. Frank Church to be our principal speaker at a mass rally, held in February, 1981 at the Ethical Society Meetinghouse. More than 1600 people packed the main hall and wired lecture rooms of the Society, with hundreds of others turned away. Recently defeated for reelection by an anti-abortion crusade, Sen. Church warned us that the nation was in for a period of repressive legislation and hate-driven politics. Church readily consented to be the first name on our National Advisory Board and was an enthusiastic supporter until his death from cancer not long after.

As a result of these and other efforts, we were able to expand our network of concerned activists from the Atlantic states to California. Only then we chanced to learn that Rabbi Sherwin Wine and a supportive group in Michigan—during the same interval—were engaged in a virtually identical effort. Although Rabbi Wine and I had known each other in earlier years, neither of us knew of the other's undertaking. Once we discovered the coincidence, it was short work to agree that the two efforts should be merged. Americans for Religious Liberty is the outcome of that resolution.

But the crowning stroke of serendipity occurred at the very conference that united our endeavor. Edd Doerr—already recognized as one of the leading champions of church-state separation in the nation—stepped forward and volunteered to direct a fully professional national office in Washington Both Rabbi Wine and I had previously known and worked with Edd on public affairs issues. There was no question that his leadership would bring success and distinction to the new organization.

But our combined budget was sufficient only to cover printing costs and mailings, since all previous services had been rendered by volunteers. Despite this, Edd generously offered to accept the post of full-time executive director without compensation until such time as a salary could be gradually phased in. Without this devoted sacrifice by Edd, his wife, and their family, we would not today enjoy the dynamic national presence that ARL has attained. Our staff has been augmented by Edd's capable assistant Marie Gore and indefatigable researcher-writer Al Menendez.

As we look back upon the decade that has transpired since ARL's beginning, it is fully evident that the concern that motivated us to organize was fully justified. Two consecutive presidents have assiduously aided and abetted the Radical Right's social agenda. Piecemeal undermining of the First Amendment by crippling equivocation is required of judges to be considered for appointment to the Supreme Court. The lower courts – from which future Supreme Court justices will be selected – are being filled with right-wing ideologues who must pass the litmus tests of anti-abortion, school prayer, and Willy Horton jurisprudence. The Chief Justice, zealous pointman for the assault on First Amendment freedoms, has contemptuously shrugged off Jefferson's "wall of separation" between church and state as bad history and bad law. Justice Rehnquist obviously pretends never to have read Madison's historic *Memorial and Remonstrance Against Religious Assessments,* when he perversely claims "original intent" to justify breaching that wall.

Those who contended a decade ago that we were overreacting to the danger posed by the Extreme Right—and many in the liberal, moderate, and responsible conservative communities made that mistake—have been proved grievously, perilously wrong. The constitutional barbarians were even then at the gates. They now occupy the inner temple.

Those who love "freedom, tolerance, and diversity in moral, religious, and intellectual life"—the announced values of our fledgling grassroots organization —need Americans for Religious Liberty more than ever before. On ARL's tenth anniversary, which roughly coincides with the two-hundredth anniversary of the Bill of Rights, Americans are faced once again with the necessity to struggle to regain lost ground and safeguard our imperiled human rights.

Sherwin T. Wine

Ten years ago the Voice of Reason was established in Michigan to fight Jerry Falwell and the Moral Majority. Reagan was our new president. The invasion of Afghanistan had revived the Cold War. Political fundamentalism was feeling the euphoria of political victory.

Jerry Falwell assaulted the foundations of the secular state. He demanded prayer in the public schools. He called for the purification of educational literature. He insisted that creationism belonged in the science classroom. He equated the neutral stand of state secularity with a religion called "secular humanism" and insisted that it receive no more state support.

We were frightened because political fundamentalism is different from religious fundamentalism. Religious fundamentalism is a religious option and has been around for many centuries. As long as the state did not interfere with its freedom of action it was willing to accept the secular state. In fact, its historic dislike for the Catholic Church made it an ardent defender of the secular state against Catholic Church encroachment. But political fundamentalism is different. It is a deliberate campaign by radical conservative Protestants to take over the government of the United States and to remold the lives of Americans to conform to fundamentalist ideals. Religious neutrality is anathema to political fundamentalists. They want a "Christian America," using their own constricted definition of "Christian."

In 1981 everything seemed to be going well for the supporters of the Radical Religious Right. They had a painful recession. They had a resurgent aggressive Communism. They had crime and moral decay in the cities of America. They had a disillusioned progressive movement exhausted from the Vietnam War. They had a declining and confused Protestant establishment. They had a secure base in a revived South, angry over Black power, affirmative action and civil liberties.

They brought to these unearned assets their own genius and commitment—a simple explanation for complex ills, absolute certainty on moral and life style issues, armies of well-trained and enthusiastic volunteers, the willingness to infiltrate the Republican Party and to elect its own spokespersons, and the foresight to blend the message of the past with the media technology of the future.

In the end, political fundamentalists did not achieve their political goal. They failed to take power. The campaign of Pat Robertson was their final gasp of the 1980s. Scandal, the decline of communism and insufficient numbers subverted their effort. But they did succeed in changing the political leadership and the American political agenda. The demand for radical religious solutions to America's "moral decay" was still abroad. And they had managed to forge an alliance with their historic enemy, the conservative Catholics, to fight legal freedom of choice on abortion.

Today the Radical Right is making a new appearance, a more dangerous one than that of Jerry Falwell and the Moral Majority. David Duke and Patrick Buchanan have made their political debut. They add racism and chauvinism to the pleas for a Christian America. The context of their messages is an economic recession far deeper and far more serious than that of ten years ago. Americans are filled with fear about the future. And they are looking for simple and clear answers to their problems.

Ironically, the fall of Communism has not served to diffuse the fundamentalist message. It has mainly served to discredit the Left and all its causes. Secularism and socialism seem to go together in the eyes of many people. The secular state and interventionist economies are a team in the fantasies of the new propaganda. Deep religious commitment is equated with the love of freedom. Religious faith is touted as the foundation of a moral democracy. All the "crazies" of the Right—anti-Black, anti-Oriental, antisemitic—who were reluctant to speak out before have been given courage by their comrades in Eastern Europe who now openly proclaim fascist alternatives to Communism more frightening than institutional Communism.

With the absence of the Communist enemy, the new enemy of the Right in America may be a trio of "welfare Blacks," Jews and secular humanists. This odd combination may be joined by a backlash against all non-white foreigners, especially the hated Japanese. The racism of David Duke will be joined to the neo-isolationism of Pat Buchanan and the fundamentalist credo of Pat Robertson and Jerry Falwell. The code word for this terrifying mishmash will be "Christian America." The election of 1992 will be a mean election. Both establishment Republicans and Democrats will feel the fury of the revived Radical Right. And they will have a hard time resisting the demands of their opponents. The call for school prayer, "Bible values" and "right to life" will be combined with appealing cries for protective tariffs and walls against immigrants.

If ever there was a need for a voice of reason, now is the time. Hard times and the new confidence of the Radical Right will make the advocacy of a secular state difficult and controversial. We have no choice but to speak out as we spoke out ten years ago.

The secular state, which we offer as the alternative to the vision of the proponents of a "Christian America" rests on four foundations. The first is personal freedom, the right of individuals to choose their life style, with no interference from government or private associations. The second is religious freedom, the refusal of the state to endorse or support any particular religious or anti-religious movement and the refusal of the state to participate in the affairs of any denomination. The third is the defense of science and rational inquiry from the encroachments of religious dogma, especially in public schools and universities. And the fourth is the promotion of civic virtue through the public teaching of responsible self-discipline, compassion and tolerance, these values deriving their authority not only from religious faith but also from shared reason and common sense.

The secular state will not cure our economic woes. But it will protect our human dignity. Both the American Bill of Rights and the French Declaration of Human Rights were its founding documents. Although they have just celebrated their 200th anniversaries, the political vision they offer is still extremely vulnerable. They need our help to survive.

ARL Signs Freedom Statement

On September 20 at the National Press Club in Washington, Americans for Religious Liberty joined more than 150 civic, labor, civil liberties, religious, and other groups, along with 300 law professors and 40 computer scientists, in expressing support for the following declaration:

In Defense of Freedom

1. On September 11, 2001, thousands of people lost their lives in a brutal assault on the American people and the American form of government. We mourn the loss of these innocent lives and insist that those who perpetrated these acts be held accountable.
2. This tragedy requires all Americans to examine carefully the steps our country may now take to reduce the risk of future terrorist attacks.
3. We need to consider proposals calmly and deliberately with a determination not to erode the liberties and freedoms that are at the core of the American way of life.
4. We need to ensure that actions by our government uphold the principles of a democratic society, accountable government and international law, and that all decisions are taken in a manner consistent with the Constitution.
5. We can, as we have in the past, in times of war and of peace, reconcile the requirements of security with the demands of liberty.
6. We should resist the temptation to enact proposals in the mistaken belief that anything that may be called anti-terrorist will necessarily provide greater security.
7. We should resist efforts to target people because of their race, religion, ethnic background or appearance, including immigrants in general, Arab Americans and Muslims.
8. We affirm the right of peaceful dissent, protected by the First Amendment, now, when it is most at risk.
9. We should applaud our political leaders in the days ahead who have the courage to say that our freedoms should not be limited.
10. We must have faith in our democratic system and our Constitution, and in our ability to protect at the same time both the freedom and the security of all Americans.

Chapter 8
Obituary Tributes

We have been privileged to work with so many outstanding men and women from many walks of life who have supported our efforts to preserve religious liberty for future generations of Americans. The following is a selection of obituary tributes of many of our founders, friends and fellow activists.

Sherwin Wine, 1928-2007

Rabbi Sherwin T. Wine, who founded Americans for Religious Liberty with Edward L. Ericson in 1982, died in an automobile accident in Morocco on July 21. Wine, who lived in Birmingham, Michigan, was on vacation when a vehicle hit the taxi in which he and his partner Richard McMains were riding. McMains survived but the taxi driver was also killed.

Rabbi Wine, a native of Detroit, founded the first congregation of Humanistic Judaism in 1963 and helped establish the Society for Humanistic Judaism six years later. The movement, which now has 40,000 members, was described in a 1965 *Time* magazine article. Wine received the Humanist of the Year award from the American Humanist Association in 2003, the same year he retired. Wine was the author of several books, most recently, *Staying Sane in a Crazy World.*

Tributes to Sherwin T. Wine

The strength and energy of Sherwin Wine's life and thought rested firmly on his commitment to enlightenment principles. When reason was out of fashion, he stood by it. When science was scorned, he upheld it. When secular democracy was attacked, he defended it.

He saw clearly that theocracy is one of the worst of all possible forms of government and that every step toward the establishment of religion, however disguised or rationalized, must be vigorously rejected. The tradition that stretches from Voltaire, Paine, Jefferson, and Madison to Hugo Black and John Kennedy provided Sherwin's platform: Democratic liberty and freedom of conscience are grounded in the separation of church and state. The framers of the Constitution mandated that separation, and we must preserve it.

As an individual, Sherwin was indefatigable. He undertook several major responsibilities at the same time, and performed amazingly well in all of them. His aims were undivided, even as his contributions were various. Highly gifted intellectually and an ever eloquent and entertaining speaker, he drew a wide audience. But unlike many other charismatic personalities, Sherwin's arguments exhibited rigorous thinking, well-reasoned organization and emotive balance.

In his sudden death, all who care about the future of a pluralistic, open society have lost a friend and a champion. He leaves a body of work and a cause that will continue to inform and inspire us.

— *Edward L. Ericson*

Edward L. Ericson, co-founder of Americans for Religious Liberty, is former president of the American Ethical Union, an Ethical Culture leader, a retired Unitarian Universalist minister, and author of Religious Liberty and the Secular State *and other books.*

Rabbi Sherwin Wine was a man of vision. He saw clearly what could be and he harnessed his enormous intellect and energy to achieve it. Personal sacrifice, public attacks, uncertainty about the future—nothing could deter him from his course.

As a college student, and even earlier, Sherwin adopted a secular and humanistic worldview. He went on to develop a new version of Judaism consistent with his beliefs and those of many others, a Humanistic Judaism in which secular people would be able to say what they really believed without reciting traditional religious language whose content they were uncomfortable with. The Humanistic Judaism movement that Sherwin founded now includes numerous congregations throughout North America and has a growing presence in Israel and elsewhere.

As an innovator and a rebel, and as someone who grew up in an era of open antisemitism, Sherwin was totally committed to the free society. As if the task of creating a new, nontheistic form of Judaism wasn't enough for one person, he was also a leader in promoting freedom – particularly religious freedom. In response to the increasing threat of religious entanglement with government in the early 1980s, personified by the rise of the Rev. Jerry Falwell, Rabbi Wine and others created the Voice of Reason organization, which then merged with the newly formed Center for Moral Democracy to become Americans for Religious Liberty. In the Detroit area where he lived and worked, Rabbi Wine founded the Conference on Liberal Religion, an association of liberal religious professionals, in 1985, and an advocacy group called Clergy and Citizens United in 1995. He understood that both religious and secular leaders need to work together to preserve our religious freedom.

In 1982, Rabbi Wine founded the North American Committee for Humanism, a confederation of the six major humanist organizations in North America, and The Humanist Institute, a graduate school in New York for training humanist leaders. He served as president of both of these organizations from 1982 until 1993.

The American Humanist Association honored him as Humanist of the Year in 2003.

Sherwin was a brilliant speaker, whose incisive reasoning and humor could mesmerize any audience. I remember when he was visiting us in the Washington, DC, area a number of years ago, I mentioned to him in a conversation just a few minutes before his major lecture that I thought it was important for people in our Humanistic Judaism movement to know more about Ahad Ha'am, who, about a century ago, had put forward a vision of Zionism quite different from the political version that ultimately prevailed. Sherwin proceeded to wrap his presentation around a discussion of the life and work of Ahad Ha'am, mentioning specific meetings and writings and ideas, as if he had spent hours preparing a lecture on the topic. He was able to talk spontaneously on a huge variety of topics with specificity and substance.

Those of us who had the opportunity to learn from Sherwin will always remember the unique insights and clarity that he brought to any subject. A couple of years ago I attended a weekend seminar he gave in New York on the rise of Christianity. Over the course of three days, he spoke for hour after hour with no notes on the lives of Jesus and his early followers. He successfully conveyed an understanding of modern scholarly views on this topic. He also said some things you would not be likely to hear from many other rabbis, if any, concerning the reliability of some of the more controversial New Testament accounts. His unique and convincing perspective on the story of the developing church was, as always, directed only by his commitment to intellectual integrity.

More recently, my wife and I were on a trip he led in Rome. Each morning he gave our group a one-hour lecture—again with no notes—on the history of Rome from the beginnings of the Roman empire right up to the present. Here he was, at age 78, explaining from memory the importance of a vast number of emperors, popes, and other political and military leaders without hesitating or getting a name wrong – and, most importantly, putting thousands of years of history into a framework that made sense. Then we would go out and see the Roman ruins or buildings that related to what he had talked about that morning. He was an extraordinary intellect and teacher.

But most of all, it was his personal warmth and ever-present humor that no one could resist. Sherwin genuinely cared about each person. Those of us who were fortunate enough to have known him couldn't get enough of him. His death leaves an enormous gap in each of our lives. At the same time, the values he cherished are made stronger in each of us by our memory of him. Our finest tribute can only be to live those values each day and to nurture them in others as he nurtured them in us.

— Michael Prival

Michael Prival is a member of the board of directors of Americans for Religious Liberty and a Certified Leader in the Secular Humanistic Judaism movement, in which he has been active for close to 30 years. He is a retired research microbiologist.

Robert Drinan, 1920-2007

Robert Drinan was many things, and he did them all well: member of Congress, law school professor, author, Jesuit priest, and stalwart opponent of the Religious Right. The first Roman Catholic priest elected to Congress, in 1970, Drinan, even as a freshman, led the fight against a school prayer amendment that was designed to reverse the Supreme Court's quite proper 1962 ruling against mandatory, devotional prayer in U.S. public schools. Drinan took an active role in helping to defeat this egregious assault on religious liberty.

In his decade-long career as a representative from Massachusetts, Drinan was a foe of the Vietnam War, an advocate of stronger civil rights and civil liberties laws, and later was pro-choice on abortion. As a member of the House Judiciary Committee, he was the first to file a resolution of impeachment against President Richard Nixon. Drinan left the House in 1981 after the Vatican ruled that no priest could hold a government position in any country, an action that may have been directed primarily at the government of Nicaragua but also cost Drinan his seat.

He spent the last 26 years of his life as a professor at Georgetown University Law School just a few blocks from the Capitol. The law was his first love. Before his election to Congress, he had been dean of the Boston College Law School. Georgetown Law Center established the Robert Drinan Chair in Human Rights last year. Drinan founded the Lawyers' Alliance for Nuclear Arms Control, the National Interreligious Task Force on Soviet Jewry and Georgetown's *Journal of Legal Ethics*. He also served as vice chair of the National Advisory Council of the American

Civil Liberties Union.

Author of a dozen books, Drinan received more than 20 honorary degrees, the ABA Medal, and the Congressional Distinguished Service Award. Rep. Ed Markey (D-Mass.) called Drinan "the conscience of the House of Representatives." Even in his last column for *National Catholic Reporter*, published in the February 2 issue, Drinan again urged the U.S. Senate to ratify the U.N. Convention on the Elimination of All Forms of Discrimination against Women, which has been approved by 185 nations, but not by the United States.

A poignant tribute came at Drinan's February 1 funeral service in Washington, when a packed crowd of mourners rose for a standing ovation to bid farewell to a man who made his mark on the U.S. legal and political system for decades.

In this age of religious extremism and the retreat of those who stand for religious liberty, Father Drinan will be long remembered as an advocate of human rights, and freedom of conscience for all.

— Al Menendez

Robert S. Alley, 1932-2006

One of America's most distinguished church-state scholars, Robert Sutherland Alley, died in Richmond, Virginia, on August 15 at age 74. Alley was professor emeritus at the University of Richmond and the son of a Baptist minister and journalist.

Alley was author of *James Madison on Religious Liberty, School Prayer* and many other titles in the field of church-state relations. One of his earliest books dealt with religion and the U.S. presidency and compared the religious views of presidents from Washington to Nixon. He was the executive director of the James Madison Memorial Committee, a contributing editor of *Free Inquiry*, and a member of the Council for Secular Humanism's Committee for the Scientific Examination of Religion.

In 1996 ARL published Alley's book, *Public Education and the Public Good* (available from ARL for $10, including postage.)

Alley was a close friend of Americans for Religious Liberty, and a personal friend of both Edd Doerr and Al Menendez. His contributions to the preservation of religious freedom for all were enormous, and he will be greatly missed.

— Al Menendez

Vashti McCollum, 1912-2006

Vashti McCollum, the courageous Illinois woman who won the landmark 1948 Supreme Court ruling in *McCollum v. Board of Education* (333 U.S. 203), died on August 20 at the age of 93. The late Robert Alley, who also died in August, wrote in his book on leading church-state cases, The *Constitution and Religion* (1999), that "The *McCollum* decision was the first Supreme Court case to erect barriers against those who wished to employ the public schools for proselytizing".

Vashti was the author of *One Woman's Fight* in 1950, served as president of the American Humanist Association, and is honored in the Women's Hall of Fame in Seneca Falls, New York. It was my privilege to have known and worked with Vashti and also with her father, Arthur Cromwell, and her sons James and Dannel.

— Edd Doerr

Hans Bethe, 1906-2005

Nobel laureate Hans Bethe, one of the 20th century's greatest physicists and a key figure in the development of the first nuclear bomb, died at his home in Ithaca, New York on March 6.

Like biologist Ernst Mayr who died at the age of 100 in February, Dr. Bethe was a member and supporter of Americans for Religious Liberty since the 1980s, as were such other eminent scientists as Isaac Asimov, Carl Sagan, Stephen Jay Gould, and Alfred McClung Lee.

Both Bethe and Mayr were Germans who left their native country because of the rise to power of the Nazis.

Ernst Mayr, 1904-2005

Dr. Ernst Mayr, one of the original sponsors and National Advisory Board members of Americans for Religious Liberty and a consistent supporter, died on February 3 in Bedford, MA. His last book, *What Makes Biology Unique?* (Cambridge University Press), was published last August, one month after he turned 100.

In his nine decade career, Dr. Mayr became the most important evolutionary biologist of the 20th century. He was the architect of the evolutionary "modern synthesis," which the late Stephen Jay Gould, another member of ARL's National Advisory Board, called "one of the half-dozen major scientific achievements in our century." He reconciled Darwin's work with the newer science of genetics. He is also credited with creating a philosophy of biology and founded the field of the history of biology.

Dr. Mayr was the first scientist to win biology's "Triple Crown," the 1983 Balzan Foundation Prize, the 1994 Japan Society for the Promotion of Science International Prize for Biology, and the 1999 Royal Swedish Academy of Sciences Craboord prize. He won the U.S. National Medal of Science in 1970 and has been named one of the 100 most influential scientists of all time.

Dr. Mayr's 2001 book, *What Evolution Is*, was reviewed in the summer 2002 issue of this newsletter, No. 79.

Francis Crick

Francis H.C. Crick, who shared a Nobel Prize in 1962 as the co-discoverer with James D. Watson, of the DNA genetic blueprint for life, died on July 29 at the age of 88.

My first contact with Dr. Crick occurred when we sat together at an awards banquet in Sacramento in 1985. (The awardee was Planned Parenthood president Faye Wattleton.) Crick impressed me as warm, funny, easy-going. Three years later I had the privilege of attending another awards banquet at Harvard, where I was to introduce Isaac Asimov. Asimov and James Watson sat on either side of me at the dinner. The conversation was quite interesting.

My next contact with Crick was in 1989, when ARL and I were coordinating an *amicus curiae* brief to the Supreme Court in an important abortion rights case. *Webster v. Reproductive Health Services*. Among the points made in the brief were: "There is no scientific consensus on when a human life begins," and "The organic capacity for human thought is absent until after 28 weeks of gestation."

The idea behind this brief was to emulate a brief to the Court two years earlier in the creationism/evolution case, which we won seven-to-two, with Rehnquist and Scalia dissenting. I had proposed getting as many Nobel laureate scientists as possible to sign the brief; 72 did, about 90% of all laureates living in the United States.

In the *Webster* case we had to limit the laureates to those in the fields of biology and medicine, so we ended up with twelve Nobel laureates, including Francis Crick, and 155 other distinguished scientists. The brief was produced in a record ten days and was hailed by the National Organization for Women as one of the best of the many briefs filed in the case. (The text of the brief and list of signers may be found in the book *Compulsory Pregnancy: The War Against American Women,* by former ARL president John Swomley, available from ARL for $12.95.)

But back to Francis Crick. Tracking down 167 scientists, showing them the text of the brief, and getting their consent to be listed was something of a mad scramble. As I had not heard back from Crick, I tried to phone him at the Salk Institute in California. Crick and his secretary were both on holiday, but Crick had had to return to his office to pick up something. He was passing his secretary's desk when the phone rang. Had I phoned a few seconds earlier or later, I would have missed him and his name would not have appeared on the brief.

Crick's most popular book was *The Astonishing Hypothesis: The Scientific Search for the Soul* (Charles Scribner's Sons, 1994).

— *Edd Doerr*

Ken Gjemre

Ken Gjemre, Americans for Religious Liberty's treasurer from 1984 to 1999, died at his home in California on May 28.

Ken co-founded Half Price Books in 1972 and built it into the nation's largest chain of used book stores. An Army captain in World War II, Ken was one of the first Americans to meet his Soviet counterparts at the Elbe River in Germany in 1945. Years later he was active in an organization of U.S. and Russian veterans who had met at the Elbe. A resident of Texas until 1998, he was an active supporter of some 90 cause organizations devoted to civil liberties, human rights, peace, church-state separation, and environmentalism.

— Edd Doerr

Stephen Jay Gould

Stephen Jay Gould, a long time member of Americans for Religious Liberty's National Advisory Board, died on May 20.

Gould, whose writing style was much admired by fellow scientist and writer Isaac Asimov, became one of the world s leading paleontologists and evolutionary biologists. His last book, *The Structure of Evolutionary Theory,* published shortly before he died, is a 1,433-page magnum opus.

No shrinking violet, Gould plunged into the struggle to block the intrusion of fundamentalist "creationism" into public school science classes. When the Kansas Board of Education voted in 1999 to remove evolution from the science curriculum, Gould made speeches in the Midwest, pointing out that "to teach biology without evolution is like teaching English without grammar." Gould was also involved in the successful Supreme Court challenge to a Louisiana creationism law in the 1980s.

— Edd Doerr

Carl Sagan

Carl Sagan, the eminent astronomer and science writer, died on December 20, just as our last newsletter was ready to go to press with an excerpt from his book, *The Demon-Haunted World.* Carl was a member of ARL's National Advisory Board, along with other prominent scientists, and a strong supporter of religious freedom and church-state separation.

An anecdote about Carl bears relating. Back in 1989 ARL was preparing an *amicus curiae* brief to the Supreme court in an important abortion rights case, *Webster v. Reproductive Health Services* (reprinted as an appendix in John Swomley's monograph, *Abortion and Public Policy*), on behalf of 167 Nobel laureates and other scientists and physicians. Before we and our attorneys decided to include only biologists and physicians, I had contacted Carl about signing on to the brief.

He said that he was not altogether sure he that he agreed with the brief's point that "Not until after 28 weeks of gestation does the fetus attain sufficient neocortical complexity to exhibit those sentient capacities that are present in full-term newborns. In lay terms, the capacity for the human thought process as we know it cannot exist until sometime after 28 weeks of gestation."

I replied to Carl that our brief was an outgrowth of ARL's 1987 conference and subsequent 1989 book on *Abortion Rights and Fetal 'Personhood,'* which had been partly inspired by the discussion of human evolution in Carl's book, *The Dragons of Eden.*

A year after the brief was filed, Carl's major article on abortion rights was read by millions in *Parade* magazine. It essentially took the position of neurobiologists that human personhood is not possible until some time in the third trimester.

— *Edd Doerr*

Corliss Lamont, Jay Wabeke, Robert M. Stein

Three important supporters of ARL and church-state separation died recently. Their contributions to this cause were significant.

Corliss Lamont, philosopher, writer, civil libertarian and philanthropist, was the lead plaintiff in the successful ARL-ACLU challenge to US tax aid to sectarian private schools overseas. Dr. Lamont was also a major supporter of ARL since the organization's founding. His international peace activities were hailed by British writer H.G. Wells in his 1933 (sic!) novel *The Shape of Things to Come.*

Jay Wabeke was a tireless activist for public education and church-state separation in Michigan. He was active in the 1970 and 1978 parochiaid referenda in that state and served on ARL's Board of Directors. He was the main catalyst behind the lawsuit that resulted in the Supreme Court's 1985 landmark ruling in *Grand Rapids School District v. Ball,* which barred publicly paid teachers from serving in sectarian private schools.

Robert M. Stein was a member of the ARL Board of Directors and staunch supporter of ARL. He was a longtime civil liberties and social justice advocate in the American Ethical Union.

James Luther Adams

James Luther Adams, 92, a long time member of ARL's National Advisory Board, died on July 26. Dr. Adams, a Unitarian Universalist minister, had a long and distinguished career as an ethicist and theologian on the faculties of the Harvard Divinity School, Andover Newton Theological School, and the University of Chicago. He served for 15 years as chair of the church-state committee of the ACLU of Massachusetts, and personally clashed with the Nazis in Germany during the 1930s.

The most recent collection of Adams' writings is *An Examined Faith: Social Context and Religious Commitment*, edited by George K. Beach (Beacon Press, 1991).

Leo Pfeffer

Leo Pfeffer, one of America's foremost scholars, authors, and jurists of church-state relations, died June 4, 1993 at the age of 83, in Goshen, New York. Born in Hungary, the son of a rabbi, he was brought to the United States by his parents when he was two years old. A graduate of the City College of New York and the New York University School of Law, he was widely recognized for more than three decades as one of the nation's outstanding authorities on church and state. His prodigious scholarship earned him the respect and stature accorded few scholars at any time, anywhere. In addition to his voluminous writings, including his classic work *Church, State, and Freedom* (Beacon Press, 1967), he probably argued more church-state cases before the United States Supreme Court than anyone else in American history. As Samuel Krislov wrote in a volume of essays written in honor of Leo Pfeffer, "No one comes to mind . . . to rival Pfeffer's intellectual dominance over so vital an area [i.e. church and state] of constitutional law for so extensive a period in this combination of pleading and intellectualizing." It was widely conceded, even by those holding sharply differing views, that it was Leo Pfeffer's view of the Establishment Clause more than any other that for almost three decades formed the Supreme Court's interpretation of it.

Admitted to the bar at the age of twenty-three, he was actively engaged in the practice of law for more than a half century, almost twenty years of which were spent with the American Jewish Congress in various capacities as director of the Commission on Law and Social Action, general counsel and finally as special counsel. In addition, he served as counsel to the New York Committee for Public Education and Religious Liberty (PEARL) and the National Coalition for PEARL from their founding until 1985. His professional responsibilities also included: Lecturer, New School of Social Research, 1954-60, and Mt. Holyoke College, 1958-60; David W. Petergorsky Professor of Constitutional Law, Yeshiva University, 1962-63; and Professor and Chairman of Political Science, Long Island University, 1964-1979, where he continued to teach until 1985.

Recognition of his work came from many and varied sources, including: the L.H.D. degree from Hebrew Union College; Trustee Award for Scholarly Achievement, Long Island University; Thomas Jefferson Religious Freedom Award, Unitarian Universalist Church; Rabbi Maurice N. Eisendrath Memorial Award, Union of American Hebrew Congregations; Citation for Contributions to Public Education, Horace Mann League; American Jewish Congress Award; and

Certificate of Merit, Council of Jewish Federations. Baylor University Press published a large volume of essays in honor of him and his life's work in 1985, to which a broad range of distinguished scholars contributed.

In Leo Pfeffer were combined the scholar and the jurist, the thinker and the participant, the theoretician and the practitioner. Scholarship, advocacy, and juridical skill were inextricably intertwined and embodied in his life work. Deeply involved in his concern for a broad range of human rights and civil liberties, he was a passionate advocate of religious liberty and an eloquent defender of the institutional separation of church and state, which he always saw as a corollary to the constitutional guarantee of "the free exercise of religion." His lengthening influence on American church-state relations and his contributions to religious liberty will long be remembered. It may well be said that the United States has lost its greatest champion of religious liberty in this century.

—*James K Wood, Jr.*

Dr. Wood is director of the J.M. Dawson Institute of Church-State Studies and Simon and Ethel Bunn Professor of Church State Studies at Baylor University in Waco, Texas, and editor of The Journal of Church and State.

Florence Flast

Florence Flast, a member of ARL's board of directors and a long time activist for public education and church-state separation, died on August 15 at the age of 74.

Mrs. Flast, a former president of the United Parent Associations of New York City, was one of the founders of the New York Committee for Public Education and Religious liberty (PEARL), formed to combat efforts to change the New York State constitution in 1966-67 to permit tax aid for sectarian private schools. The 72% to 28% defeat of the proposed new constitution, mainly on religious liberty grounds, was the subject of my 1968 book, *The Conspiracy That Failed.*

Mrs. Flast was the lead plaintiff in *Flast v. Cohen,* the case in which the Supreme Court in 1968 recognized the "standing" of taxpayers to use federal courts to challenge tax expenditures alleged to violate the First Amendment's establishment clause, a ruling which made possible the Supreme Court's series of decisions against parochiaid beginning in 1971. She was actively involved in other parochiaid challenges, such as the suit *Aguilar v. Felton,* in which the Supreme Court in 1985 ruled unconstitutional the assignment of publicly paid teachers to work in denominational schools.

Mrs. Flast was one of the founders and vice-president until her death of the National Coalition for Public Education and Religious Liberty (National PEARL) and also served on the national Church-State Committee of the ACLU.

One of her last efforts was to write a chapter, "Theocracy versus Democracy in the Empire State: Three Decades of Church-State Entanglement in the Schools of New York," in the recently published book, *Why We Still Need Public Schools: Church/State Relations and Visions of Democracy* (Prometheus Books, 1992, $17.95, available from ARL).

When Sen. Daniel P. Moynihan co-chaired a Senate hearing in 1978 on a bill to provide massive aid to denominational schools through tuition tax credits, he charged opponents of the bill with "nativist bigotry." Mrs. Flast, who had a little earlier that day presented testimony against the bill, cornered Moynihan when the hearing recessed for lunch and demanded, "I am a member of a minority religion whose parents immigrated to this country from Russia. How can you accuse me of nativist bigotry?" Moynihan, usually rather voluble, had little to say.

Florence Flast was the very model of the citizen activist She volunteered her time, energy, and eloquence for over a quarter of a century to the cause of defending public education and religious liberty, truly the "PEARL" of great price.

— *Edd Doerr*

Isaac Asimov

Isaac Asimov, this century's most prolific writer, died on April 6 after a short illness. He was the author of more than 450 books, with at least a couple dozen more still in the pipeline.

The range of his writing was astonishing—science fiction, books interpreting science for non-scientists, books of history for children, collections of limericks, mysteries, *Asimov's Guide to the Bible, Asimov's Guide to Shakespeare,* etc.

Born in Russia in 1920 and taken by his parents to the U.S. when he was two, young Isaac taught himself to read at five and graduated from high school at 15. With a PhD. in chemistry from Columbia, he taught at Boston University's School of Medicine for ten years, until he began writing full time in 1958.

Asimov was one of the earliest supporters of Americans for Religious liberty when it was started in 1981, having been recruited by ARL co-founder Edward L. Ericson. He subsequently served on ARL's national advisory board until his death. He was a plaintiff in the case of *Lamont v. Woods,* a joint ARL-ACLU federal court suit challenging U.S. federal aid to religious schools abroad (see newsletter No. 39).

Eminent zoologist Stephen Jay Gould, also a widely published science writer and member of ARL's National Advisory Board, shared this memory of Isaac Asimov with us:

"My first contact with Isaac Asimov was daunting. I picked up the phone one day, and a voice bellowed: 'Gould, this is Isaac Asimov. I hate you.' 'Oh,' I replied with astonishing lack of originality, 'Why so?' 'I hate you because you write so well,' he said. So I replied, 'and if I had written 400 books instead of ten, I wouldn't be paying such rapt attention to stylistic nuances either. 'We both laughed and became good friends. Isaac was the best (and most copious) there has ever been—ever throughout history—in the presentation of science. Only Galileo and Huxley (maybe Medawar in our generation) matched his clarity, his verve, his dedication, and, above all, his moral sense of the rightness and power of knowledge."

My own acquaintance with Asimov began when, as a kid in my first year of high school, I picked up my first science fiction magazine in October of 1944, and there was a story by Asimov. I could not have dreamt that many years later we would be associated in a venture called Americans for Religious Liberty and working together for six years as president and vice-president, respectively, of the American Humanist Association. (I once remarked in a speech that the president and vice-president of the AHA had written an average of 220 books each, Asimov's 430 and my 10.)

Even though he was a genius and one of the most celebrated writers, published in many languages (I ran across his books in Spanish in Madrid), he was as easy to talk to as the guy next door. Until near the end of his life he answered all of his own voluminous correspondence, usually on postal cards.

His sense of humor was legendary. When I had to introduce him at a conference at M.I.T. in the fall of 1988, Asimov, his wife Dr. Janet Jeppson, and I got stuck for a very long time in a limousine piloted by a chauffeur who managed to get lost in Boston. To while away the time we jointly composed limericks, though I don't know if they ever ended up in one of his books.

One of the great lights in our civilization has gone out. The chances are infinitesimal that his like will ever be seen again.

As I concluded in introducing him at the M.I.T. conference, "Isaac Asimov is not a Renaissance man; he is a one-man Renaissance."

— Edd Doerr

Alfred McClung Lee

Dr. Alfred McClung Lee, a long time member of ARL's National Advisory Board and one of the country's most eminent social scientists, died on May 19 at the age of 85. At the time of his death, Dr. Lee was professor emeritus of sociology and anthropology at Brooklyn College and at the Graduate School of the City University of New York. He also held the honorary post of visiting scholar at Drew University in his retirement

A noted sociologist and a former president of the American Sociological Association, Dr. Lee was the author of *Terrorism in Northern Ireland, The Fine Art of Propaganda, The Daily Newspaper inAmerica:The Evolution of a Social Instrument,* and 17 other books.

Dr. Lee's activity on behalf of church-state separation went back to the 1940s, when he was on the faculty at Wayne State University in Detroit and one of the founders of the Committee to Maintain Separation of Church and State, formed to defend religious neutrality in public schools.

Dr. Lee was always available for consultation with ARL's staff on church-state questions.

He is survived by his wife, Dr. Elizabeth Briant Lee, also a sociologist, a visiting scholar at Drew University, and a member of ARL's National Advisory Board, and two sons, Alfred McClung Lee and Briant Harmon Lee, five grandchildren and two great-grandchildren.

Sewall Wright

Sewall Wright, a member of the ARL National Advisory Board and the country's leading evolutionary theorist, died in Madison, WI, in March at 98 as a result of complications from a fall. Dr. Wright, a geneticist known for his pioneering studies of genetic changes in evolving species, was best known for mathematical formulations he developed to illustrate and prove the theories of Darwin and Mendel. He taught at the University of Chicago from 1924 to 1954 and then joined the faculty of the University of Wisconsin.

Joseph L. Blau

Professor Joseph L. Blau, a member of ARL since its foundation and a leader in the Ethical Culture movement, died in December. Blau, a long time professor of philosophy and religion at Columbia University, wrote and lectured often on religious liberty. He was author/editor of *Cornerstones of Religious Freedom in America,* an anthology of key documents in the development of church-state separation.

Publications by Edd Doerr and Albert J. Menendez

Books Written Jointly by Edd Doerr and Albert J. Menendez

Great Quotations on Religious Freedom
The Case Against Charitable Choice
The Case Against School Vouchers
Religious Liberty and State Constitutions
Religion and Public Education: Common Sense and the Law
Church Schools and Public Money: The Politics of Parochiaid

Books by Edd Doerr

Here I Stand
Somebody Has to Say It
My Life as a Humanist, a Memoir
Rejoyce, Rejoyce!
Six Stories and Seventy Poems
Cómo Mantener la Cordura en un Mundo Loco
Vox Populi: Letters to the Editor
Timely and Timeless: The Wisdom of E. Burdette Backus (Editor)
Catholic Schools: The Facts
Dancing on the Wall
Images
Abortion Rights and Fetal Personhood
Religious Liberty in Crisis
A Hitch in Time and Other Tales
Dear Editor
Parochiaid and the Law
Eden II
The Conspiracy That Failed

Books by Albert J. Menendez

The Geography of Presidential Elections in the United States, 1868-2004
Joy to the World: Sacred Christmas Music Through the Ages
South Carolina Trivia
Christmas Songs Made in America
Who Goes to Nonpublic Schools?
The Red Mass
Three Voices of Extremism
The Perot Voters and the Future of American Politics
Church and State in Canada
Evangelicals at the Ballot Box

Home Schooling: The Facts
New Jersey Trivia
Abortion Rights at the Polls
Visions of Reality: What Fundamentalist Schools Teach
The December Wars: Religious Symbols and Ceremonies in the Public Square
Maryland Trivia
The Subject is Murder
The Catholic Novel
The December Dilemma
No Religious Test
Religion and the U.S. Presidency
Civil War Novels
The Road to Rome
School Prayer and Other Issues in American Public Education
Religious Conflict in America
Christmas in the White House
The Dream Lives On
Mistletoe Malice
John F. Kennedy: Catholic and Humanist
Classics of Religious Liberty
Religion at the Polls
The Origins of Religious Liberty
Church-State Relations: An Annotated Bibliography
The American Political Quiz Book
The Best of Church & State
Sherlock Holmes Quiz Book
The Bitter Harvest: Church and State in Northern Ireland

This book has bee[n]
withdrawn from the
South Bend Public Library
due to:

_ deteriorated/defective condition

obsolete information

_ superceded by newer holdings

✓ excess copies / reduced demand

_ other _____

6/16 Date   Staff

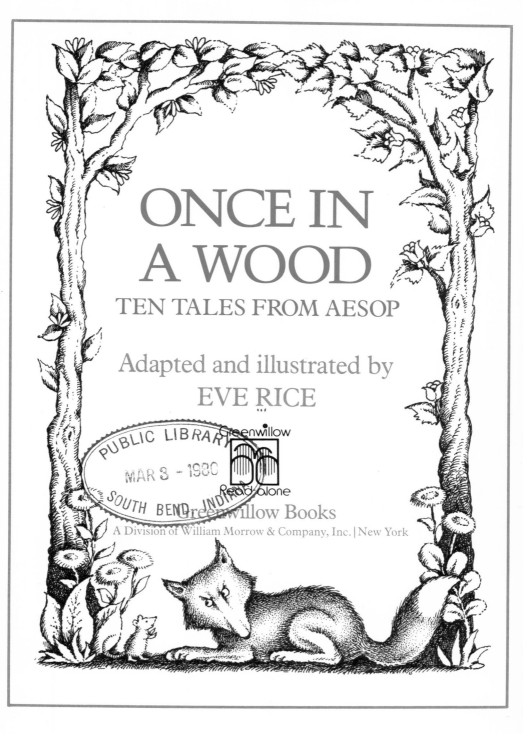

ONCE IN A WOOD

TEN TALES FROM AESOP

Adapted and illustrated by
EVE RICE

PUBLIC LIBRARY
MAR 3 - 1980
SOUTH BEND INDIANA

Greenwillow Books
A Division of William Morrow & Company, Inc. | New York

This one is for Tim

Copyright © 1979 by Eve Rice. All rights reserved. No part of this book may be reproduced or utilized in any form or by any means, electronic or mechanical, including photocopying, recording or by any information storage and retrieval system, without permission in writing from the Publisher. Inquiries should be addressed to Greenwillow Books, 105 Madison Ave., New York, N.Y. 10016. Printed in the United States of America

First Edition   1 2 3 4 5 6 7 8 9 10

Library of Congress Cataloging in Publication Data
Rice, Eve.   Once in a wood.   (Greenwillow read-alone books)
Summary: A retelling of 10 fables by Aesop including "The Fox and the Crow,"
"The Crow and the Water Jug," and "The Lion and the Mouse."   1.   Fables.
[1.   Fables] I.   Aesopus.   II.   Title.   PZ8.2.R38On   [398.2]   78-16294
ISBN 0-688-80191-9   ISBN 0-688-84191-0 lib. bdg.

CHILDREN'S ROOM

j 398
Ae 880
cop.1

CONTENTS

THE FOX
AND THE CROW

Once in a wood, long ago,

there lived a clever Fox.

One morning as Fox stepped out,

he saw the Crow fly overhead.

In her beak she held a piece

of tasty yellow cheese.

Fox licked his lips.

He had not had breakfast yet.

But Crow soon landed in a tree,

safely out of reach.

"Tree or no," said clever Fox,

"I'll have that cheese, by and by."

Then he said to Crow,

"Good morning, friend.

My! How well you look today!"

Crow flapped her wings with pride.
And Fox declared,
"Why, in my life I've never seen
feathers shine the way yours do.
And such a handsome bird as you
surely has a lovely voice.
Will you sing a song for me?"

So Crow, of course, began to sing.

She raised her beak.

"C-caw, caw-caw."

But as she did,

she dropped the cheese.

It fell right into Fox's jaws.

He ate it up and licked his lips.

And then Fox said to Crow,

"Thank you for my breakfast.

I will pay with some advice:

Beware of those who flatter

and tell lies meant to please—

and be glad, you foolish bird,

you only lost a cheese."

THE LION
AND THE MOUSE

One day, a mighty Lion was
fast asleep in the woods.
Thinking he was just a rock,
a little Mouse ran up his back.
The Lion woke at once
and took the poor Mouse
by the tail.

"How dare you wake me up?"
he roared.
"I am going to eat you!"

"Oh, please," the Mouse said.
"Let me go, and someday
  I will repay you."
"Don't be silly!" Lion roared.
"How will you repay me?

You are just a little Mouse—
too small to be
much use to me."
But then he laughed.
"All right. Go on."
He put the Mouse down and
she ran off into the woods.

When many days had passed,
the Mouse ran by that place again.

And hearing an awful roar,

she soon found Lion,

caught in a trap made of rope.

Quickly Mouse ran to the trap.

She took the rope in her teeth

and chewed and chewed until

she chewed right through the rope

and set the Lion free.

"Thank you!" roared Lion.

"You are welcome," said the Mouse.

"And now I hope that you can see

how big a help

small friends can be."

THE FOX
AND THE GOAT

Fox went walking in the woods

and fell into a well.

"This well is very deep,"

Fox thought sadly to himself.

"And I cannot jump very high.

How will I get out again?"

Just then a thirsty Goat

passed by.

"Hello, Fox," said the Goat.

"Why are you down in the well?"

"Oh, Goat," replied clever Fox,

"I came to get a drink, of course.

This water is

the finest in the wood."

"It is?" asked Goat.

"It is!" said Fox. "But come

and taste it for yourself.

I'm sure you will agree."

So Goat jumped down

into the well.

When Goat had had a drink,

he said,"This water is

as sweet as it can be.

But tell me, Fox,

how will we get out again?"

"That is easy," said the Fox.
"If you will stand very still,
   I can climb upon your back.
   And as soon as I am out,
   I will pull you up."
So Goat stood still
and Fox climbed out.

But then Fox turned

and walked away.

"Oh, please!" Goat called to Fox.

"Don't go!

How will I get out again?"

"Don't ask me," the Fox replied.

"You should have looked

before you leaped—

and asked yourself

the question then."

BELLING THE CAT

A hungry cat had come to stay
and all the mice lived in fear.
The mice decided
they would call a meeting.

When they were
all together,
the biggest mouse
stood up and said,
"There is a hungry cat about.
As long as he walks these woods,
not one of us is safe.
So I ask you all to think.
What are we to do?"
Then one mouse gave a plan.
And one mouse gave another.
And still a third had his say
and on and on until
a very young mouse spoke.

"Friends," he said.
"I think that we can
    solve this problem easily:

Hang a bell on the cat.

Then we will know when he is near

and we can stay out of his way."

"A good idea!" someone called.
And all the other mice agreed.
"We'll be safe at last!" they said
and danced around until
a very old mouse spoke.

"Friends," he said.

"One moment, please.

Things are easier said than done—
the old and wise will tell you that.
So now, will someone tell me this:
Who is going to bell the cat?"

THE FOX
AND THE STORK

Fox came to Stork and said,

"Will you come to dinner?

I will fix a tasty meal."

"How nice of you to ask,"

said Stork.

"I will be glad to come."

So Stork went to Fox's house.

And Fox cooked the dinner.

He served Stork hot soup

in a plate.

It smelled so good. . . .

But Stork, who had

a long, long bill,

could not eat soup from a plate.

And she watched while

greedy Fox ate up every bit.

"Don't you like my soup?"

Fox laughed.

And Stork went home

as hungry as she had come.

The next day, Stork went
to Fox and said,
"Will you come to dinner?"
"How nice of you to ask,"
said Fox. "Of course,
I will be glad to come."
So Fox went to Stork's house.
And Stork cooked the dinner.

She served Fox hot stew
in a tall jar.
It smelled so good. . . .
But Fox, who had no bill,
could not reach into the jar.
And greedy Fox watched hungrily
as Stork ate up every bit.
"Don't you like the stew?"
asked Stork.
"You set a fine example
when you fixed that meal for me.
I think you should be happy
that I've used your recipe."

THE HARE WHO
HAD MANY FRIENDS

The Hare had many, many friends:
the Crow, the Goat, the Cow. . . .
Everyone was Hare's good friend,
everyone except the Fox.

And every time Hare saw the Fox,
she ran to save her life.

But one day, when Fox came round,
Hare thought,
"Why should I run away?
My many friends will help me out!"
So Hare went to Crow and said,
"Please, Crow. Fox is coming!
Will you hide me in your tree?"

"Oh," said Crow.
"I'd like to help.
But this tree
is very small.
It cannot
hold us both."

So Hare went to Goat and said,

"Please, Goat. Fox is coming!

Will you butt him with your horns?"

"Hmmmm," said Goat.

"I'd like to help.

But I am very busy now.

I have a lot to do."

So Hare went to Cow and said,
"Please, Cow. Fox is coming!
Will you chase him far away?"

"Ah," said Cow. "I'd like to help.
But I cannot chase anyone.
I have hurt my leg, you know."
"Yes, I do know," said Hare.

And then with Fox right behind,

Hare ran to save her life once more.

"Alas!" she said when she was safe.

"Those in trouble soon find out

how many friends they really have.

I once thought I had so many.

But now I see that I was wrong—

for, in fact, I haven't any!"

THE LION
AND THE FOX

The Lion had decided

that he was too old to hunt.

"I cannot run well anymore.

My four old legs are tired.

But, if I use my head,

I'm sure that I can get my dinner."

So Lion went into his cave
and sent out word that
he was sick in bed.
Then one by one, the animals
came to wish the Lion well.
First the Calf came,
then the Horse came,
then the Deer, the Duck, the Pig.

And clever Fox, hearing the news,
also came to pay a call.

"Hello, Fox," Lion said,

   looking out his door.

"Won't you come in

   and stay awhile?

   We can sit and talk a bit."

"Thank you, sir," Fox replied.

"But I will not come inside."

"Afraid?" asked the Lion.

"You should not be—

   for I am old and sick,

   as you can see.

   Please, Fox. Do come in."

"What I can see," Fox replied,

"are footprints by your door.

They show that many went inside—

and none came out again.

So thank you, Lion, just the same.

Though fools may
walk into danger
when the signs are all about,
this Fox will not come in until
your other guests come out."

THE CROW AND
THE WATER JUG

One day thirsty Crow
came upon a water jug.
"Now I will have a drink,"
she thought.
She put her beak into the jug,
but the water was so low,
Crow could not get a drink.

So she reached farther in.
She flapped her wings
and stretched her neck.
But still she could not get
a single drop to drink.

"I know," she thought. "I'll turn
the jug over on its side."
And then she pushed
with all her might.
But no matter how she tried,
the jug still stood upright.
"I may as well give up," she thought.
And crow might have flown away—
but she stopped and thought again.

A moment later, Crow bent down

and picked up a pebble.

She dropped it in the jug

and then she bent

and picked another. . . .

One by one, on and on,

she dropped the pebbles in the jug.

And with each stone

that she dropped in,

the water rose a little bit

until, at last, it reached the top.

"Caw, caw!" Crow called

and had her drink.

"Caw, caw!" Crow called

and flapped her wings.

For she had learned

that many things

are better done bit by bit.

And things that can't

be done by strength,

may often be done by wit.

THE FROG
AND THE OX

A young Frog came hopping home
as fast as he could go.
"Father!" he told the old Frog
sitting by the pond.
"I have seen the biggest beast—
a beast as big as big can be!"

The young Frog pointed
toward the meadow.
"Look, Father. There he is!"
"Nonsense!" said the old Frog.
"That is just the Ox.

And he is not so big at all.

Why, with a breath of air or two,

I could be about his size.

Watch me. I will show you."

With that, the old Frog took a breath

and puffed up his chest.

"Am I as big as the Ox?"

"No, Father," said the son.

"I'm sure the Ox is bigger still."

So the old Frog breathed again

and puffed himself up some more.

"Am I as big as the Ox?"

"Oh, no," replied the son. "Not yet.

The Ox is bigger still."

At that, the old Frog took a breath
and puffed himself up even more.
"Am I as big as the Ox?"
"No, Father," said the son.
"I fear the Ox is bigger still."
"Nonsense!" cried the old Frog.
"I must be bigger than the Ox!"

And then, like the fool he was
(fools try to be what they are not),
he breathed in all the air he could.
He took more air
than he had room.
"I must, I must,
I must, I... Oh!"
And then
the old Frog burst:
KER-BOOM!

THE COCK, THE DOG, AND THE FOX

The Cock and the Dog
set off through the woods together.
When darkness came, they found
a tree where they could stop
and spend the night.
Cock climbed up to the top
while Dog made a bed below.

And so they slept till dawn
when Cock awoke and crowed,
"Cock-a-doodle-do!
Cock-a-doodle-do!"
Now clever Fox,
who was nearby,
thought,
"Aha!
It is the Cock.
What a meal
he will make!
I'll just use
a trick or two
to get
him down
from that tree."

So Fox went round and called,

"Who was that?

Who sang so well to greet the day?

I'm sure I'd like to greet the singer."

"It was I," replied the Cock.

"Cock-a-doodle-do!"

"Who?" asked Fox. "It is too dark.
Come down so I may see you."
"Oh, I'll come down," Cock replied.
"But you must ask the doorkeeper
if he will open up the door.

You'll find him
underneath the tree."
"Of course," said Fox and
smacked his lips.
"I will ask him right away."

So Fox walked around the tree...
but he only found the Dog.
And Dog bit him on the leg.
"Oooch! Please, don't!
Oh, stop!" cried Fox
as he ran off into the woods.

Cock laughed to see him go.

"Good-bye, you silly Fox!" he called.

"You know at least a hundred tricks,

but now you've learned

something new:

Even the Fox can be outfoxed!

Cock-a-doodle-doodle-do!"

EAST

j398 Ae88o   CR   cop.1
Rice, Eve
Once in a wood

EASY

Public Library
South Bend, Ind.

Central Building
122 West Wayne Street